New Casebooks

POETRY

YEOVIL COLL

...ed by Valerie Allen and Aries Axiotis
COLERIDGE, KEATS AND SHELLEY Edited by Peter J. Kitson
JOHN DONNE Edited by Andrew Mousley
SEAMUS HEANEY Edited by Michael Allen
PHILIP LARKIN Edited by Stephen Regan
PARADISE LOST Edited by William Zunder
DYLAN THOMAS Edited by John Goodby and Chris Wigginton
VICTORIAN WOMEN POETS Edited by Joseph Bristow
WORDSWORTH Edited by John Williams

NOVELS AND PROSE

AUSTEN: *Emma* Edited by David Monaghan
AUSTEN: *Mansfield Park* and *Persuasion* Edited by Judy Simons
AUSTEN: *Sense and Sensibility* and *Pride and Prejudice* Edited by Robert Clark
CHARLOTTE BRONTË: *Jane Eyre* Edited by Heather Glen
CHARLOTTE BRONTË: *Villette* Edited by Pauline Nestor
EMILY BRONTË: *Wuthering Heights* Edited by Patsy Stoneman
ANGELA CARTER Edited by Alison Easton
WILKIE COLLINS Edited by Lyn Pykett
JOSEPH CONRAD Edited by Elaine Jordan
DICKENS: *Bleak House* Edited by Jeremy Tambling
DICKENS: *David Copperfield* and *Hard Times* Edited by John Peck
DICKENS: *Great Expectations* Edited by Roger Sell
ELIOT: *Middlemarch* Edited by John Peck
E. M. FORSTER Edited by Jeremy Tambling
HARDY: *Jude the Obscure* Edited by Penny Boumelha
HARDY: *The Mayor of Casterbridge* Edited by Julian Wolfreys
HARDY: *Tess of the D'Urbervilles* Edited by Peter Widdowson
JAMES: *Turn of the Screw* and *What Maisie Knew* Edited by Neil Cornwell and
    Maggie Malone
LAWRENCE: *Sons and Lovers* Edited by Rick Rylance
TONI MORRISON Edited by Linden Peach
GEORGE ORWELL Edited by Byran Loughrey
SHELLEY: *Frankenstein* Edited by Fred Botting
STOKER: *Dracula* Edited by Glennis Byron
STERNE: *Tristram Shandy* Edited by Melvyn New
WOOLF: *Mrs Dalloway* and *To the Lighthouse* Edited by Su Reid

DRAMA

BECKETT: *Waiting for Godot* and *Endgame* Edited by Steven Connor
APHRA BEHN Edited by Janet Todd
(continued overleaf)

REVENGE TRAGEDY Edited by Stevie Simkin
SHAKESPEARE: *Antony and Cleopatra* Edited by John Drakakis
SHAKESPEARE: *Hamlet* Edited by Martin Coyle
SHAKESPEARE: *King Lear* Edited by Kiernan Ryan
SHAKESPEARE: *Macbeth* Edited by Alan Sinfield
SHAKESPEARE: *The Merchant of Venice* Edited by Martin Coyle
SHAKESPEARE: *A Midsummer Night's Dream* Edited by Richard Dutton
SHAKESPEARE: *Much Ado About Nothing* and *The Taming of the Shrew*
  Edited by Marion Wynne-Davies
SHAKESPEARE: *Romeo and Juliet* Edited by R. S. White
SHAKESPEARE: *The Tempest* Edited by R. S. White
SHAKESPEARE: *Twelfth Night* Edited by R. S. White
SHAKESPEARE ON FILM Edited by Robert Shaughnessy
SHAKESPEARE IN PERFORMANCE Edited by Robert Shaughnessy
SHAKESPEARE'S HISTORY PLAYS Edited by Graham Holderness
SHAKESPEARE'S TRAGEDIES Edited by Susan Zimmerman
JOHN WEBSTER: *The Duchess of Malfi* Edited by Dympna Callaghan

GENERAL THEMES

FEMINIST THEATRE AND THEORY Edited by Helene Keyssar
POSTCOLONIAL LITERATURES Edited by Michael Parker and Roger Starkey

New Casebooks Series
Series Standing Order
ISBN 0-333-71702-3 hardcover
ISBN 0-333-69345-0 paperback
(outside North America only)

You can receive future titles in this series as they are published by placing a standing order. Please contact your bookseller or, in case of difficulty, write to us at the address below with your name and address, the title of the series and the ISBN quoted above.

Customer Services Department, Macmillan Distribution Ltd
Houndmills, Basingstoke, Hampshire RG21 6XS, England

New Casebooks

DYLAN THOMAS

EDITED BY JOHN GOODBY AND CHRIS WIGGINTON

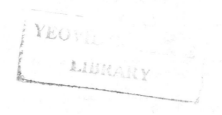
palgrave

First published 2001 by
PALGRAVE
Houndmills, Basingstoke, Hampshire RG21 6XS and
175 Fifth Avenue, New York, N. Y. 10010
Companies and representatives throughout the world

PALGRAVE is the new global academic imprint of
St. Martin's Press LLC Scholarly and Reference Division and
Palgrave Publishers Ltd (formerly Macmillan Press Ltd).

ISBN 0-333-80394-9 hardback
ISBN 0-333-80395-7 paperback

This book is printed on paper suitable for recycling and
made from fully managed and sustained forest sources.

A catalogue record for this book is available
from the British Library.

Library of Congress Cataloging-in-Publication Data

Dylan Thomas / edited by John Goodby and Chris Wigginton.
          p. cm. -- (New casebooks)
     Includes bibliographical references (p.) and index.
     ISBN 0-333-80394-9 (cloth)
          1. Thomas, Dylan, 1914-1953 – Criticism and interpretation.
     I. Goodby, John, 1958-II. Wigginton, Chris, 1972-III. Series.

     PR6039.H52 Z6238 2001
     821'.912-dc21

10   9   8   7   6   5   4   3   2   1
10   09   08   07   06   05   04   03   02   01

Printed in China

For Charles and Jenny,
and Ken and Edna

Contents

Acknowledgements   ix

General Editors' Preface   xi

Abbreviations   xiii

Introduction: JOHN GOODBY and CHRIS WIGGINTON   1

1.   'The little arisen original monster': Dylan Thomas's
Sour Grapes   20
STAN SMITH

2.   'The Lips of Time'   46
STEWART CREHAN

3.   'Daughters of Darkness': Dylan Thomas and the
Celebration of the Female   65
KATIE GRAMICH

4.   'Birth and copulation and death': Gothic Modernism and
Surrealism in the Poetry of Dylan Thomas   85
CHRIS WIGGINTON

5.   The Poetry of Dylan Thomas: Welsh Contexts,
Narrative and the Language of Modernism   106
WALFORD DAVIES

6.   'Death is all metaphor': Dylan Thomas's Radical
Morbidity   124
IVAN PHILLIPS

7. 'Shot from the locks': Poetry, Mourning, *Deaths and Entrances*   140
    STEVE VINE

8. Questions of Identity: The Movement and 'Fern Hill'   158
    JAMES A. DAVIES

9. 'Oh, for our vanished youth': Avoiding Adulthood in the Later Stories of Dylan Thomas   172
    JENI WILLIAMS

10. 'Very profound and very box-office': the Later Poems and *Under Milk Wood*   192
    JOHN GOODBY

Further Reading   221

Notes on Contributors   225

Index   227

Acknowledgements

The editors wish to thank Aeronwy Thomas, Dave Woolley, Jeff Towns, Richard Chamberlain and The Dylan Thomas Society of Great Britain for their help with, and support of, our interest in Dylan Thomas's work. In addition, our thanks must also go to all of the contributors, to the series editors, Martin Coyle and John Peck, and to Margaret Bartley, Beverley Tarquini, and Judy Marshall for their help at every stage.

The editors and publisher wish to thank the following for permission to use copyright material:

Dylan Thomas Estate, for extracts from *Collected Poems*, *Collected Stories* and *Under Milkwood* by permission of JM Dent and David Higham Associates and New Directions Press.

Stewart Crehan, for 'The Lips of Time', first published in Dylan *Thomas: Craft or Sullen Art?*, ed. Alan Bold, St. Martin's Press (1990), pp. 35–65, by permission of the author; Walford Davies, for material from *Dylan Thomas*, Open University Press (1986), pp. 94–123, by permission of the author; John Goodby and Chris Wigginton, for 'Shut in a Tower of Words: Dylan Thomas's Modernism' from *Locations of Literary Modernism*, ed. Alex Davis and Lee Jenkins (2000), by permission of Cambridge University Pres; James A. Davies, for material from *A Reference Companion to Dylan Thomas* by James A. Davies (1998), pp. 196–204, by permission of Greenwood Publishing Group, Inc.

General Editors' Preface

The purpose of this series of New Casebooks is to reveal some of the ways in which contemporary criticism has changed our understanding of commonly studied texts and writers and, indeed, of the nature of criticism itself. Central to the series is a concern with modern critical theory and its effect on current approaches to the study of literature. Each New Casebook editor has been asked to select a sequence of essays which will introduce the reader to the new critical approaches to the text or texts being discussed in the volume and also illuminate the rich interchange between critical theory and critical practice that characterises so much current writing about literature.

In this focus on modern critical thinking and practice New Casebooks aim not only to inform but also to stimulate, with volumes seeking to reflect both the controversy and the excitement of current criticism. Because much of this criticism is difficult and often employs an unfamiliar critical language, editors have been asked to give the reader as much help as they feel is appropriate, but without simplifying the essays or the issues they raise. Again, editors have been asked to supply a list of further reading which will enable readers to follow up issues raised by the essays in the volume.

The project of New Casebooks, then, is to bring together in an illuminating way those critics who best illustrate the ways in which contemporary criticism has established new methods of analysing texts and who have reinvigorated the important debate about how we 'read' literature. The hope is, of course, that New Casebooks will not only open up this debate to a wider audience, but will also encourage students to extend their own ideas, and think afresh about their responses to the texts they are studying.

John Peck and Martin Coyle
University of Wales, Cardiff

Abbreviations

Quotations from the poetry of Dylan Thomas are taken from *Collected Poems 1934–53*, ed. Walford Davies and Ralph Maud (London, 1988); the abbreviation *CP* will be followed by the relevant page number. Quotations from the letters are from *Dylan Thomas: The Collected Letters*, ed. Paul Ferris (London, 1985); the abbreviation *CL* will be followed by the relevant page number. Quotations from the short stories and fictions are taken from *Collected Stories*, ed. Walford Davies (London, 1995); the abbreviation *CS* will be followed by the relevant page number. Quotations from *Under Milk Wood* are from *Under Milk Wood*, ed. Walford Davies and Ralph Maud (London, 1995); the abbreviation *UMW* will be followed in the text by the page number.

Introduction

JOHN GOODBY and CHRIS WIGGINTON

I

All readers of Dylan Thomas, if they wish to progress beyond initial acquaintance with his work, are forced to confront the problem of the yawning gap between his popular and critical reputations. On the one hand, here is a lyric poet of unignorable inventiveness, energy and resonance, one who also happens to be the author of short fictions, letters and film and radio scripts of singular imagination and humour. Several of Thomas's poems are anthology staples, and few readers can fail to have been impressed by lyrics such as 'And death shall have no dominion', 'Poem in October' or 'Do not go gentle into that good night', while lines like 'After the first death there is no other' and 'The force that through the green fuse drives the flower' are part of the common currency of twentieth-century English language poetry. *Under Milk Wood*, an enormously popular radio 'play for voices', has been adapted for several media – stage, film and cartoon – and is still regularly performed and broadcast. Yet when new readers look for critical accounts to guide them further they find very little in the way of recent criticism. Moreover, what exists is almost entirely innocent of the wide-ranging and excitingly various approaches – feminist, New Historicist, psychoanalytic, Marxist, poststructuralist, postcolonial, and so on – which have transformed literary studies over the last 30 years. As a result, speculation, gossip and rehashed biography (which, of course, accumulate around all authors) continue to shape the reception of Thomas to an inordinate degree. In this sense he differs from almost any other canonical author of stature, from William Shakespeare to Virginia Woolf, Jane Austen to Philip Larkin, likely to be encountered either within the higher education system

1

or beyond it. For example, the bibliography in what is still the best short introduction to Thomas's poetry, Walford Davies's 1986 *Dylan Thomas*, lists no criticism written after the mid-1970s, and certainly nothing influenced by contemporary critical activity. Equally revealing of the state of Thomas studies is the fact that the standard poem-by-poem glossary for the *Collected Poems*, William York Tindall's *Guide*, could be reissued in 1996 unrevised from its first publication in 1962. Why have the intervening 40 years had no impact upon the standard readings of Thomas's poetry? Precisely how and why was it preserved, as if in a sealed time capsule, from the upheaval which has altered almost every other aspect of literary studies? And why, finally, should this be the case with a writer whose work, on the face of it, is both stylistically radical *and* has so much to recommend it to the non-academic reader?

It is the contention of this volume of essays that recent critical developments have an enormous amount to offer our understanding of Thomas's work (we would also argue that his writing has much to offer literary theory itself, many of whose insights are indebted to modernism's strategies of hermeneutical suspicion), and that it is a peculiar set of circumstances, rare, but not unique, which have delayed the encounter between the two. This delay, we would argue, is not merely an unfortunate critical oversight but has material causes. Within his lifetime Dylan Thomas's work faced divided responses similar to those which operate today; these continue to dog interpretation, and the forces which gave rise to them remain in place half a century after his death in 1953. Consequently, no twentieth-century poet of comparable reputation has generated such lasting and violent differences of opinion. Chief among these 'forces' has been the problem of separating the presumed excess of Thomas's lifestyle from the apparent excess of his style of writing. Its baroque richness of imagery and verbal playfulness, its declamatory, gothic and sentimental qualities, have made it all too easy, for detractors and champions alike, to read the writing in terms of the life, and vice versa. As a result, most Thomas criticism has been implicitly or explicitly moral in its assumptions, whether in aggressive or defensive mode. This applies particularly to the crude psychoanalytic readings which were legion from the 1950s to the 1970s, and most notably in three book-length studies by David Holbrook, a critic for whom Thomas was virtually the root of all evil.[1] Holbrook's treatment of Thomas as a psychotic case history is adequately disposed of by Walford Davies in his introduction to Thomas's *Selected Poems*, but it is worth noting that – personal animus apart – the distinguishing characteristics of Holbrook's use of a psychoanalytic model were its unexamined linkage of text and life (as if poetry passively 'reflected' a writer's circumstances), and its profoundly reactionary politics. In terms which recall F. R. Leavis at his most rebarbative, Thomas is served up in Holbrook's account as the product of a regressive and infantile modernity which he is simultaneously accused of helping to create.

Holbrook's work was damaging because it gave the impression that a psychoanalytic approach to Thomas could only ever be a negative one. Yet, as Stan Smith (essay 1) shows, a properly historicised understanding of Freud reveals Thomas using his own complex personality to diagnose the neuroses of his era in as thoroughgoing a manner as Auden. Similarly, for Stewart Crehan (essay 2), there are urgent parallels to be drawn between Thomas's making a 'Freudian exemplar' of himself and his dialectical method of composition as a species of resistance to the 'stalled dialectic' of the polarised situation in the 1930s. Crehan outlines Thomas's bravura display of linguistic and psychic structures, and the ways in which these bear on the formation of the self, and hence on all forms of authority. Thomas's own radical use of psychology is followed through from the early poems to 'Fern Hill' in order to refute Russell Davies's notorious jibe that the poem is 'about as political as a mountain goat'.[2]

The distinctiveness of Crehan's essay, which allows for the overdetermined character of Thomas's writing – the way in which gender, politics and language can only be read in terms of each other – can be seen when it is set against the way that interpretations of Thomas, even in the 1990s, continued to mimic Holbrook's tendency to slip from text to author. Only Neil Corcoran in his *English Poetry Since 1940* (1993), registers the possibilities offered by a newer form of criticism; as he acutely observes, 'The way the world is read through, or dreamed across, the human body in this poetry surely makes Thomas overdue for a contemporary Bakhtinian reassessment.'[3] Indeed, as Corcoran implies, confusion of work and writer, or even dislike of his introspection, can only afford a partial explanation of the general indifference, or casual dismissiveness, of critics (most, but not all, non-Welsh) to Thomas's work. To explain these responses more fully, it is necessary to consider the larger institutional and social forces which have shaped its reception.

II

Many earlier commentators focused on the importance of Thomas's Welshness: indeed, this – together with speculation concerning the 'true' original of Llareggub, the town in *Under Milk Wood* – has now become one of the dominant and more depressing features of the cottage industry which is Dylan Thomas in Wales today. This is, of course, a critical approach which – like the focus on the character of the poet it resembles in some ways – is dangerously susceptible to simplification and stereotyping. For if it can be shown that Thomas was in some way 'essentially' Welsh, much of the need for close critical understanding disappears; Thomas wrote like this, or acted like that, because he was a Welshman. A reductive politics of race and place complements a dot-to-dot psychoanalysis in which pre-determined drives 'explain' everything, overriding more complicated understandings of the self as produced by, and interacting with, complex societies historically mutating through time. Both societies and selves are structures which are defined by their capacity for change, and claims for their fixed character must be treated with suspicion. This granted, however, it may still be that a more subtly nuanced comprehension of the way Thomas's locations shaped his writing and its reception provides one way out of the critical deadlock.

This becomes clearer if we look at the historical circumstances in which Thomas's work was received. Following his death, what had, in the 1930s, been described as 'formless' writing – H. G. Porteus, reviewing *The Map of Love*, had spoken of 'an unconducted tour of Bedlam'[4] – was more widely acknowledged to be tightly controlled and shaped. Crucial to this process was the publication of Thomas's letters to his fellow Swansea poet Vernon Watkins in 1957. These showed Thomas to be a painstakingly conscientious craftsman striving deliberately, even agonisingly, for his effects. These letters were complemented by a sympathetic and illuminating study by Ralph Maud, one of the doyens of Thomas criticism, *Entrances to the Poetry of Dylan Thomas*, in 1963, and by his publication of Thomas's early notebooks in 1968 (*Poet in the Making*). The notebooks are an extraordinary record of poems written between the ages of 16 and 20, revealing the strikingly precocious, yet consistent, evolution of the unique stylist and craftsman-poet. (The notebooks, though, also gave credence to the immaturity argument which fuelled moralistic critical responses; the revelation that over half the poems in the 1952 edition of the *Collected Poems*, or versions of them, had been written before Thomas was 20, reinforced charges that he was a writer who, like some kind of poetic Peter Pan, simply refused to grow up.) A *Selected Letters*, edited by Constantine FitzGibbon in 1967, and a *Collected Letters*, edited by Paul Ferris in 1985, added further weight to the argument that Thomas was thoroughly aware of what he was doing, even in his most seemingly obscure pieces. Nevertheless, earlier biographies of the poet by the same writers (in 1965 and 1977, respectively) partly pre-empted some of the potentially beneficial effects of the publication of the letters. FitzGibbon's, in particular, mythologised the Fitzrovia bohemian scene in which Thomas was 'famous among bars', while Ferris's, in mirror image fashion, gave a more finely detailed account of the poet's life, yet was deeply judgemental of it. Neither had much to say about the poetry, which Thomas himself considered to be the central fact of his existence.

If the differences between Ferris's and FitzGibbons's accounts of Thomas's life illustrate something of the ambivalence of the Welsh (or 'Celtic') attitude to Thomas, far less ambiguous responses had always been available in other quarters. During his lifetime, Thomas had suffered virulent attacks from the dominant English poetry critic of the period, Geoffrey Grigson (summarised in his essay 'How much me now your acrobatics amaze'[5]), and not long after his death his reputation was subjected to an assault by Robert Graves in his Oxford poetry lectures.[6] Elsewhere, Graves damned Thomas as 'a demagogic Welsh masturbator who failed to pay his bills',[7] a sentence which lays bare the class and national prejudice – 'Taffy was a Welshman, Taffy was a thief' – at the heart of much English hostility to Thomas. It also illustrates a patriarchal link between masculine sexual and poetic potency and phallic aggressiveness which, as Katie Gramich shows in her feminist reading (essay 3), Thomas was capable of querying throughout his career and which, near the end of his life, he would transcend in the 'erotic celebration of female sexuality' of 'In the White Giant's Thigh'. James A. Davies (essay 8) points out that the tradition of abuse was perhaps most notoriously kept alive by Kingsley Amis, who would write (in 'A Poet's Epitaph' in 1956): 'They call you "drunk with words"; but when we drink / And fetch it up, we sluice it down the sink. / You should have stuck to spewing beer, not ink.'[8] Davies also notes that Amis caricatured Thomas by placing 'demagogic', beer-sodden Welsh poets in two of his novels. That the last of these, *The Old Devils*, appeared as late as 1986 – it was Amis's final work – says much about the staying-power of this strain of denigration. Such persistence, we now see, points not so much to Thomas's weaknesses as to the obsession of a particularly English sensibility which felt itself under threat (it is ironic indeed that – as Geoffrey Thurley has noted – the stereotype of Thomas was precisely that of the kind of poet Graves continually exalted in his own tight-lipped yet Goddess-worshipping poetry[9]). Evident in such responses is what, until recently, would have been critically invisible because of the assumption that the subject position of the English, Oxbridge-educated, middle-class male was the norm from which all 'British' poetry could be judged. In addition, it was Thomas's misfortune to die just at the moment when a backlash against the New Apocalypse writing of the 1940s, with which his own was associated (although it was unlike it in most significant aspects), was developing.

'The Movement' is the typically low-key, yet ironically aggrandising label ('*The* Movement') applied to themselves by a group of poets who emerged in the early 1950s, among them Philip Larkin, D. J. Enright, Donald Davie, Anthony Thwaite, and Kinsley Amis himself. Their reaction against their 1940s predecessors was manifested in a plain style, a disdain for rhetoric or ostentation and a commitment to discursive realism – all clearly at odds with most of what Thomas seemed to stand for. Such responses never entirely held the field, not least because Thomas had powerful champions, among them Louis MacNeice and William Empson (and, as James A. Davies [essay 8] notes, there was an undercurrent of sympathy for Thomas as a 'Bubbles who fell among literary touts', to cite Enright's striking phrase). Among younger critics, and countering Davie's Movement advocacy of classicist values for English poetry in *Articulate Energy* (1955), John Bayley's *The Romantic Survival* (1957) included a positive chapter-length discussion of Thomas. Nevertheless, and despite a partial rehabilitation at the hands of Al Alvarez in the Introduction to his influential anthology *The New Poetry* in 1963, Thomas's critical reputation entered a period of decline even as – in the 1960s at least – his popularity as a writer and romantic icon was firmly established. Unacknowledged at the time, but clearer in hindsight, is that at stake was the nature and responsibilities of poetry to an *English* identity and culture. Thus, when English poetry thawed, dividing between the 'cool' of Larkin and a 'hotter' style, associated with Ted Hughes and US Confessional and experimental poetry in the 1960s, there still remained little space for Thomas. These poetics represented an internal division in English poetry, predicated on a consciousness (and also a repression) of national post-imperial decline. Forty years on, in a multiethnic United Kingdom, the investigation of what Englishness might be – that term which, within 'Britishness', always usurped the peripheral identities of the United Kingdom – is developing apace.

Nevertheless it has to be acknowledged that Thomas's Welsh readers have been scarcely more understanding of Thomas's significance. If Leavisite poetics (however leavened with radicalism) are the outcome of one development in British post-war higher education, then this has had its Welsh equivalent, equally damaging to critical understanding. For if Thomas's death coincided with the rise of the Movement, and an empiricism which dominates British poetry even now, it also coincided with the developing debate over what a 'Welsh' literature in English might be defined as, and how best it should be taught and propagated. Among Thomas's generation of Welsh-born writers the division between those writing in Welsh and those writing in English had been bitter. It had, however, largely been confined to the literary realm – to cultural journals, publishers and the writers themselves. But the massive post-war expansion of higher education made these differences institutional on a large scale, even if professionalisation seemed to take some of the personal edge off the debate. With the development of a critical industry, as it were, labelled 'Anglo-Welsh Writing', writing on Thomas gradually narrowed, in the 1960s and 1970s, to a kind of ring-fenced parish patrolled by academics who were largely Welsh themselves, and based in universities and colleges within Wales. For courses on 'the Anglo-Welsh literary tradition' (one which is – like Anglo-Irish writing – overwhelmingly twentieth-century), Thomas was a dangerously slippery figure. Too important to be ignored – he was its one unignorable and internationally renowned figure, after all, unless the adoptive Welshman David Jones was counted – he could figure both as a major writer whose claims could be advanced, or as a stage Welshman who had pandered to all the worst stereotypes of the drunken Celt abroad. The debate was, in most instances, bound up in a selective view of Thomas's writing which focused on its middle and later phases. At the heart of this approach was an identitarian politics, which necessarily had to ignore the difficult issues raised by Thomas's debt to modernism, and its attendant complex linguistic and philosophical issues (very little Welsh writing was formally modernist). It adhered, in other words, to a basically reflectionist, realist model of literature. (Similar attitudes can be traced in the hostile attitude of Irish academia, until the 1960s, towards Yeats, Joyce and Beckett, who only belatedly made it onto university curricula.) Thomas, in this reading, became the *enfant terrible* who had shaken off his callow experimentalism to become the 'mature' poet of the natural world. Taken out of the context of the larger debate about the fate of modernism in mid-century, however, inordinate emphasis on 'Fern Hill' and *Under Milk Wood* could make Thomas appear a merely provincial writer.

Outside Wales, the general trend from the late 1960s was to leave Thomas to what was assumed to be his own. The issue of who and what his 'own' were, of course, had never been satisfactorily settled. A leading Welsh language writer of the twentieth century, Saunders Lewis, had in the 1930s castigated such South Walian, English language writers as Thomas as the inauthentic, un-Welsh product of English linguistic colonisation: 'there is nothing hyphenated about him', Lewis remarked in 1939, '[h]e belongs to the English.'[10] For Lewis, writers such as Thomas had turned their backs on the Welsh language within which was contained the essential core of Welsh identity. Thomas, by virtue of his bad eminence, was targeted as the chief offender. At the time of Thomas's death, Lewis was more generous;[11] but the terms of the debate established by him, and other critics and writers in the 1920s and 1930s, continued to haunt post-war attempts to define a canon of Welsh literature. Even now, the hyphen in 'Anglo-Welsh' points to an insecurity and defensiveness. In this it resembles 'Anglo-Irish', a label which, until the mid-1980s, was used to distinguish Irish literature written in English from that written in the Irish language. In Ireland, however, a new sense of confidence and self-assurance has led to the dropping of the term, with its pejorative (or triumphalist) associations, and the use of 'Irish' to denote all writing by Irish-born, or Irish-located writers, in whatever language (although 'Anglo-Irish' may still be applied as a neutral historical term to those writers who belonged to the Ascendancy gentry class). Such disputes, apparently hair-splitting, have a great deal of bearing on the ways in which literature is read. For, as theorists have argued, the notion of a pure, unitary national identity (and the concomitant rejection of 'bastard' or 'hybrid' terms) stems from a unitary conception of the human subject itself.

It is precisely the notion of unitary subjectivity which is so problematised in Thomas's writing, particularly in the early poetry and short fictions. This is one major reason why the whole tenor of the critical attack on Thomas rested on the notion of him as an imposter, as inauthentic. From the English point of view, this was largely because his rhetorical strategies could be adduced to some stereotype of 'Welshness'. (Typical is Julian Symons's claim in 1940 that 'frequently [Thomas's] poems are jokes, rhetorical and intellectual fakes of the highest class'.[12]) But in a Wales still suffering from its dependent position within the British State, that supposed inauthenticity took (and still takes) a different form. Nevertheless – and this is the critical rub – it was precisely the concept of the unitary self, the 'I' as coherent and issuing from an organically whole identity, which the new literary theory problematised. At precisely the time, that is, when Thomas's work could have been read as anticipating such ideas, in the early 1970s, it was being isolated and sidelined in a debate about belonging and identity which were inappropriate to its strategies. As a result, the encounter between theory and Thomas was postponed until the 1990s. In the meantime, many advances were made. The establishment of sound texts, the rebuttal of the worst, quasi-racist attacks on Thomas, took place. In particular, critics such as Walford Davies, John Ackerman and James A. Davies, provided a clear case for taking Thomas seriously as a writer. Yet their defence rarely rose beyond a wary and lucid empiricism to consider those aspects – of gender, the body, language and the unconscious, the split between high and low culture, for example – which Thomas's work, in the new critical climate, might have invited.

III

In one sense, the critical encounter we are talking about could not take place until new critical light had been shed on conceptions of national identity and cultural otherness, and the ways these shifted the larger framework within which Thomas was viewed. This did not happen until some time after the theoretical sea-change in the academy, the key text being Edward Said's *Orientalism* (1978). Virtually every previous discussion of Thomas's 'Welshness', as we have claimed, had failed to pass beyond the terms of an identity assertion which more or less inverted the dominant rhetoric of Englishness (and anti- or pro-Welshness), or 'Britishness', which it sought to displace. But neither as the bardic other of the thin-lipped

London literati (or, more convincingly, as Auden's main chal-
lenger), nor as the mongrel Welshman who welshed on his
birthright for a mess of BBC pottage (or, alternatively, blathering
Celtic imposter) – as none of these things could the persistent energies of Thomas's work be explained, let alone explored. With Said's
work, and following him that of Homi Bhabha, among others,
more nuanced ways of reading marginalised or non-metropolitan
writers could occur. Said had written of the ways in which the West
had established, over the course of centuries, a specific 'discourse'
for dealing with the East by marginalising it as an 'Other', perceived – often in self-evidently contradictory terms – as exotic, ener-
vatingly decadent, barbarous, cowardly, obscurantist and so on.
The appositeness of Said's model was not lost on critics of what are
known as postcolonial literatures, those of the recently decolonised
(or decolonising) nations of Africa and Asia. For Bhabha, however,
unlike Said, the central term in analysing postcolonial literatures is
'hybridity'. Writings which are 'hybrid' cannot be described in
terms of a discourse and the counter-discourse it invites; as Bhabha
points out, to simply oppose the dominant 'discourse' is to risk remaining trapped within its binary structure, opposing the identity
imposed upon you with another of your own construction.
Inverting the binary terms of an unequal relationship between cultures and nations, however unequal that relationship may be, is to
remain within the limits set by those terms. Abandoning the
either/or, coloniser/colonised dichotomies of Said, Bhabha argues
that postcolonial writing derives from a refusal to belong to any essential identity and not from a compromise between cultures; a
recognition that such a concept of identity is an imperial or metropolitan construct in the first place. Rejecting this kind of conceptual
mirror-imaging for a kind of subversive mimicry, literary 'hybridity'
for Bhabha 'represents the ambivalent "turn" of the discriminated
subject into the terrifying, exorbitant object of paranoid
classification – a disturbing questioning of the images and presences
of authority . . . [which] is not a third term which resolves the
tension between two cultures.'[13] If 'a disturbing questioning of the
images . . . of authority' can be applied readily enough to Dylan
Thomas's writings, then 'terrifying', 'exorbitant' and 'paranoid
classification' irresistibly suggest the reaction to them of Amis,
Holbrook and Graves.

In a less densely theoretical way, the terms of this debate can be
detected in *Frontiers in Anglo-Welsh Poetry* (1997), by the distin-

guished Welsh critic and poet Tony Conran. He explains in his Preface that:

> The book's title includes the word 'frontiers' because Anglo-Welsh poetry is the product of three kinds of frontier between the Welsh and their dominant partners in Great Britain. First, a frontier between two peoples, two ways of life. The Welsh way of life is or was a close-knit structure essentially emanating from the Methodist Awakening of Wales in the eighteenth century. Second, a frontier between two civilisations. Welsh civilisation built upon the ruins of Celtic Christianity to achieve classical status in the fourteenth and fifteenth centuries. It was more or less moribund by the seventeenth, but has since been the subject of several renaissances. Third, a frontier between two languages. Welsh is a modern tongue derived from the Celtic that the Britons spoke in Roman times. It is very different from the Low German speech, 'creolised' by Norman French, of their Norman neighbours.
>
>   These three frontiers are related but in themselves very different, and Anglo-Welsh poetry responds to the stresses they occasion in different ways. None of them, however, is to be identified with the historical frontier, the Marches or geographical borderland between Wales and England. Nowadays anywhere in Wales is frontier country.[14]

Conran's suggestive notion of all of Wales as a 'frontier country' is analogous in many ways to what Bhabha has called the 'interstitial space'[15] between well-defined cultures, within which postcolonial writing occurs (a phrase whose applicability to Thomas's writing James A. Davies usefully explores in his discussion of 'Fern Hill' [essay 8]). As the terms in the Conran passage reveal, however, the usefulness of 'frontier country' as a critical concept is finally weakened by being wedded to an essentialist notion of national identity. '*The* Welsh way of life', for example, is remarkably totalising, assuming as it does a single, easily definable way of life in Wales distinguishable from that in England. Like many other Welsh commentators on Welsh identity, Conran overlooks powerful, material, historical determinants in favour of spiritual or idealistic ones, observing a silence on the Industrial Revolution which so profoundly transformed Wales in order to attribute national difference to 'the Methodist Awakening' (which, in any case, occurred with similar force in Cornwall and Yorkshire and could therefore be categorised as a regional, rather than a national, phenomenon). Did not the 'close-knit structures' of community he sees as specifically

Welsh emerge elsewhere in Britain (the North-East coalfields, Clydeside shipyards, etc.) as the result of near-identical circumstances? What are we to make of the inverted commas surrounding 'creolised' in this passage, which, like a pair of surgical forceps, seem to grasp – only in order to disdainfully separate – the author from a condition of which he disapproves? Or the fact that the third most spoken language in 'modern' Wales is Sylheti-Bengali, a Bhabhaesque 'third term' which – reflecting past Welsh involvement in the British empire – destabilises, rather than resolves, the binary linguistic relationship observed by Conran? It is revealing that although Conran's interesting chapter on Dylan Thomas identifies (and in a non-judgemental sense) a 'schizoid' modernist aspect to his writing, the insight cannot be pursued further.

The need for caution becomes more pronounced later in Conran's book when he claims that Anglo-Welsh poetry 'is like English poetry written by Irishmen or Indians'.[16] This, we would argue, runs the risk of a kind of self-aggrandising self-victimisation. The point is not, of course, that Welsh writing and culture *cannot* be defined as in some way colonial or postcolonial – on the contrary, this is part of the case we are arguing. It is, rather, that it is simplistic to make these claims in such general terms, conflating Ireland and India, and both of them with Wales, as Conran does. Here a further irony comes into play, since Bhabha's model of the postcolonial is very specifically an Indian one, drawn from the Indian Subaltern Studies Group of critics who in the 1970s and 1980s furnished a series of readings of texts emanating from the boundaries between the provincial and the outright colonial – that is, from places where (as in India and Wales) an indigenous culture had not been totally extirpated by colonialism, and actually interacted with it in highly complex, often parodic, ways.[17] Conran's other comparison – Ireland – illustrates even more clearly the potential a more nuanced definition offers for a postcolonial redefinition of Welsh literature.

Discussing Irish literature, Colin Graham has written of how postcolonial theory strives to fragment and disintegrate the monologism of cultural affiliation and to rethink such notions as irony, mimicry and hybridity 'out of a recognition of the claustrophobic intensity of the relationship between Ireland and Britain'.[18] The distinctiveness of the Welsh as opposed to the Irish situation lies not just in its dormancy (this is how a traditional nationalist would read it; a 'national spirit' waiting to be aroused), but in its differently impacted, 'claustrophobic' relationship with England and the rest of the United Kingdom. This has become particularly apparent over the last few years, of course, when the loosening of ties within the United Kingdom – as identified in books such as Tom Nairn's *The Break-Up of Britain: Crisis and Neonationalism* (1977) – has entered a new phase with the establishment of a Scottish Parliament and Welsh Assembly in the late 1990s. In this sense – again, we think especially of the early writing – Thomas can be seen as paradoxically far more 'Welsh' than those who orient their writing according to an image of pure Welshness (or, better, towards Welshness as itself a kind of purity), since his work articulates precisely a 'claustrophobic intensity' in its compromised, impacted sense of identity, at the deepest, genetic level of style. Indeed, the mockingly authoritative tones of Thomas's poetry announce the kind of interstitial, parodic, hybrid writing which confounds more binding notions of identity, not only of Welshness – and this is the point – but also of Englishness/Britishness.

IV

What Thomas always threatened to upset, both in the 1930s and in later assessments of the decade's poetry, was the centrality of W. H. Auden. It is in this frame that the 'oedipal' struggle between Thomas and Auden should be placed. The 'ruin' pursued by both poets even as they fled it, was, as Smith shows (essay 1), differently inflected by virtue of differing class, national and sexual allegiances. If the Northern Irish MacNeice was marginalised for decades because of his similarity to Auden, so Thomas was marginalised by virtue of his difference from him. The virulence of this process in Thomas's case, however, stemmed from the very profound and radical antipathy to the *New Country* poetics which both Auden and MacNeice shared, an antipathy discussed by Chris Wigginton (essay 4), who stresses the modernist inheritance of Thomas's writing which has been partially concealed in the confusion of man and work. Similarly, for Wigginton, the issue of whether Thomas is a surrealist or not has been falsely couched in either/or terms; Thomas's liminal position meant that surrealism was for him a way of both accessing and mocking the avant-garde metropolitan cultural *zeitgeist*, just as his gothicism allowed a specifically Welsh twist to be given to Eliotic modernism. Indeed, like the essays by Gramich (essay 3) and Crehan (essay 2),

Wigginton's description of Thomas's obsessive use of rhetorical devices and wordplay within traditional forms as a kind of imploded, simulacrum modernism, directs us to those ways in which Thomas faced both forwards and backwards at the same time. All of these contributors are a reminder of Bhabha's point that what most deeply disturbs the metropolitan centre is less outright opposition than the adoption of postures it views as self-evidently sham – those which, in the act of imitation, mock the fixed, binary categories of identity, of putatively coherent individual and national 'essences', through a calculated misappropriation of them. In Bhabha's formulation, '[Hybridity's] threat ... comes from the prodigious and strategic production of conflictual, fantastic, discriminatory "identity effects" in the play of a power that is elusive because it hides no "essence", no "itself" '.[19]

Such mimicry, gothicism and anguished yet playful reinscriptions of modernism are nowhere more apparent than in Thomas's response to the Second World War, the central historical event of his lifetime, and one from which, in Vernon Watkins's words, 'he never completely recovered'.[20] In a series of elegies – more properly anti-elegies – Thomas registered the impact of the London Blitzes of 1940–1 and 1944–5 in a language which fused the densely metaphysical manner and bodily awareness of his earlier style with a more public concern for witness which had begun to develop at the end of the 1930s. Again, there is a sense in which Thomas's hybrid allegiances and poetic strategies suited him for this role; it is notable that the outstanding literary responses to London under attack were by outsiders – T. S. Eliot in *Little Gidding* (1943), his compatriot Hilda Doolittle (H. D.) in 'The Walls Do Not Fall' (1944) and the Anglo-Irish Elizabeth Bowen in a number of short stories, as well as in her greatest novel, *The Heat of the Day* (1949). There are several critics who consider Thomas's war poems to be his major achievement; and, without necessarily endorsing this, it is clear that the poems in question perform the extraordinary feat of holding, under enormous pressure, sexual rapture and jealousy, the self as performance and physical destruction within – a telling wartime coinage – the 'theatre of war'. It is as if Thomas's earlier poetics of analysis, dismemberment, conflict and (attempted) synthesis and resurrection had become terrifyingly literalised under wartime conditions, forcing a final flowering of the modernist style he had said farewell to in 1939 with *The Map of Love's* 'Once it was the colour of saying' and 'How shall my animal'. As Bowen's haunted fictions testify, this was a time when the worlds of the living and the dead seemed to merge, while the contemporary catch-phrase 'careless talk costs lives' became as applicable to the many illicit sexual encounters conducted under the cover of blackout and dislocation as it was to secret military information. Ivan Phillips (essay 6) reminds us that the war years were a period of constant travel and displacement, marital stress and hackwork for Thomas. Moreover, in placing his poetry in the same context as the war poets, Alun Lewis, Keith Douglas and Sidney Keyes, who were direct combatants, Phillips emphasises that in this war, for the first time in British history at least, the 'home' front shared the risk of sudden death with those actual ones in North Africa, Europe or the Far East. Crucially, he sees the war as sharpening the self-cancelling qualities in Thomas's poetry, and connects this with the relative silence of the final years in a way which amplifies Watkins's claim for the lasting psychic damage wrought by the war, its permanently traumatising effects. At the same time, however, he finds a 'demo-cratic and complex reaction', one taken up in Steve Vine's analysis of the ways in which Thomas's poetry, conspicuously, 'refused to mourn' (essay 7).

For Vine, tracing the implications of the title of *Deaths and Entrances* (1946), in which the wartime poetry was collected, Thomas's work of these years is also about the unrepresentable, the impossibility of making death *mean* in language. Incursion and violent irruption are seen as characterising Thomas's poetry generally, in fact, with the poems viewed as traumatic sites where different selves interpenetrate, perilously balanced against the 'warring flux' from which they emerge, a process given fresh intensity by the all-per-vasive war raging around the poet. Yet at the same time, these poems refuse the standard and frequently specious consolation of losing themselves wholly in the mourning of melancholy; death suspends such work of mourning 'because no symbolic compensation' is capable of answering it. Thus, for Vine, 'Ceremony After a Fire Raid' attempts to resolve the problem of interposing the poem between us and the fact of the death of the child by dissolving the authorial ego and offering the child's body as that which exceeds the poem's own grasp, as an instance of what the theorist Jacques Lacan calls the 'Real' beyond language.[21] In this reading, the extravagant language of the poem is seen as being deliberately directed *away* from the child in order to open up an ethical distance between the poem and the unincorporated reality of the bodily 'husk' which is its subject. Language itself, that is, is left to outface death on behalf of the child and, by implication, humanity.

The centrality of the figure of the dead child to the two best known of Thomas's war poems points us to a group of themes common to every phase of his writing. From the very early poems to the final stories and the incomplete *In Country Heaven* sequence, Thomas was preoccupied with conception, the life of the child in the womb, with growth and with adolescence. For Gramich (essay 3), these concerns embody the drama of acquiring a gender; within the womb (and beyond it) nothing is fixed and identity remains fluid. This, as she points out, 'is a source of anxiety and even anguish', a far cry from the view that Thomas is merely 'immature' in dwelling on such subjects, as if a thematics of growth and development confirmed a use of language deemed morbid or sentimental, or essentially adolescent in some way. And yet – to return to the notion of Thomas as a transgressive, hybrid, marginalised writer – it could be argued that nothing could better exemplify the postcolonial condition, in however impacted, complex and oblique a form, than a thematics and stylistics of infantilism and return to origins, or a concern with revenants and spectres. Like much postcolonial writing, Thomas's work mediates its insecurities via the Oedipal family romance; obsession with castration, absent fathers (and gods), mothers reduced to biological function, confused sibling relationships. Stan Smith (essay 1) traces the ways in which an anxiety concerning a father and with becoming a father works itself out at the level of literary influence; and family relationships are everywhere in the poetry, from 'my father's ghost' in 'I fellowed sleep' to the ambiguous daughter/wife figure of 'In Country Sleep'. It could be argued, then, that the womb voices of poems such as 'I see the boys of summer' and 'Before I knocked', discussed respectively by Gramich and Wigginton (essays 3 and 4) articulate also the desire of the excluded writer to recapitulate his dubious, unstable origins at the most material level of phylogeny (we might recall the 'Oxen of the Sun' chapter in James Joyce's *Ulysses* [1922], which matches the evolution of the English language with that of the child in Mrs Purefoy's womb, an affectionate yet mockingly virtuosic seizure of the language of dispossession). Similarly, if Smith (like Neil Corcoran) finds 'narcissism' in Thomas's many poems on births and birthday, a less personalised reading would see them as rather (or also) encoding South Walian outsiderness, as mediating a radically insoluble doubt over identity and belonging.

Jeni Williams (essay 9) discusses two of Thomas's last fictions, 'A Story' and 'The Followers', in the light of an understanding of his marginal status. For Williams, a more general sense of Thomas's irresponsibility (which she shares with Smith) is therefore complicated by his tangled origins. What the English George Orwell saw as the 'child-ishness'[22] of Welsh writing of the time can be regarded, in Thomas, as the granting to women of a certain agency (as opposed to the men, who are overgrown children), and thus as a challenge to the masculine self and the linear plotting of conventional fiction; but, at the same time Williams, like Gramich, notes the elements of asexual misogyny and escapist regression displayed in the stories. The virtue of 'The Followers' is that it articulates the dilemma of a male gaze forever excluded from an authority which is at once metropolitan and, according to the inversions of gender politics, female. The same attention to cultural contexts in these late works is also displayed by John Goodby (essay 10) in his analysis of the last poems and *Under Milk Wood*. While acknowledging the slow silencing which marks Thomas as a poet in the post-war period, Goodby sets this in the context of a highly fraught Cold War political climate which led Thomas to ruralist themes and more discursive, 'realist' modes of representation. Rather than viewing this as representing a decline, he notes the way in which it matches general trends in writing of the time towards pastoral and parable. Similarly, Thomas's use of folk-lore, fairy story and the natural world is seen as a problematic, elaborate exploration of the nature of innocence, an exploration pursued most fully in *Under Milk Wood*. As Goodby points out, this work – Thomas's last – is more fruitfully related to contemporary radio comedies such as 'ITMA' and 'The Goon Show' than to stage drama, by whose criteria critics have so often sought to judge it (although, as he points out, its static world of fixed 'characters' looks forward to the soap opera genre which began a few years later with 'Coronation Street'). He suggests that it is clearly possible to read *Under Milk Wood* in terms of linguistic play, voice and a problematised notion of stereotype, according to which official authority and rationality are subverted by clowning and a celebration of excess. This materiality also serves as a reminder of how insistently Thomas's writing was, among other things, always 'about' language, a reflection on its own medium.

The question of the use of language – always the most distinctive feature of Thomas's writing, for all media – returns us to the basic issue of modernism, critical neglect and popularity. Walford Davies (essay 5), one of the first critics to note the importance of Thomas's debt to modernism, traces the specifically Symbolist strand within this inheritance and shows how vital syntax and narrative – as well as the distinctive vocabulary – are to his impact. Davies focuses on the early poetry to show just how seriously we should take Thomas's claim that his poetry was to be read 'literally', rather than unpacked for its discursive content. An understanding of the earlier modernism is important to an appreciation of Thomas's later work, one of the most notable features of which was increasing prominence as a broadcaster and reader of poetry, latterly on the US lecture circuit. Can the shift from modernism, finally and briefly, be related to this evolution in his critical and popular fortunes? The critic Andreas Huyssens has written of later modernism, after the 1920s, being defined by a split between the political and the aesthetic avant-garde.[23] However, this fairly straightforward model has now been made much more complex with a realisation of the many regional locations in which modernist writing developed, and the absence of any single, dominant modernist style or centre. The certainty with which a writer like Thomas would once have been placed in the 'aesthetic' camp now seems presumptuous. Certainly, by broadening definitions of both the 'political' and the 'aesthetic' in mid-century poetry and stressing the hybrid qualities which his various locations enjoined on Thomas, it is possible to see his work as problematising this kind of division. Thomas remains a central and awkward fact of the period; in him modernist difficulty, parodic-bardic persona and suburban Swansea petit-bourgeois produce what might be seen as a supplement which would complete and simultaneously undermine the standard, 'audenary' histories of British poetry. It is a guarantee of Thomas's continuing importance that his work has still found no adequate critical assessment 50 years after his death, and that – oscillating subversively between inclusion in, and exclusion from, the canon of twentieth-century poetry – it retains all of its power to challenge and entrance us.

NOTES

1. David Holbrook, *Llareggub Revisited: Dylan Thomas and the State of Modern Poetry* (London, 1962); *Dylan Thomas and Poetic Dissociation* (Carbondale, IL, 1964); *Dylan Thomas: The Code of Night* (London, 1972).

2. Russell Davies, 'Fibs of Vision', *Review* (Autumn/Winter 1971–2), 75.

3. Neil Corcoran, *English Poetry Since 1940* (London, 1993), p. 43.

4. Hugh Gordon Porteus, 'Map of Llareggub', *New English Weekly*, 7 September (1939), pp. 269–70.

5. Geoffrey Grigson, *The Harp of Aeolus and Other Essays* (London, 1948), pp. 151–60.

6. The Clark Lectures are included in Robert Graves, *The Crowning Privilege* (London, 1955).

7. See Chris Wigginton's essay, below, p. 96.

8. Kingsley Amis, *A Case of Samples: Poems 1946–1956* (London, 1956), p. 53.

9. Geoffrey Thurley, *The Ironic Harvest: English Poetry in the Twentieth Century* (London, 1974), p. 131.

10. Saunders Lewis, *Is There An Anglo-Welsh Literature?* (Caerdydd, 1939), p. 5.

11. Lewis wrote 'We have lost the most splendid English speaking child Wales has ever produced.' Saunders Lewis, 'Dylan Thomas', *A Dylan Thomas Number*, special issue of *Dock Leaves*, 5: 13 (Spring, 1954), 9.

12. Julian Symons, 'Obscurity in Dylan Thomas', *Kenyon Review*, 2:4 (Winter 1940), 71.

13. Homi K. Bhabha, *The Location of Culture* (London, 1994), p. 113.

14. Tony Conran, *Frontiers in Anglo-Welsh Poetry* (Cardiff, 1997), p. vii.

15. Bhabha, *The Location of Culture*, p. 3.

16. Conran, *Frontiers in Anglo-Welsh Poetry*, p. 1.

17. See Peter Childs and Patrick Williams, *An Introduction to Post-Colonial Theory* (Hemel Hempstead, 1997), pp. 36–9, 160–4.

18. Colin Graham, ' "Liminal Spaces": Post-Colonial Theories and Irish Culture', *The Irish Review*, 16 (Autumn/Winter 1994), 41.

19. Bhabha, *The Location of Culture*, p. 90.

20. *Letters to Vernon Watkins*, ed. Vernon Watkins (London, 1957), p. 19.

21. See Steve Vine's essay, below, p. 150.

22. See Jeni Williams's essay, below, p. 172

23. See *Modernism and Ireland: The Poetry of the 1930s*, ed. Patricia Coughlan and Alex Davies (Cork, 1995), p. 46.

1

'The little arisen original monster': Dylan Thomas's Sour Grapes

STAN SMITH

> The fathers have eaten sour grapes and the children's teeth are set on edge.
>
> (Ezekiel 18: 1–2)

BOY BUSHRANGERS

Among the 'Sixteen Comments on Auden', mostly reverential though a few disapproving, in the *New Verse* Auden Double Issue in November 1937, one stands out:

> I sometimes think of Mr Auden's poetry as a hygiene, a knowledge and practice, based on a brilliantly prejudiced analysis of contemporary disorders, relating to the preservation and promotion of health, a sanitary science and a flusher of melancholies. I sometimes think of his poetry as a great war, admire intensely the mature, religious, and logical fighter, and deprecate the boy bushranger.
>
> I think he is a wide and deep poet, and that his first narrow angles, of pedantry and careful obscurity, are worn almost away. I think he is as technically sufficient, and as potentially productive of greatness, as any poet writing in English. He makes Mr Yeats's isolation guilty as a trance.

P.S. – Congratulations on Auden's seventieth birthday.[1]

The author of this parodically judicious, affectionately patronising assessment, so much in the mock-pompous mode of the early Auden, is not, as one might think, some *grand seigneur* of the literary establishment, a little put out by the overnight fame of callow youth (in 1937 Auden had just turned 30), but graciously admiring of its promise. He is, in reality, an even callower youth, all of 23, whose second slim volume had appeared only a year earlier. It is, of course, Dylan Thomas, whose trademark is revealed in that gnomic remark about Yeats, 'guilty as a trance' (what *does* he mean?), and in the scatological play that goes from 'sanitary science' to 'flusher of melancholies', and whose own bushranger boyishness comes out in that parting shot: Auden is already, at 30, a grand old man of letters, assuming the *dignitas* of an unimaginably older generation. (Yeats was to die two years later, aged 74.) But, if Auden is a premature patriarch, who, by implication, is the young pretender who will supplant him? The answer is obvious. The facetious birthday greeting conceals a deeper message: The king is almost dead. Watch out, Wystan!

It is Thomas's condescending discrimination of 'the mature, religious, and logical fighter' (an odd mélange) from the 'boy bushranger' which is most interesting. What, precisely, does this last phrase mean? The second edition of the *Oxford English Dictionary*, published in 1936, defines 'bushranger', with a first usage in 1817, as 'An escaped convict living in the bush, and subsisting by robbery with violence'. Now I can see the point of this; but read on. The dictionary then proffers the related word 'Bushwhacker' (US 1809):

> *lit.* One who beats bushes; hence 1. A backwoodsman, a bush-ranger. 2. In the American Civil War, irregular combatants who took to the woods, and were variously regarded as patriot guerrillas, or as banditti 1862. 3. An implement used to cut away brushwood 1858.

Not to beat about the bush, I'd suggest that all these meanings are lurking in Thomas's usage. The variously defined 'irregular combatants' are picked up in his image of Auden the guerrilla fighter, a persona adopted in *The Orators: An English Study* in 1932, with its swithering uncertainty about loyalties in the perennial *Kulturkampf* of the generations in the poem, 'To My Pupils' (later called 'Which side am I supposed to be on?'). The cutter-away of brushwood comes out in the emphasis on the cleansing and clearing of disorder, summed up by that sharp question in *The Orators*, addressed by an old boy at a school prize day to the young boys gathered respectfully, sceptically, in front of him: 'What do you think about England, this country of ours where nobody is well?'[2]

Thomas has indeed assumed here the parodic mantle of Auden's old boy, whose speech begins with the words 'Commemoration. Commemoration. What does it mean? What does it mean? Not what does it mean to them, there, then. What does it mean to us, here, now? It's a facer, isn't it boys? But we've all got to answer it'[3] – rather like Thomas himself compelled to answer the request from Geoffrey Grigson for a comment on Auden at 30. For celebration of this kind comes very close to *commemoration*, in which 'eulogistic mention' of the living (one meaning of the word in the 1936 *OED*), turns into its more usual meaning, 'A calling to remembrance by some solemnity or celebration . . . A service, or a prayer, in memory of a saint or of a sacred event.' Thomas's reaction to the solemnity of this tribute to Auden is apposite, then. The old boy is already posthumous, even though he doesn't know it. And the young boys down there, giggling behind their hands on the floor of the hall on this solemn Prize Day, have a different agenda, a different war to wage.

There is a strange reduplication and projection in these mediations of the boy Wystan and the boy Dylan. Wystan, a mere 'boy bushranger', is mocked because he appears to endorse the process whereby his admirers treat him as already a grand old man. Dylan, denouncing the emperor's new clothes like any iconoclastic teenager, nevertheless speaks in the mock tones of a gerontocrat. This *double* double-take is clearly something of which Thomas was half-aware. A revealing acknowledgement of it can be found in the flippant parenthesis he added to a bout of adolescent soul-searching in a letter to Trevor Hughes in 1933:

> I shall [never] know the answer to the looking-glass question, 'Why is this me?' . . . Sometimes only a worm is companion, its grey voice at your ear the only voice. (This, too, you might laugh off. 'Juvenilia.' A shrug. A slight condescension. Boys will be old men.)
>
> (CL, 19)

In this reduplication, boy and old man are simultaneously distinguished and identified in a perpetual war of the generations. A more serious instance of the ultimately Freudian paradigm can be found in a very interesting poem of Thomas's from September 1934, 'Do you not father me'. Here the conjugations of consanguinity seem like a deliberate meditation on the dilemma of Sophocles' (and Freud's) Oedipus, at once father and sibling of his own children, summarised in the line: 'Am I not father too, and the ascending boy . . . ?' (*CP*, 42).

OLD BOYS

Wyndham Lewis, recalling the interwar years in *Rude Assignment: An Intellectual Autobiography* in 1950, cites some Sorelian second thoughts of 1925:

> That we are witnessing the *ruin of the modern world* – ruin which the 'great war' (1914–18) will have helped not a little to precipitate and to consummate – about this there can be no doubt in the mind of any well-informed person.[4]

What Lewis identifies here is an ideology of ruin which runs through the work of the young writers who emerged in the aftermath of the Great War and the Modernist revolution. In a letter to Pamela Hansford Johnson which refers appreciatively to Wyndham Lewis's *Tarr* and *The Apes of God*, and penned, he says, on Armistice Day 1933, Dylan Thomas wrote of the decline of the West, consummated by that war, in terms which recall both Lewis and Spengler, but rapidly mutate into the pulpit/soapbox oratory of the streetcorner communist:

> The state was a murderer, and every country in this rumour-ridden world, peopled by the unsuccessful suicides left over by the four mad years, is branded like Cain across the forehead. What was Christ in us was stuck with a bayonet to the sky, and what was Judas we fed and sheltered . . . Civilisation is a murderer. We, with the cross of a castrated saviour cut on our brows, sink deeper and deeper with the days into the pit of the West . . .
>   This is a lament on the death of the West. Your bones and mine shall manure an empty island set in a waste sea. The stars shall shine over England, but the darkness of England and the sarcophagus of a spoonfed nation, and the pitch in the slain souls of our children, will never be lit.
>
> CL, 54–5)

The imagery here suggests, for all his later disclaimers, a political unconscious to Thomas's recurrent trope of a crucified and castrated Christ. But out of this necessary ruin can come renewal. The rhetoric leads, predictably, to an attack on the Old Men responsible for the War, in a line that runs from Pound, through Lewis and Lawrence, to Auden's *Orators*:

> The old buffers of this world still cling to chaos, believing it to be Order. The day will come when the old Dis-Order changeth, yielding to a new Order. Genius is being strangled every day by the legion of old Buffers, by the last long line of the Edwardians, clinging, for God and capital, to an outgrown and decaying system. Light is being turned to darkness by the capitalists and industrialists. There is only one thing you and I, who are of this generation, must look forward to, must work for and pray for, and, because, as we fondly hope, we are poets and voicers not only of our personal selves but of our social selves, we must pray for it all the more vehemently. It is the Revolution. There is no need for it to be a revolution of blood. We do not ask that. All that we ask is that the present Dis-Order, this medieval machine which is grinding into powder the bones and the guts of the postwar generation, shall be broken in two, and that all that is in us of godliness and strength, of happiness and genius, shall be allowed to exult in the sun.
>
> (CL, 55)

This goes on (and on), to a climactic vision of some Nietzschean/communist thaumaturge, in part a projection of his own self-aggrandising fantasy, a 'new Christ [crying] in the wilderness', proclaiming 'the huge, electric promise of the future' and the death of the old order, 'And we, who have not been long enough alive to be corrupted utterly, could build out of its manuring bones the base of an equal and sensible civilisation' (CL, 56).

There is, of course, a subliminal sexual undercurrent in all this, with its Lawrentian attack on marriage as 'a dead institution . . . the old rigid monogamous lifelong union of male and female', and its conclusion that 'The precious seeds of revolution must not be wasted, though I do not think they will be in you' (CL, 55–6). He is, after all, writing to a young woman whose conversion to the Revolution may also get her into bed. But one shouldn't underestimate the politics. Two months later he would write to her that

> [Y]ou know as well as I do that patriotism is a publicity ramp organised by holders of excess armament shares; you know that the Union Jack is only a national loin-cloth to hide the decaying organs of a diseased social system; you know that the Great War was purposely protracted in order for financiers to make more money . . . that

> Kipling ... is ... an 'I gave my son' militarist; that the country which he lauds and eulogises is a country that supports a system by which men are starved ... not allowed to work, to marry, to have children; by which they are driven mad daily; by which children are brought into the world scrofulous; by which the church is allowed to prevent the prevention of sexual disease ....
>
> (*CL*, 88)

A country, in fact, where nobody is well.

Clearly Bert Trick, the 'communist grocer' who gave Thomas's rebelliousness a direction, lies behind the bar-room brawling vehemence of this. But Thomas's 'Revolution' had little, really, in common with the hardline politics of the Comintern in its intransigent Third Period. In the same letter which indicts Kipling he observes that 'Every thinking man – that is, every man who builds up, on a structure of tradition, the seeds of his own revolution' must 'gradually form a series of laws for living', not as dogma or theory, but as sensuously apprehended, intuitive 'impressions'; while his Armistice Day letter promised 'Later ... a more reasoned outline of revolution, the hard facts of communism – which is above communism for it holds the individual above everything else' (*CL*, 56).

For such a credo, Thomas has other, more directly literary mentors, foremost of whom is the poet whose slim volume, called simply *Poems*, he carried around in his pocket until it fell to pieces, the poet invoked in a letter he wrote to Hansford Johnson towards the end of 1933, apologising for 'sending those three sheets of socialism', and adding 'I am not going to indulge in any more propaganda in this letter; I shall keep two or three red hot notes – along with a note on W. H. Auden, the Poet of Revolution – & send them to you next time' (*CL*, 64).[5]

RUINED BOYS

There is an ambiguity in Thomas's use of the Old Boy motif. On the one hand, he is the despised representative of 'the Old Gang' – a phrase from Auden's revolutionary/apocalyptic poem '1929', which Thomas used in a letter to Bert Trick in 1935, dismissing both 'the new Vanocs of Socialism and the bollocks of the old gang' (*CL*, 190). (In Arthurian legend, Vanoc was Merlin's son and successor.) But he can also assume a more endearingly raffish aspect. To

Trevor Hughes, Thomas wrote in 1934: 'There's muck in the soul of man, and a devil in his loins. God was deposed years ago, before the loin-cloth in the garden. Now the Old Boy reigns, with a red-hot pincers for a penis. Here's to him' (*CL*, 162). Thomas's Old Boy here is in reality the Old Adam, merged with Old Nick – more colloquially, and *pace* Edward Thomas's poem 'Old Man', a user-friendly way of referring to the phallus.

The same ambiguity obtains in the poem which opens Thomas's first volume, *Eighteen Poems*, published in December 1934. According to Bert Trick, 'walking on the beach, Thomas referred to middle-aged men in Corporation bathing suits as "boys of summer in their ruin" ' (*CP*, 178n.). The animus towards the 'boys of summer' is certainly in part a rejection of the generation of old buffers responsible for the War, 'clinging, for God and capital, to an outgrown and decaying system' (*CL*, 55), turning light into darkness, laying barren the harvest, freezing the soil, drowning the apples, curdling the milk and souring the honey. But it is more complex than a simple indictment of the Old by the New Boy. The poem was written in the spring of 1934, and first published in Geoffrey Grigson's *New Verse* in June of that year, a year after the second edition of Auden's *Poems*, which appeared in 1933. Its vision of desolation most immediately recalls the opening lines of a separately published sestina of Auden's of May 1933, 'Hearing of harvests rotting in the valleys'.[6] Thomas would have found particularly appealing the poem's incitement to rebel: ' "Now is the time to leave your wretched valleys ... forget your sorrow, / The shadow cast across your lives by mountains." '[7] In October 1933 a self-justifying letter to Hansford Johnson commended Auden as a model of 'conscious obscurity', writing 'valuable things, so complicated that even he who writes of them does not comprehend what he is writing', and went on, in a vein reminiscent of Auden's sestina, to attack farmers staring into their fires, 'thinking of God knows what littleness, or thinking of nothing at all but their own animal warmth', the 'miserably wet fields', and 'the industrial small towns ... each town a festering sore on the body of a dead country', concluding:

> All Wales is like this. It's impossible for me to tell you how much I want to get out of it all, out of narrowness and dirtiness, out of the eternal ugliness of the Welsh people, and all that belongs to them ... I shall have to get out soon or there will be no need. I'm sick, and this bloody country's killing me.
>
> (*CL*, 30)

But there are other precedents in Auden for the complex shifts which the phrase 'the boys of summer' effects. Syntactically, it moves from a dismissive third person (I see *them*) to a self-implicating first person plural in its second section, admitting that '*We* are the dark deniers . . . *We* summer boys', before, in its one-stanza conclusion, establishing a kind of vocative relation between seer and seen ('*I* see *you* boys of summer in *your* ruin'). This rhetorical address then forms the basis for a wider admission of personal complicity, compounding the generations, old boys and new boys, in a universal conjugation of ruin: '*I* am the man your father was. / *We* are the sons of flint and pitch' (*CP*, 8) (my emphasis).

'I see the boys of summer in their ruin' was placed first, a keynote text, in *Eighteen Poems*. It derives its central, determining trope – indeed, its first line – from the penultimate poem in Auden's even more laconically entitled *Poems*: 'Consider this and in our time'.[8] Auden's poem, like Thomas's, confuses its addressees and disorientates its speaker. Its opening lines address us, ordinary readers and citizens of Britain in the early 1930s. Its contempt for the smart women in furs, and the men in uniform seen through the plate-glass windows of the Sport Hotel, supplied with their feelings by an efficient band, would have spoken directly to Thomas, the sterile artificiality suggested by those carefully chosen words, 'Supplied' and 'efficient', sharpening a Lawrentian class loathing to which Thomas's bosom, more provincial and more lower middle class than Auden's, would have returned an immediate echo.[9] But, calling up our resentments, sense of exclusion and contempt in the first paragraph, the poem turns in its second section to a rather different addressee, a 'supreme Antagonist' who, long ago, in the high far places of Britain – Cornwall, the Mendips, the Pennines – led 'the highborn mining-captains', by his rebuffs to 'wish to die / Lie since in barrows out of harm'.[10] This 'supreme Antagonist' is none other than Thomas's 'Old Boy', that daemonic life-force which ensures that 'the old Dis-Order changeth, yielding to a new' (*CL*, 55).

Auden's supreme Antagonist, like Thomas's devilish Old Boy, is an amoral life-force that can never be finally defeated. He is already talking to his agents of revolt, by silted harbours, derelict works, in strangled orchard or silent combe, organising the ill – that is, the disaffected, the unreconciled – to attack, visiting the ports and – something that would have struck a chord with Thomas – 'interrupting / The leisurely conversation in the bar';[11] everywhere beckoning his chosen out. But isn't Auden himself the Antagonist here, his poem buttonholing Thomas like that bar-room mentor, Bert Trick, with apocalyptic talk of riot and revolution? Isn't Thomas himself one of 'Those handsome and diseased youngsters'[12] – well, in his own estimate, diseased, at least – summoned by this suasive voice? Isn't *he* one of the Revolution's 'solitary agents in the country parishes', himself one of the 'powerful forces latent / In soils that make the farmer brutal'?[13] Even the symptoms of a diseased body politic Auden evinces would speak to Thomas's hypochondria: immeasurable neurotic dread, fugues, irregular breathing, the explosion of mania, a classic fatigue.[14] The rumour of revolution, spreading, becomes 'a polar peril, a prodigious alarm' in Auden's poem, and is transformed into 'the poles of promise in the boys' (*CP*, 8) in Thomas's.

Auden's addressees change for a final time at the end of the poem, mutating into the financiers, college dons, all those affluent cultured types sleeping with people and playing fives whom Thomas also loathed, to whom it can be confidently proclaimed: 'The game is up for you and for the others'.[15] For:

> It is later than you think; nearer that day
> Far other than that distant afternoon
> Amid rustle of frocks and stamping feet
> They gave the prizes to the ruined boys.[16]

'That day': how Thomas's Chapel ancestry would respond to that phrase, in a country, in his words, 'where the Bible opens itself at Revelations' (*CL*, 557)! For what is 'That day' except the 'Dies Illa' of *Revelation*, 'Dies Irae', that day of wrath and retribution which in 1930 had a great deal more immediacy than St John's turgid imaginings, discussed so recently by Lawrence in his posthumously published book *Apocalypse*. (Both Latin phrases also provided the titles for poems in Lawrence's last collection of verse.) There is – on the surface – the idyllic, prelapsarian 'distant afternoon' of the school prize day, with the parents admiring their faultless hero sons. But, inside all this, there is already *ruin*, the boys corrupted both politically and sexually by their public school education, the Old Boy rampant.[17] The real lesson Thomas draws from Auden's volume lies in 'Consider''s fine's rapid telescoping of addressees, which he reproduces in 'I see the boys of summer'. It is not a matter of us and them: we *are* them. It is in our very ruin that, as he put it to Hansford Johnson, at once Cain and Judas, 'We, with the cross of a castrated Saviour cut on our brows', can become the 'manuring bones' of a new civilisation (*CL*, 54–6).

PERMANENT ADOLESCENCE

Thomas thought 'I see the boys of summer', along with 'When, like a running grave', 'the best poems in my book' (*CL*, 208). Significant, then, that the dominant trope in the latter should trace its lineage to another poem of Auden's, 'The Witnesses', first published in *The Listener* – a weekly Thomas read and was soon to publish in – in July 1933. The line 'Comes like a scissors stalking, tailor age' (*CP*, 19), in its syntactic inversions, echoes the cadences of early Auden. More significantly, 'The Witnesses' offers a specific warrant for its deployment of the story of *Struwwelpeter*. Thomas records variously his early acquaintance with that nightmarish story, writing of '*Struwwelpeter* – oh! the baby-burning flames and the clacking scissorman!' in 'Memories of Christmas', as well as in 'Return Journey' in *Quite Early One Morning* (see *CP*, 188n.). Auden too, in various memoirs, records his childhood fascination with the fate of 'little Suck-a-Thumb', with its veiled castration threat to masturbators and nail-biters alike. But 'The Witnesses' gave the story a new and contemporary urgency, as the emblem of a generation's angst, anxiety and anger: 'now with sudden swift emergence / Come the women in dark glasses, the hump- / Backed surgeons / and the scissor-man.'[18] Auden's poem opens with a jeering call to dowagers, peers, solicitors and bishops, reporters coming home at dawn, etcetera, to consider the story of Prince Alpha, the boy who had everything – hero, adventurer, lover – but who finally sank down in the desert, to ask, despairingly, why he was born if it 'was it only to see / I'm as tired of life as life of me?'[19] Disaffected from his very identity, Prince Alpha gives up, and dies. He is, in fact, the archetypal ruined boy of summer. In the same way, the self of Thomas's poem 'Stride[s] through Cadaver's country in [his] force', only to confront failure in 'Love's twilit nation and the skull of state', for this 'Sir, is your doom' (*CP*, 20); and the poem ends, like Auden's, with an apocalyptic generalising of that doom. 'When like a running grave', inspired by the insistent vocatives of Auden's first volume, fulfils the concluding command of that volume, in 'Sir, no man's enemy', to 'Harrow the house of the dead':[20]

When like a running grave, time tracks you down,
Your calm and cuddled is a scythe of hairs,
Love in her gear is slowly through the house,
Up naked stairs, a turtle in a hearse,
Hauled to the dome,

Comes, like a scissors stalking, tailor age . . .
(CP, 19)

For Thomas, however, the house of the dead is not simply the external world, where we are dying as we live, but the body itself, Hopkins's 'bone house, mean house',[21] worn as the turtle wears its shell (for a hearse is yet a home). The running – that is, the living – man ('There is a book who runs may read')[22] is his own running grave, never stepping twice in the same running temporal stream. The naked stairs he climbs are those of the body, ascending to the dome of the skull, taking death for companion, for he is at once 'Chaste and chaser' (CP, 20) (an ingrown virgin / a hunter of self), 'barer' (more naked) and 'bearer' (carrier) of his own death (CP, 19). Time/death is not only a tailor, measuring one's final suit with his 'footed tape' (CP, 19); he is also a midwife and, even, a thaumaturge/saviour, as with that repeated call to 'Deliver me, my masters, head and heart' (CP, 19–20).

If 'The Witnesses' provides a key figure for 'When, like a running grave', Auden's 'Doom is dark' feeds into its overall narrative strategy, tone and vocabulary, particularly in its closing appeal to protect 'His anxious house where days are counted' from 'gradual ruin spreading like a stain', and to 'Bring joy, bring day of his returning, / Lucky with day approaching, with learning dawn'.[23] Thomas's poem, however, rejects the possibility of 'joy'. Joy is simply 'the knock of dust' (CP, 20), dusty death knocking to enter, the knock on the door at midnight, but also, playing on the colloquial sexual meaning of knocking ('knocked up', 'knocking shop'), reworking the Renaissance trope of the sexual act as a *petite mort*, a little death, each act a step on the winding stair of the great big death outside. 'Cadaver's shoot / Of bud of Adam' (CP, 20) is then both a bud of Adam's stock and a spurt of Adam's seed.

According to Walford Davies and Ralph Maud, the keystone of Thomas's second volume, 'I, in my intricate image', first printed in *New Verse* in autumn 1935, grew out of 'When, like a running grave'. Its opening stanza is full of echoes of early Auden, particularly in its persona of 'the brassy orator, / Laying my ghost in metal'

(*CP*, 33), which recalls not only Auden's *Orators* (of 1932 and 1934), but also the 'communist orator' of 'The chimneys are smoking', published in *New Country* in 1933.[24] It also develops the theme of striding to a doom:

> I, in my intricate image, stride on two levels.
> Forged in man's minerals, the brassy orator
> Laying my ghost in metal.
> The scales of this twin world tread on the double.
> My half ghost in armour hold hard in death's corridor,
> To my man-iron sidle.
>
> Beginning with doom in the bulb, the spring unravels . . .
> (*CP*, 33)

But there are even richer echoes and allegiances here. The image of the human subject as some kind of ghost, so frequent in these poems, is ubiquitous in early Auden, quintessentially so in the verse charade from *Poems*, 'Paid on Both Sides', which sees each new-born son as a 'new ghost' inserted into the patriarchal culture, 'Learn[ing] from old termers what death is, where'.[25] From 'Paid on Both Sides' comes, too, the emphasis on duality, also to be found in 'The Witnesses' and in one of the most contortedly Hopkinsian poems of *Poems*, 'Bones wrenched', which speaks of the self constructed out of a 'two-faced dream'.[26] Linking all three poems of Thomas's already mentioned is a passage in 'Paid' which casts the son as a conscripted victim of the patriarchal culture to which he is born, in John Nower's central, self-discovering soliloquy beginning 'Always the following wind of history'. Here, speaking of coming upon pockets of silence where 'Is nothing loud but us', beyond the lies 'Our fathers shouted once', the young Nower envisages 'that soon-arriving day' when it will no longer be possible to gaze in delight on a face or an idea, as did the 'simpleton' who lived

> Before disaster sent his runners here;
> Younger than worms, worms have too much to bear.
> Yes, mineral were best . . .[27]

In response to the vision of a once 'lively world' now rendered 'Sterile as moon', the Chorus interrupts to proclaim that

> The Spring unsettles sleeping partnerships,
> Foundries improve their casting process . . .

> . . . In summer boys grow tall
> With running races on the froth-wet sand . . .[28]

The boys of summer, loud and brassy orators, wait in their ruin in the unravelling spring for 'that soon-arriving day' (note too the imagery of worms, minerals and forging metal), listen impatiently for the approach of disaster's runners.

Looking back on the decade in 1938, Auden's friend, and subsequently Thomas's, Cyril Connolly in *Enemies of Promise* adumbrated a 'Theory of Permanent Adolescence' to account for the decline of the West, detecting among his contemporaries, products of the great public schools, a state of arrested development which left 'the greater part of the ruling class . . . adolescent' and, already, in their early thirties, 'haunted ruins'.[29] But if there is going to be a race for ruined boys, the grammar school Dylan can outrun, out-ruin, the public school Wystan any day.

A BOY WHO HAD LITERARY PRETENSIONS

Fashionably 'ruined boys', however, turn into unfashionable ruined men. In 1933, contemplating in *The Use of Poetry and the Use of Criticism* the addictions in which poets flee their talent, T. S. Eliot wrote of Coleridge as 'a haunted man, a ruined man'; but added, with a knowing twinkle, 'Sometimes, however, to be a "ruined man" is itself a vocation'.[30] Or, as Thomas wrote in 'I make this in a warring absence', 'Ruin, the room of errors . . . is my proud pyramid' (*CP*, 69).

As Constantine Fitzgibbon notes of Thomas, the image of himself as the damned and dying boy-poet of romantic tradition had a great appeal to him, an appeal he made the most of to impress others, though often for Thomas it was couched in a distinctly modern, mock-heroic mode. He wrote to Pamela Hansford Johnson in May 1934 'to think of me today not as a bewildered little boy writing an idiot letter' (*CL*, 136). But even while playing the ruined boy, Thomas was aware of the prospect Eliot had delineated, by turns contemptuous and brazen about his own posturing. To Trevor Hughes he wrote in January 1934, 'Once upon a time there was a boy who had Literary Pretensions'; but 'The boy, very suddenly, became disgusted with the mental disease of his country, the warped apathy of his countrymen, and of the essentially freakish nature of himself' (*CL*, 90). To Henry Treece in June 1938 he objected, he said, not to Michael Roberts's comment in the *London*

Mercury about him making a ' "schoolboy exhibition", for I'm not afraid of showing off or throwing my cap in the air', but to the 'patronising "pity" ' of Roberts's piece (*CL*, 301). In May 1939 he had second thoughts about schoolboy exhibitions, writing to Treece of an interview he had given, 'cut out that remark of mine about "I have a beast and an angel in me" or whatever it was; it makes me sick, drives me away from drink, recalls too much the worst of the fat and curly boy I know too well, he whose promises are water and whose water's Felinfoel, that nut-brown prince' (*CL*, 373) (Felinfoel is a Welsh beer). The 'ruined boy' soon transmutes into what Constantine Fitzgibbon calls 'the pattern of the *enfant terrible*', which in turn spawns 'that of the boy with the load o' beer'.[31]

To establish his literary pretensions as the new boy of poetry, Thomas had to slay the poetic father; which meant Auden. His thirties letters are full of the note of repudiation. He wrote to Trevor Hughes in January 1934, picking up the last words of 'Sir, no man's enemy': 'Does one need "New styles of architecture, a change of heart"? Does one not need a new consciousness of the old universal architecture and a tearing away from the old heart of the things that have clogged it?' (*CL*, 93).

On New Year's Eve 1938 he penned a new year resolution which declared its independence of Auden in more concrete terms, as it simultaneously refused to sign the New Apocalypse manifesto sent him by Treece:

> I cannot see how Auden is unaware of Donald Duck, unless Donald Duck is supposed to be a symbol and not a funny bird. Donald Duck is just what Auden is aware of . . . Auden often writes like Disney. Like Disney he knows the shapes of beasts . . . Unlike Lawrence, he does not know what motivates or shapes those beasts. He's a naturalist who looks for beasts that resemble himself, and, failing that, he tries to shape them in his own curious image.
>
> (*CL*, 348)

And, he adds, by way of an afterthought, still thinking about Lawrence, 'I like the title "Apocalypse: The Dissolute Man" more than yours.' It's a good point about Auden, but its main function here is symbolic assassination, overthrowing the unitary ego of those cryptic, self-circling early Auden poems – which seek in the external world fit emblems of their own inner state – with a more open, dissolute being. It's here that Thomas's idea of ruin goes beyond Auden's. Far from being a necessary *prelude* to revolution and renewal, ruin *is* the new order of things, a state of permanent, fecund anarchy for a subject that has overthrown the superego's internal patriarch, and realised that state of being of which he wrote to 'Comrade Fisher' in 1935, in which poetry would be 'as orgiastic and organic as copulation, dividing and unifying, personal but not private, propagating the individual in the mass and the mass in the individual' (*CL*, 182).

It might seem presumptuous for Thomas, of all people, to accuse Auden of obscurity; but presumption, for an heir presumptive, is the name of the game. Writing to Glyn Jones in March 1934, he attacks, 'As a Socialist myself', Auden's most recent poems as 'neither good poetry nor propaganda', and, in discussing the ways various modern writers have dislocated language, he accuses Auden of having neglected his audience, cutting out all words that seem unnecessary, and producing poems 'written in an imaginative shorthand' (*CL*, 97–8). This approach he compares with that of Arthur Rimbaud, who has, he says, 'introduced exclusively personal symbols and associations so that reading him and his satellites, we feel as though we were intruding into a private party in which nearly every sentence has a family meaning that escapes us' (*CL*, 98).

This is not a fortuitous linking. From Donald Duck to that old *canard*, 'the Rimbaud of Cwmdonkin Drive' is not far, as the duck waddles. For all his periodic denials of knowing any French poetry, Thomas on various occasions implies an at least superficial knowledge of Rimbaud, and I'd concur with Davies's and Maud's conviction, in the notes to the *Collected Poems*, that he had 'undoubtedly read Norman Cameron's translation of Rimbaud's "*Bateau ivre*" ("The Drunken Boat") in *New Verse* (June–July 1936)' (*CP*, 247n.), which they see as an influence on his 'Ballad of the Long-legged Bait'. But, if Rimbaud assumes any significance for Thomas, I would suggest, it is one mediated by Auden's ideology of ruin.

[NB: A section on Rimbaud's influence on Dylan Thomas, as mediated by Auden, has been omitted at this point for reasons of space.]

VOYAGE TO RUIN

What 'Poem on his Birthday' (published in *In Country Sleep* in 1952) calls 'The voyage to ruin I must run' (*CP*, 146) took on a new urgency in the last decade or so of Thomas's life. The original version of the poem 'When I woke', written for the little magazine *Seven* in the autumn of 1939 (but not finished in time to appear in that issue), ended, as war approached, with a vision of collective ruin:

> Shaking humanity's houses:
> Wake to see one morning breaking:
> Bulls and wolves in iron palaces;
> Winds in their nests in the ruins of man.
>   (CP, 244n.)

The postwar version, in *Deaths and Entrances*, substitutes a more upbeat personal ending, in which the coins on his eyelids, signifying death, break into new life and '[sing] like shells' (CP, 112). This bravado is recurrent.

The punning play on 'prodigal son' is one Thomas made himself in 'Holy Spring', sent to Vernon Watkins in November 1944 as a poem 'which I started a long time ago but finished very recently' (CL, 532). Davies and Maud trace its origin to a notebook of February 1933, and it exhibits many signs of the Auden ethos of sons wounded and ruined by the struggle of the generations:

>   And ruin and his causes
>   Over the barbed and shooting sea assumed an army
>   And swept into our wounds and houses,
>   I climb to greet the war in which I have no heart but only
>   That one dark I owe my light,
>   And I am struck as lonely as a holy maker by the sun.
>   (CP, 133)

The last line of this first stanza, as published in *Deaths and Entrances*, foregrounds aloneness, and 'maker' alludes not only to God but to the old Scottish term for poet (a 'makar'). 'Sun' here leads on to the punning play of the second, final stanza, with its cluster of Biblical allusions, one of them mediated by Anthony Trollope's joke about that prodigal and prolific father, the reverend Quiverfull:

>   My arising prodigal
>   Sun the father his quiver full of the infants of pure fire,
>   But blessed be hail and upheaval
>   That uncalm still it is sure alone to stand and sing
>   Alone in the husk of man's home
>   And the mother and toppling house of the holy spring,
>   If only for a last time.
>   (CP, 133)

But if the sun father is prodigal in his bounty, the son is a prodigal, wasting his gifts. ('Prodigal', applied to the father rather than the son, finds its precedent in Auden's appeal to the patriarch in 'Sir, no man's enemy' to 'be prodigal'.[32]) In a variant printed by Davies and Maud, that line concerns not the loneliness of the long-distance maker, but Thomas's deepest terror – being silenced: 'And I am struck as dumb as cannonfire by the sun' (*CP*, 248n.). In this variant the singing of stanza two is followed not by a further reference to aloneness, but by a reiterated anxiety about being struck

> Dumb by the chanted blaze
> By the mother and showering voice of the mortal spring
> Hail and upheaval of the judge-blown drowned of the sun
> (*CP*, 249n.)

The prodigal son, in collusion with the mother, judges and drowns the father, cancels his singing. But this son is not principally the boy Dylan. In the poem's palimpsest of complexes, Oedipus has given way to Chronos. The rebellious 1930s prodigal has taken on the chronic anxiety of the 1940s patriarch, 'fathered' (that is, turned into a father) by the birth of a son who is a rival for the mother's love.

Judged and found wanting, the father stands alone in the possession of a 'toppling house' (*CP*, 133), and, Chronos-like, contemplates the symbolic infanticide of the rising generation. The myth of Chronos, in which Time devours his children to avoid castration and usurpation by them, lies behind much of the imagery of the early poems. In particular, it elucidates the cryptic and apparently contradictory reference in 'Then was my neophyte' to 'the masked, headless boy' (*CP*, 57). The allusion is, I think, to Goya's famous picture of Chronos devouring a son, 'headless' because his head is already 'masked' by the father's jaws. The poem adopts the persona of the neophyte, ending 'I saw time murder me' (*CP*, 58), and in all these early poems, though the son acknowledges that he is father and 'ascending boy' (*CP*, 42) in one, it is the latter whose voice takes precedence. From the birth of Thomas's son Llewelyn onwards, however, it is the distraction of the declining father which dominates the poems, whether in those numerous narcissistic birthday odes for himself – almost a separate genre in Thomas's work – which chart his years to heaven, or projecting a vicarious frisson on to his grief for a dying father, or imparting a disturbing animus to those in which he addresses with fatherly benediction an infant son.

Symbolic infanticide: strong words. But 'This side of the truth', for a poem addressed to a six-year-old child, is disturbingly replete with presage of the boy's death. Its first stanza stresses the child's ignorance 'That all is undone' already, and ends amidst 'the dust of the dead' (*CP*, 88–9). The second opens with 'two ways / Of moving about your death' (*CP*, 89) which, tellingly, point forward to the idiom of 'Do not go gentle':

> Go crying through you and me
> And the souls of all men
> Into the innocent
> Dark, and the guilty dark, and good
> Death, and bad death
>
> (*CP*, 89)

The final stanza speaks of 'the wicked wish' which is 'cast before you move', concluding that 'all your deeds and words . . . / Die in unjudging love' (*CP*, 89). Though the last word of the poem is 'love', I cannot myself avoid the suspicion of a darker, Chronos-like animus towards the usurping child in that 'Die', isolated almost as a command. The father who wishes to remain a boy half admits to a 'wicked wish' for the death of this challenge to his patriarchal authority. His consolation is that the king is not yet dead, for his son is as yet a puny pretender, no more than 'king of your six years'. Paul Ferris, Thomas's biographer, confirms this filicidal rivalry in Thomas, observing, of his second son, Colm, 'his new-born son he "detested", because he was jealous of him'.[33]

'This side of the truth' comes immediately after 'A Refusal to Mourn' and 'Poem in October' in *Deaths and Entrances* and it throws a retrospective light back on both, suggesting that their pairing is not merely fortuitous. For if the death of the child in 'A Refusal' at the hands of a 'Fathering and all humbling darkness' (*CP*, 85) is not something to be mourned, the anti-elegist's outliving of the child is clearly a cause for celebration (which is what the poem becomes). The 'elegy of innocence and youth' (*CP*, 86) refused here finds full throat in 'Poem in October' – another birth-day poem in which, in his thirtieth year to heaven, the lost boy is reborn, to delight that, in the twice-telling of the bardic voice, once again 'the true / Joy of the long dead child sang burning / In the sun' (*CP*, 88).

The hidden agenda of all these poems is indicated in the first poem Thomas wrote for an as yet unborn Llewelyn in late 1938. 'A saint about to fall' evokes the neoplatonism of Wordsworth's 'Immortality Ode' (the only Wordsworth poem he admitted liking); for, as Thomas wrote to Desmond Hawkins, it concerns 'a saint about to fall, *to be born*, to fall from a visionary heaven into original sin', so that the heavenly apartment houses are 'all discoloured by the grief of his going, ruined for ever by his departure (for heaven must fall with every falling saint)' (*CL*, 398). Yet the son's 'making and unmaking' is also 'the dissolution of his father's house', 'the last feathers of his fatherlands' (*CL*, 398). The making of the child, that is, is the unmaking of the father who, no longer a boy, confronts his own supersession. One can chart this evolution by contrasting the 1933 poem about Thomas's own prenatal existence, 'Before I knocked', with, a mere six years later, 'If my head hurt a hair's foot', which reruns this prenatal scenario for the unborn Llewelyn. In 'Before I knocked' the embryo Dylan is metaphorically a suit of armour forged on the anvil of the mother's womb by 'the rainy hammer / Swung by my father', a 'mortal ghost' whose 'last / Long breath . . . carried to my father / The message of his dying christ' (*CP*, 11–12). 'If my head . . .', however, is couched as a dialogue between mother and unborn child from which the father is conspicuously absent, and the 'fathering worm' of the earlier poem has transmogrified into 'the worm of the ropes' (*CP*, 80) of the umbilical cord. The father has absconded, denying paternity claims. Today, he would have had a Poetic Child Support Agency knocking at the womb door.[34]

THE HELL WITH HIM

In May 1934, having estranged Pamela Hansford Johnson, to whom he was then engaged, with a boastful confession of sexual misdemeanour, Thomas whined in self-exoneration, 'I'm in a dreadful mess now . . . I'm absolutely at the point of breaking now . . . with my nerves oh darling absolutely at the point of breaking into little bits . . . It's *all* nerves and more . . . I'm just on the borders of D.T.s darling' (*CL*, 139–40). In a sense, the case of Dylan Thomas *is* a case of the DTs, insofar as such extremities of addictive self-

abuse, in our postmodern age classed along with such other symptoms as self-mutilation, bulimia, anorexia nervosa, etcetera, arise
from a deep discontent in the very construction of the subject, an
autodestructive punishment of self just for being which is the
obverse of that revelling in ruination, disassemblage and decon-
structive plurality with which Thomas's poetry runs riot. The title
poem of *In Country Sleep* writes large that insidious agent of self-
destruction, *Struwwelpeter*, as the Thief that comes in the night.
According to Paul Ferris, Thomas explained to a New York jour-
nalist: 'Alcohol is the thief today. But tomorrow he could be fame
or success or exaggerated introspection or self-analysis. The thief is
anything that robs you of your faith, of your reason for being.'[35]
   The immediate source of the image is, of course, Paul's first letter
to the Thessalonians (1, 5:2): 'For yourselves know perfectly that
the day of the Lord so cometh like a thief in the night.' It is, in fact,
'that day', *dies illa*, the day of reckoning for every fallen saint.
Thomas spelt it out in a prose note for the poem:

> If you believe (and fear) that every night, night without end, the
> Thief comes to try to steal your faith that every night he comes to
> steal your faith that your faith is there – then you will wake with
> your faith steadfast and deathless.
>   If you are innocent of the Thief, you are in danger. If you are inno-
> cent of the loss of faith, you cannot be faithful. If you do not know
> the Thief as well as you know God, then you do not know God well.
> Christian looked through a hole in the floor of heaven and saw hell.
> You must look through faith, and see disbelief.
>
>   (CP, 251–2)

Which is to say that to avoid final ruination you have perpetually to
court ruin, to sink into ruin, for renewal is only possible through
self-destruction. But that identification of the Thief not only with
alcohol or (in another explanation) jealousy but with 'fame or
success or exaggerated introspection or self-analysis' – the latter
close, in Thomas's early letters, to self-abuse – suggests other links,
recalls, most pointedly, 'that day far other . . . / They gave the prizes
to the ruined boys'.
   If, as has been suggested by various critics, this poem is addressed
to his wife Caitlin and not his daughter Aeronwy, it would confirm
my suspicion that one of the texts it echoes is Auden's 'A Bride in
the 30s'. The latter speaks of the bride's 'flesh and bone / These
ghosts would like to make their own'. It sees the 'innocent' 'wooed'
by forces of betrayal, and laments the power that corrupts 'all who

long for their destruction, / The arrogant and self-insulted'. It imagines love's looks being fed in 'the sterile farms'.[36] Thomas's poem contrariwise refers to 'the rind / And mire of love' 'in the ruttish farm' (*CP*, 140). It speaks of the bride's face as 'The pool of silence and the tower of grace',[37] and Thomas's call to 'lie in grace' is associated with similar imagery. And it ends with fear of betrayal, the presage of doom, and the Pauline image of love moving 'Crooked . . . as a moneybug or a cancer'[38] – recalled, I would suggest, in Thomas's 'Be you sure the Thief will seek a way sly and sure' (*CP*, 140). But this is mediated, compounded, by another poem of Auden's, first published in *New Country*, with the 'communist orator' landing at the pier,

> And since our desire cannot take that route which is straightest,
> Let us choose the crooked, so implicating these acres,
> These millions in whom already the wish to be one
>   Like a burglar is stealthily moving.[39]

Auden's 'ungovernable sea'[40] in this poem is directly reversed in Thomas's phrase, 'the dew's ruly sea' (*CP*, 142), while Auden's 'We ride a turning globe'[41] is converted into 'the turning of the earth in her holy / Heart! Slyly, slowly, hearing the wound in her side go / Round the sun' (*CP*, 142).

In Auden's poem, Eros, the life force, moves slyly and crookedly like a thief in the night, and *that day* will come for all, whether ushered in by alcohol, fame or success, when this cupidity will stand forth not as Eros but as Thanatos, the death drive. Ruin itself, in fact, *is* the ultimate prize awaiting the ruined boys. With a certain romantic melodrama, Constantine Fitzgibbon places at the end of his *Selected Letters of Dylan Thomas* a letter which, he concedes, may not have been written in 1953 at all, but in either of the two preceding years, and may not even have been sent. It is yet another of Thomas's apologies to the Princess Caetani for his insufferable rudeness in not replying to her letters or producing the work he had promised, and been paid for, for her journal *Botteghe Oscure*. Whenever it was written, its suggestion of an escapologist at the end of his tether means that it can only read now like a last will and testament, or even a deathbed confession:

> Why do I bind myself always to these imbecile grief-knots, blindfold my eyes with lies, wind my brass music around me, sew myself in a sack, weight it with guilt and pig-iron, then pitch me squealing to

sea, so that time and time again I must wrestle out and unravel in a panic, like a seaslugged windy Houdini, and ooze and eel up wheezily, babbling, and blowing black bubbles, from all the claws and bars and bars and breasts of the mantrapped seabed? . . .

What can I tell you? Why did I bray my brassy nought to you from this boygreen briny dark? I see myself down and out on the sea's ape-blue bottom: a manacled rhetorician with a wet trombone, up to his blower in crabs.

Why must I parable my senseless silence? My one long trick? My last dumb flourish? . . . no, I must blare my engulfment in pomp and fog, spout a nuisance of fountains like a bedwetting what in a blanket, and harangue all land-walkers as though it were their shame that I sought the sucking sea and cast myself out of their sight to blast down to the dark. It is not enough to presume that once again I shall weave up pardoned, my wound dim around me rusty . . . as musical and wan and smug as an Orpheus of the storm: no, I must first defeat any hope I might have of forgiveness by resubmerging the little arisen original monster in a porridge boiling of wrong words and make a song and dance and a mockpoem of all his fishy excuses.

The hell with him.

(CL, 915–16)[42]

Ultimate self-disenchantment, or another mockpoem of excuses? But note that play on Orpheus/orphan of the storm: the disassembled poet, his senses systematically deranged by drink, now only, in Rimbaud's terms, 'a manacled rhetorician' blowing his own trombone, finding his vocation in ruin. This ruined boy is a ruined boyo, yes, but he is also an aborted being, down with all the other self-slaughtered embryos in the 'boygreen briny dark' – for what is this sea, what is this sack of the self in which he is sewn, Houdini-like, except a strangling birth caul, become a shroud, that image from his earliest poems? And his life, this 'one long trick', 'a blind bag' in which he is 'lashed and bandaged', is that of a 'bedwetting what', something he cannot even name – a child or an old man, or just a speechless, blind imbecile of a grown man – a ruined boy, orphaned, drowned, 'the little arisen original monster'.[43]

NOTES

[Stan Smith's essay began life as a keynote paper presented at the Dylan Thomas Conference held in Swansea in 1998 and has already appeared in the Delhi journal, *In-between*, 7:1 (March 1998), published in December 1999. In it Smith argues that the young Thomas cast himself in consciously

Freudian terms as the new, 'ascending boy' overthrowing, but in the process becoming, the 'Old Boy' Auden – his future ruin, as patriarch, thus latent in his present, neophyte state – and traces the implications of this paradigm in a wide-ranging and sophisticated intertextual discussion. Thomas's and Auden's early poetry is forced to yield a dense network of allusions, parallels, shared tropes and items of vocabulary. Beginning with Thomas's literary relations with the poetic father/brother Auden, the essay moves to a more general exploration of the father/child nexus in the poems. This looks back to Thomas's own dominating schoolmaster father and forward to the threat which, for Smith, Thomas found in his own son, indicating the kind of crisis of 'permanent adolescence' identified by Cyril Connolly in all writers of the 1930s and discerned in Thomas's prose writings by Jeni Williams (essay 9). For Smith, the 'revelling' in ruin which characterises the earlier work has as its 'obverse' an addictive and self-punitive urge, Eros becoming Thanatos (or the 'Thief' of 'In Thomas's 'In country sleep'), which emerges to dominate fatally Thomas's last years. In his impressive, historicist study of twentieth-century poetry *Inviolable Voice: History and Twentieth Century Poetry* of 1982, Smith had made no provision for Thomas in his discussion of mid-century poetry. In this essay, however, while continuing to stress the centrality of Auden to our understanding of the time, he corrects that omission. In doing so he gives a new (and characteristically stylish) extension to his coverage of the dynamics of the period, one which remains informed by a detailed awareness of historical crisis and the complexity of its literary mediations. Eds]

1. The comments were included with a letter of 7 September 1937, to the editor of *New Verse*, Geoffrey Grigson, for inclusion in the forthcoming Auden issue: the postscript is taken from the letter itself (*CL*, 259).

2. W. H. Auden, *The English Auden: Poems, Essays and Dramatic Writings 1927–1939*, ed. Edward Mendelson (London, 1977), p. 62.

3. Ibid., p. 61.

4. *Rude Assignment: An Intellectual Autobiography* (1950), reprinted, ed. Toby Foshay (Santa Barbara, CA, 1984), p. 37. A confusion in Wyndham Lewis's annotations makes the attribution of this quotation unclear. His text attributes it to the Sorelian Edouard Berth, but a confused and clearly incorrect footnote attributes it to Georges Sorel himself, in *Les illusions du progrès*, while a footnote over the page cites *La Ruine du Monde Antique* (Paris, 1925), p. xxiv. For the purposes of this argument the attribution is neither here nor there.

5. Thomas's identification with Auden in this capacity is indicated by a letter to Pamela Hansford Johnson in October 1934, about a reading he gave to Swansea's John O'London's Literary Society: 'The Chairman, a big-bellied bore, introduced me as a Young Revolutionary (I was becomingly clad in red) . . . The more I see of

Wales the more I think it's a land completely peopled by perverts. I don't exclude myself' (*CL*, 171–2).

6. Auden, *The English Auden*, p. 135.

7. Ibid., p. 136.

8. Ibid., p. 46.

9. He wrote apologetically to Geoffrey Grigson, in August 1933: 'I have developed, intellectually at least, in the smug darkness of a provincial town' (*CL*, 19).

10. Auden, *The English Auden*, p. 47.

11. Ibid.

12. Ibid.

13. Ibid.

14. Ibid.

15. Ibid.

16. Ibid.

17. I have discussed this aspect of Auden's work in Stan Smith, 'Ruined Boys: Auden in the 1930s', in *British Poetry, 1900–50: Aspects of Tradition*, ed. Gary Day and Brian Docherty (London, 1995), pp. 109–30.

18. Auden, *The English Auden*, p. 130.

19. Ibid., pp. 126–8.

20. Ibid., p. 36.

21. Gerard Manley Hopkins, 'The Caged Skylark', in *Gerard Manley Hopkins: Poems and Prose*, ed. W. H. Gardner (Harmondsworth, 1987), p. 31.

22. The reference is to Habakkuk, ii, 2: 'And the LORD answered me, and said, Write the vision, and make *it* plain upon tables, that he may run that readeth it', meaning that the works of God (that is, the world) make his glory so plain that even a 'running' man cannot help but be aware of it. It is the first line of the well-known hymn 'Creation and Providence'; see also 'Run' in *Brewer's Dictionary of Phrase and Fable*.

23. Auden, *The English Auden*, pp. 55–6.

24. Ibid., pp. 116–18.

25. Ibid., p. 2.

26. Ibid., p. 21.

27. Ibid., p. 7.

28. Ibid.

29. Cyril Connolly, *Enemies of Promise* (Harmondsworth, 1979), p. 271.

30. T. S. Eliot, *The Use of Poetry and the Use of Criticism: Studies in the Relation of Criticism to Poetry in England* (London, 1933), p. 69.

31. Dylan Thomas, *The Selected Letters of Dylan Thomas*, ed. Constantine Fitzgibbon (London, 1966), p. 140.

32. Auden, *The English Auden*, p. 36.

33. Paul Ferris, *Dylan Thomas* (London, 1978), p. 266.

34. A letter cited by Vernon Watkins in *Dylan Thomas: Letters to Vernon Watkins* (London, 1957), p. 55, suggests how closely the birth of a son and the death of the poet-patriarch were associated in Dylan's mind. Writing on 1 February 1939, four days after Yeats's death, he pronounces the interloper's patronym in a brutally unpaternal and dismissive neuter, moving instantly to his own deeper preoccupation, the always premature death of poets, and their unborn poems lost in the womb of time: 'This is just to tell you that Caitlin & I have a son aged 48 hours. Its name is Llewelyn Thomas . . . It does not like the world. Caitlin is well, & beautiful. I'm sorry Yeats is dead. What a loss of the great poems he would write. Aged 73, he died in his prime.'

35. Paul Ferris, *Dylan Thomas*, pp. 226–7.

36. Given as 'XXII' in 'Poems 1931–1936', Part IV of *The English Auden*, pp. 154, 152.

37. Ibid., p. 153.

38. Ibid., p. 154.

39. Ibid., p. 118.

40. Ibid.

41. Ibid., p. 116.

42. This seems to recall consciously or unconsciously what now seems like a prophetic letter to Pamela Hansford Johnson, on Christmas Day, 1933: 'I should like to be somewhere very wet, preferably under the sea, green as a merman, with cyclamine crabs on my shoulders, and the skeleton of a commercial magnate floating, Desdemona-wise, past me; but I should like to be very much alive under the sea, so that the moon, shining through the crests of the waves, would be a beautiful pea-green' (*CL*, 82).

43. I should record, however, that Paul Ferris transcribes what Fitzgibbon reads as 'what' ('a bedwetting what in a blanket') as 'whale', which

certainly makes sense in context, but lacks the chutzpah of Fitzgibbon's version (*Dylan Thomas*, p. 325). Whether there is any subliminal significance in the fact that both versions share the initials of the name W. H. Auden, by this time another beached and boozy leviathan, now lies beyond conjecture.

2

'The Lips of Time'

STEWART CREHAN

How does one begin to contextualise the poetry of Dylan Thomas? Or is such an enterprise not wholly perverse? What are the social and historical dimensions of his poetry? Or is historicising what has successfully defied history not a repressive and destructive activity? A poet does not, of course, have to refer in the manner of a John Betjeman or a Philip Larkin to 'unpoetic' items such as dancing pumps and cycle clips in order to prove his social awareness, or write about pylons and express trains like Stephen Spender, or, to quote an extreme example of despondently humdrum English realism, write a poem like Alan Brownjohn's 'A202', praised as a 'fine poem' by Jonathan Raban for the way it mimics, 'like an indifferent mirror, suffocating in its own realism', the 'sludgy progress' of the road itself.[1] Still, as Elder Olson put it, the age demanded poetry with a social reference, and 'the poetry of Thomas, quite obviously, had no social reference'.[2]

From the outset, Dylan Thomas rejected the poetic model whereby rhyme and metre, image and metaphor are employed primarily as a means of shaping and 'dressing' – as one might dress a hedge, or a person – observations and reflections derived from ordinary experience. Thomas's poetic creed was to make poems *out of* words rather than working *towards* words; to bring to light a submerged, 'unsentimental' reality through his 'craft or art' rather than using poetic devices to shape and dress essentially mundane or prosaic thoughts. Instead of describing visual objects, the true poet for Thomas treats words themselves as objects. Obsessive themes run through Thomas's first three collections, yet only two poems, 'My world is pyramid'

46

and 'After the funeral (In memory of Ann Jones)', have thematic titles. The titles of the others are taken from the first lines, few of which really tell us what the poem is 'about'. Thomas seems to have embarked on many of his poems equipped, not with a preconceived theme or subject, an 'idea for a poem', but with intrinsically poetic material: with words and phrases, sounds and sound patterns, images and image clusters that emanated from deep psychic sources, and which formed part of an evolving symbolic universe. The charges of escapism and what Vernon Watkins called a 'rooted opposition to material progress'[3] also fit in well with the picture of a man given to nostalgic indulgence, 'pitying himself for ever growing up', fixated on the delights of an over-protected infancy and childhood and therefore unable to bear 'that pain of coming-to-terms with the conditions of life that maturity is',[4] a picture which David Holbrook painted in 1962. The fascination with the sound of words from the time of innocence[5] is explained as the irresponsible fixation of a man who, at heart, remained a babbling infant: 'in its very oral sensationalism, in its very meaninglessness, [poetry] represented for him and his readers a satisfying return to infancy'.[6] Analogously, his disdain for 'poets in uniform' (CL, 310) like Auden might be compared with John Malcolm Brinnin's conclusion that, while Thomas 'was actually far more censorious of the *status quo* than any of the other British poets', his 'emotional identification with the lowest stratum of society' [was a gesture] 'uncontaminated by the *realpolitik* of the twentieth century' and 'unsupported by knowledge'.[7]

The view that Dylan Thomas's poetry tells us nothing of value about the contemporary world rests on four assumptions. The first is that Thomas's subject-matter (birth, death, man and the cosmos) is purely metaphysical. The second is that poetry 'expresses' its author. The legend of Dylan Thomas as the wild bohemian, in part a self-protective public persona, deceived many of those ignorant of his meticulous working methods into believing that his poetry was a spontaneous and irrational outpouring. He told Henry Treece: 'My selfish carelessness and unpunctuality I do not try to excuse as poet's properties. They are a bugbear and a humbug' (CL, 347). Yet some critics and commentators insisted on the formula: bad man = bad art. The 'recurring slide from text to author'[8] noted by Catherine Belsey as characteristic of Leavis's criticism is seen in Holbrook's condemnation of Thomas's irresponsibility, lack of control, and failure to 'organise deeply felt experience', Leavisite categories whose moralistic animus could take in the man, his public image, his work and his working methods in one fell swipe: 'Dylan Thomas's attitude to his work was a struck pose of careless-ness, and frenzied spontaneity, at least in public.'[9]

The third assumption is that social and moral awareness (imply-ing social and moral responsibility) lies not only in the choice of theme but in precise descriptive reference, producing a referential effect that distinguishes subject from object, feelings and thoughts from external stimuli. Apart from a few famous exceptions, little of Thomas's poetry can be read in terms of its referential effect. His modernist lyricism creates its own world rather than describing the world we know, while subject and object are frequently fused, as in 'Light breaks where no sun shines', where a mysterious, elemental grandeur is generated through the identification of natural and bodily processes. Taking as its vocabulary words that relate to natural and cosmic phenomena, the human body and the emotions, Thomas's poetry steers clear of social registers and the kind of local, period references that might date it. Images that come 'from the cinema & the gramophone' (*CL*, 310) ('the gunman and his moll' [*CP*, 17] in 'Our eunuch dreams', 'the wax disc' in 'I, in my intricate image' [*CP*,35]) are treated as intruders from mundane reality that have to be transformed if they are to be successfully woven into the surrounding poetic tissue. In Spender's 1933 poem, 'I think continually of those', the plea 'Never to allow gradually the traffic to smother / With noise and fog the flowering of the Spirit'[10] achieves its smothering opposite in the bathos of its inert imagery. By contrast, the assertion in Thomas's 'When, like a running grave' that joy is not 'city tar and subway bored to foster / Man through macadam' (*CP*, 20) combines pun, allusion and alliteration to produce not just a monologic statement about urban life but a play of meanings from the literal facts.

The fourth assumption extends the principle of mimesis to syntax. In 1955 Donald Davie argued that syntax was a source of poetic plea-sure and that (following Fenollosa) verbs were preferable to nouns since a true noun did not exist in nature. Thus 'one superiority of verbal poetry as an art rests in its getting back to the fundamental reality of time'.[11] Subjective syntax follows the form of thought in the poet's mind; dramatic syntax, the form of thought in another's mind; and objective syntax, a form of action. Dylan Thomas's syntax, even when formally correct, 'cannot mime, as it offers to do, a movement of the mind'; his sentences do not drive forward in time, being an 'endless series of copulas'.[2] In other words, Thomas's poetry privileges spatial and associative relations over temporal and syntagmatic ones.

Yet lying behind these criticisms and prejudices is a case that was mounted, not just against Dylan Thomas's poetry, but against his *poetics*; against the aesthetic principles upon which his poetry is based. Bardic mysticism, Welsh *hywl* and the neo-romanticism of the 1940s were bundled into the past along with wartime passions, paving the way for the welfare-state Augustanism of the Movement, but in some ways, due to their eagerness to dismantle, Thomas's detractors began to strike at the roots of poetry itself. When mimesis is granted its own indispensable aesthetic value, a realist epistemology may become more important than artistic form; common-sense principles assume the reins, while semantic rules and the laws of representation are enthroned as the arbiters of poetic language and syntax. What, then, is poetry? In its essence it is a species of literary art that exploits the musical potentialities of language, repeating identical or similar patterns of sound and rhythm in order to achieve a pleasing affect. For its various semantic effects it relies less on the syntagmatic axis – the temporal linearity of grammatical chains of words – than on the paradigmatic or associative axis, aiming for what Thomas called 'that momentary peace which is the poem' (*CL*, 282).

As *Wortkunst* or 'word art', poetry has its origins in wordplay, which treats words as things, independently of the way signifier and signified 'are held in relation by the "social fact" of language'.[13] Sound reaches the ear before meaning is understood: 'As far as the social fact of discourse is concerned the bond of the signifier and signified ceases to be arbitrary; but it never ceases to be arbitrary for the subject.'[14] The dead generations bequeath words and their meanings to the living, who must re-tongue them and learn their meanings as the dead decreed, but it is through this very process of language acquisition that the 'I', the human subject, is born, as Thomas's poem 'From love's first fever' tells with its Blakean echo:

> And from the first declension of the flesh
> I learnt man's tongue, to twist the shapes of thoughts
> Into the stony idiom of the brain,
> To shade and knit anew the patch of words
> Left by the dead who, in their moonless acre,
> Need no word's warmth.
>
> (*CP*, 22)

One can perhaps argue for certain radical social implications, then, in Thomas's intention to stir in us a flagrant enjoyment of word sounds and patterns. What begins as a spontaneous pleasure in infancy and childhood becomes repressed to an extent that depends on the pleasure obtained – which for Thomas was probably greater than for most of us – by the social rules that line up signifier and signified; the pleasure later re-emerges as a kind of defiance, or outlet for the defiance of these and other social rules, so that an element of anarchic resistance springing from the child's initial pleasure is never far away in Thomas's poetry, even in those poems with a public-sounding, incantatory resonance such as 'And death shall have no dominion' and 'A Refusal to Mourn the Death, by Fire, of a Child in London'. When I first read the line, 'All all and all the dry worlds lever' (*CP*, 29) I took shameless oral (and aural) pleasure in declaiming it and the poem in private, only to learn later that if 'it is possible to exult diabolically' in reading Thomas's poetry aloud, 'it is a shallow and sickly pleasure that uses the poss-ibilities of sound to thrust back sense from its only appointed place, within words'.[15] My own pleasure was not, I thought, shallow and sickly (though I was by no means sure of the meaning), but was secret enough, and hence suspect, that being told it was could make it so. Yet my censor is guilty of a cardinal fallacy. The 'appointed place' of meaning is not '*within* words' at all, as phonetic entities. Meaning is an arbitrary, socially-agreed bond between the signifier and the signified. These bonds are systematically internalised along with countless other social rules. Those who have successfully re-pressed their own pre-moral experience tend to see meaning as natural and transparent, as lying wholly '*within* words'. The con-ventional way to resolve the issue is to provoke a double, though not necessarily more intense pleasure by fusing sound and sense, which is invariably a mimetic pleasure, whereas some of Thomas's obscurity is calculated to foreground sound and its pleasures before the meaning sinks in.

The issue of neo-romanticism leads us to the suggestion that Dylan Thomas's poetry actually does address twentieth-century realities. Alex Comfort articulates the facile optimism of a macho-romantic ideology:

> It is from this metaphysical idea of conflict, of principles which are maintained only by struggle, that romanticism draws the tremendous force of its social and philosophical criticism, and the equally tremen-

dous emotional and intellectual appeal of its artistic statements. It is a force which alone among artistic forces seems to preserve perpetual virility and perpetual youth.[16]

Certain lines of Thomas, even certain poems, do express a virile, youthful energy, an active spirit of renewal that might be equated with revolutionary optimism. There is the poem 'All all and all', with its commitment to the real ('Fear not the working world, my mortal' [*CP*, 29]) and its last stanza, whose first line could almost have been taken up as a libertarian slogan in the 'flower power' '60s. There are the famous rhetorical challenges to death and to conventional ways of mourning in 'And death shall have no dominion', 'Do not go gentle into that good night', 'After the Funeral', and 'A Refusal to Mourn'; there is the youthful affirmation of life in 'Find meat on bones', where the father's advocacy of rebellion 'against flesh and bone' is spurned with:

> I cannot murder, like a fool,
> Season and sunshine, grace and girl,
> Nor can I smother the sweet waking.
> (*CP*, 54)

and there is the last stanza of 'When once the twilight locks', with its rejection of moony introspection:

> Awake, my sleeper, to the sun,
> A worker in the morning town,
> And leave the poppied pickthank where he lies;
> The fences of the light are down,
> All but the briskest riders thrown,
> And worlds hang on the trees.
> (*CP*, 10)

This conclusion vindicates the birth process despite earlier implications that the human body has a 'carcase shape' (*CP*, 10). Such images have sometimes been glossed as the product of self-pitying, adolescent morbidity, a self-conscious dramatising tendency eager to shock and sensationalise, or a recognition of 'the horrifying fact of death in eternally self-renewing nature'.[17] Really, we should take the opposites together. What we have then is not Comfort's cliché of 'struggle', but something more complex and ambiguous, a contradiction that informed Thomas's own poetics.

A touchstone is the poem 'The force that through the green fuse', which has lent itself to straightforward interpretations: the forces of life and death, of growth and decay that are at work in nature are also actively present in the poem's speaker. The paradoxical duality of existence is mirrored not only within each stanza but in the poem's structure: the first two stanzas articulate the same basic idea with comparable vigour, but the somewhat contrived imagery of stanza three ('The hand that whirls the water in the pool', 'the hangman's lime' [CP, 13]) dissipates some of it. This relaxed, entropic effect is partly brought about by a loss of polysemy in the language used: more meanings are possible in 'green fuse' and 'mouthing streams' in stanzas one and two than in 'quicksand' or 'blowing wind' (CP, 13). The romantic (or rather neo-romantic) myth of 'perpetual virility', the idea that Shelley's West Wind never flags or dies down, is drastically modified in Thomas's poem: the poet's creative powers are no less subject to decay than the forces of natural growth. The energy is renewed, however, with the line, 'The lips of time leech to the fountain head' (CP, 13). Various meanings are possible here: that the infant mouth sucks like a leech from the breast (in 'When once the twilight locks' 'The mouth of time sucked, like a sponge, / The milky acid on each hinge, / And swallowed dry the waters of the breast' [CP, 9]), and that when it is sated, the mother is relieved ('Love drips and gathers, but the fallen blood / Shall calm her sores' [CP, 13]); that the poet's lips, which are subject to creative as well as physical decline, must drink or suck at the renewing, inspirational source; or, like a sucking mouth, that time itself – the natural cycle – must periodically return to the fountain head for the process of organic growth to be repeated; or that time, like water percolating ('leaching') down, cumulatively makes the child in the womb ('the fountain head') by dripping blood through the umbilical cord, or, like a bloodsucking worm ('leech'), through a build-up of force sucks the child from the aquatic womb, calming the mother's birthpangs after release of blood. The possibilities do not end there. If the poetic voice seeks inspiration from 'the fountain head' (evoking both 'maidenhead' and, since 'fountain' rhymes with 'mountain' in stanza two, the *mons veneris*) of sex, then male desire is in play: it is the erect penis, filled with blood like a bloodsucking worm ('lips' suggesting the prepuce) that seeks vagina and womb; sexual desire 'drips and gathers', but after ejaculation ('the fallen blood' signifying the flaccid member) desire is assuaged, the force spent, the pain of frustration ('sores') calmed. Female desire may also be there: the female labia ('lips') are attracted towards and suck in the head of the male member, whose seminal spurt ('fountain'), like the vagina's own lubricants, is the moist gathering and concentration of sexual passion. Thomas may have chosen the word 'sores' (risking unpleasant associations) because it is a near-homophone of 'source'; the giving and desiring female source, towards which male desire gravitates, is also assuaged. The resulting calm contrasts with the blasted roots, dried streams, hauled shroud and hangman's lime of the first three stanzas, but is immediately followed by a repetition of 'And I am dumb to tell' (*CP*, 13), paradoxically hammering home in a kind of conceit the poet's verbal impotence (refuted in the poem's compressed potency). Death returns in the last two lines, which compare the post-coital bed ('the lover's tomb') both with the poet's lonely bedsheet on which his repressed libido (the Blakean 'crooked worm' [*CP*, 13]) leaves its tell-tale stains, and with the sheet of paper on which his pen-holding finger has left its involuted eloquence.

The slippery instability of meaning, the restless fluidity not only of individual words but of whole syntactic units, may annoy the reader who expects there to be one meaning only, and each concrete image to remain itself: milk must always be milk (not semen), a cloud a cloud. Yet if Thomas's words and images are susceptible to alarming fluctuations of meaning, if his signifieds keep sliding under their signifiers (which is more likely to happen with a word like 'lips' than with a word like 'gramophone'), there still remains, in the lines we have examined, an anchoring signification within an achieved poetic form, with syntax that is not merely 'pseudo'. Had this not been the case, the syntactic polysemy, condensing so much into one grammatical statement, would not have given that statement the universality it has.

The poem's opening speaks not of energy building up and subsiding but of a violent reversal of forces:

> The force that through the green fuse drives the flower
> Drives my green age; that blasts the roots of trees
> Is my destroyer.
>
> (*CP*, 13)

Like the refrain 'And I am dumb to tell', regretting the separation of the speaking self from physical realities or an inability to express those physical realities (an issue grappled with in the magnificent

'How shall my animal') – like this refrain, which suppresses the
validity of the assertions articulated in the first three lines of each
stanza, these opening lines contain a strong assertion which is then
negated by its contrary, the second stronger than the first. But, it
might be objected, why must there be a negation at all?

Thomas's theme of 'doom in the bulb' (*CP*, 33), of death as continually present in life, not merely the end of life; the realisation
that '[nothing] can endure as itself for more than an instant',[18]
which is a dialectical insight, is reflected in his poetics:

> I let, perhaps, an image be 'made' emotionally in me and then apply
> to it what intellectual and critical force I possess – let it breed
> another, let that image contradict the first, make, of the third image
> bred out of the other two together, a fourth contradictory image, and
> let them all, within my imposed formal limits, conflict.
>
> (*CL*, 281)

Each image, says Thomas, 'must be born and die in another'
(*CL*, 281). Negation and denial are therefore an essential part of
the creative process:

> The origin of poetry is the negation of poetry, 'destructive and con-
> structive at the same time', and it is this negation to which poetry
> must testify at the same time that it testifies to the inexhaustible
> fecundity of the source. Poetry, like its origin, must be 'creative
> destruction, destructive creation'.[19]

Some of the complexity of Dylan Thomas's poetry lies in the fact
that it goes beyond intellectual paradox by expressing the conflict
between an erupting unconscious and a restraining ego; between a
passive, 'surrealist' receptivity to whatever the unconscious pushes
up ('I let, perhaps, an image be "made" emotionally in me') and
conscious, formal control ('my imposed formal limits'). This gives
us a clue as to the nature of the force or forces being referred to in
'The force that through the green fuse'. First, however, let us see
how far the themes we have discussed can be contextualised, and
how far they relate to neo-romanticism.

On the one hand, there is the way in which Thomas associates
womb, birth, childhood and youth with death and mortality. On
the other hand, there is 'the inexhaustible fecundity of the source'.
Whether this is a timeless matrix which will apparently survive even
the 'all humbling darkness' (*CP*, 85), or the universal 'Love' (*CP*,

74) which the poet waits for Ann Jones's stuffed fox to cry, or an 'unjudging love' (*CP*, 89), or the unconscious, this source has nothing to do with God or morality. Thomas's poetry testifies to deeper needs, qualities and resources within the human spirit than can ever be contained by, and hence which must always rebel against, the rules and restraints of conventional morality.

Taking it in its larger context, the theme of life's transience, including in earlier periods (A. E. Housman), is invariably elegiac. But when there is no longer a God or a real heaven (other than the illusory heaven that time has 'ticked . . . round the stars' [*CP*, 13]); when the physical world is all that one has, ideality and permanence have to be somehow siphoned back in. If the only immutable law of physical existence is the mutability of all things, including ideas, one may begin to see, if not good, then vitality even in the profligate louts in 'I see the boys of summer'. If all nature is *energised*, there is no need for an immaterial heaven.

Thomas's poetry, like that of the Romantics, is much concerned with creation and origins, and hence with conception, birth and infancy. But if the Romantic dawn was the birth of a new era, the twentieth-century births to which Thomas's poetry implicitly bears witness have the smell of death about them. I shall offer three approaches to the problem. First, the process poem bequeathed by Romanticism explores the processes of creation and growth as an organic unfolding. The narrative mirrors the process it describes, beginning at the beginning and moving on from there, whether as a sequence of events or as a sequence of thoughts. Interest in the fecund source, in birth, origins and creation, becomes an interest in *growth*, in temporal, linear processes. In Thomas's poems about birth, temporal logic is overthrown. 'A process in the weather of the heart' is a series of assertions (or possibly instantaneous insights) that there are no orderly seasonal changes in human perception or in the human temperament, only sudden, often unpredictable transpositions and changes of mood: 'the quick and dead / Move like two ghosts before the eye', and 'A weather in the quarter of the veins / Turns night to days' (*CP*, 11, 10). In Thomas's dialectic, opposites interpenetrate and poles cross with alarming, almost cinematic rapidity.

Second, the poetics of an evolutionist liberalism in which crises are resolved, of peaceful linear processes that so easily become routine and commonplace, gives way in Thomas to radically honest, excoriating self-analysis and to a multiple array of futuristic perspectives, a kind of 'permanent revolution' where each contradictory moment breeds not only its own dissolution but an incalculable number of future possibilities. No sooner has time resolved one of these possibilities into a solid fixity than this in turn must dissolve, die and produce something new, since death is ever-present (not a 'horrifying fact'[20]) in all physical processes, which include the acts of speaking, reading and writing. A poem for Thomas is not a 'piece of experience placed nearly outside the living stream of time from which it came' but 'a watertight section of the stream that is flowing all ways'.[21]

Third – and this brings me to the heart of my contextual argument – Thomas's dialectic, together with his rejection of 'regimented thinkers and poets in uniform' (which we can connect with his 'emotional identification with the lowest stratum of society') is, if anything, even more relevant today than it was in the 1930s, looked at from a standpoint critical of the Stalinism the 'intellectual communists' (*CL*, 185) of Thomas's day were propagating. In 1989 everyone (not just a few Trotskyists, which was the case in the 1930s) saw that Stalinism, that grotesque, autocratic, sclerotic product of a genuine revolutionary transformation, had sown the seeds of its own violent and bloody overthrow. The newborn baby of 1917 was, in fact, already dead as a revolutionary force by 1930. Looking for a force for change, any politically aware young man living in South Wales in the interwar years and comparing the Labour Party of 1920 with that of MacDonald in 1931 would have seen how *that* force had died. The twentieth century has devoured ideologies, theories, governments, parties, programmes, policies, fashions and artistic movements faster than any other century; almost, indeed, as fast as its inexhaustibly fecund matrix has produced them. 1789 may have led to Napoleon, but it initiated a new bourgeois era, whereas in the twentieth century the socialist revolution has been repeatedly stillborn, strangled at birth or has died in infancy, negated by bureaucrats and dictators.

Thomas's poetics were based, as we have seen, on the dialectic. The dialectic in its Marxist guise that Hitler tried to murder in 1933, Stalin tried to absorb into 'Socialist Realism', the doctrine of art officially promulgated at the Soviet Writers Congress in 1934, when *18 Poems* was published. Thomas was keeping alive imaginatively what fascism and dogmatism had apparently succeeded in killing politically. The rich polysemy and fluidity of his poetic language undermine the apparent fixity of the idea; they show the idea in its abstract form to be merely a string of signifiers, not a reliable truth, so that abstract pseudo-truth is replaced by the verbal image. Nor is the image fixed either. Only when the image does its work at an emotional level, as a material signifier within an associative process originating in the unconscious, and then, crucially, within a contradictory process where the id and the ego battle it out in a 'war' whose imaginative resolution is the 'momentary peace' of an achieved poetic form – only then does the image resist decay, remaining the last graspable straw in a world of drowning truths. As sounds, words are among the most perishable man-made things, dying on the breath as soon as breath gives them birth. Thomas's poetry recognises, however, that if it is as sounds that words die, it is as sounds that they live. Out of that contradiction his poems seek to be monuments of sound, which is why the speaker in 'The spire cranes' advocates 'songs that jump back / To the built voice' and warns: 'But do not travel down dumb wind like prodigals' (CP, 73).

Thomas's vision is not, in essence, escapist. Nor is the rejuvenation of the language irrelevant here. Thomas's poetic technique does not – as Holbrook charged – consist in a repertoire of tricks: of clever juxtapositions, novel collocations and ingenious transpositions. It grapples with experience, not according to the principles of mimetic or expressive realism, but at the highest imaginative level.

Without sliding too loosely from the man to the text, I wish to conclude by placing Thomas's poetry in its Freudian context, bearing in mind that the 'political' 1930s were also a Freudian decade. (To call Thomas a 'Poet of the 40s' misrepresents a poet whose recurrent subject was his own personal psychology by associating him with poets whose primary imaginative stimuli were myths and Jungian archetypes.) Any suggestion that Freudian psychology is tangential to social and political concerns is refuted by the very terms Freud used, such as 'censor' and 'repression'. Thomas's lower middle-class background in cramped, chapelled Wales was, it seems, a rich spawning ground for unresolved complexes. One has only to look, for example, at the way he repeatedly details his own faults and inadequacies, a habit which dates from his sexually self-conscious adolescence. Despite an impeccable and often humorous self-awareness, he never seems to have made any real effort to mend his ways. A Freudian might conclude that, like the boy in Freud's celebrated case study, *An Infantile Neurosis*, Thomas was being consistently 'naughty' so that he could be punished by his father. His self-castigating critiques went, we know, with bouts of melancholy. Freud explains melancholia as a state brought on by a super-ego that 'becomes over-severe, abuses the poor ego, humiliates it and ill-treats it, threatens it with the direst punishment'.[22] The super-ego internalises parental and social authority, especially the authority of the father. The implications of this are not discussed by Paul Ferris, who simply says:

> He had never ceased to regard his father with understanding and respect, and the pattern of his life was in some measure a response to D. J. Thomas and his wishes. For the early books that Dylan Thomas read, the rhythms he absorbed, and probably for his obsession with the magic of the poet's function, he was indebted to D.J. There was something about his father, the man of letters, to which he aspired.[23]

Indebtedness to one's father may guarantee respect and admiration at the conscious level, but as Freud has shown and as Dylan Thomas's poetry reveals, the unconscious does not let matters rest there. In any case, Dylan was nothing like his father. For all his role-modelling and strong identification, Dylan was hardly a copy of cold-lipped Jack. Pamela Hansford Johnson was quick to notice something odd about Thomas's relationship with his father. She wrote in her diary: 'That fearful D.J. is his best friend!'[24] Thomas's terrified state of mind in the last eighteen months of his life had more to do with his father's illness and death than Ferris allows.

Thomas made a Freudian exemplar of himself, as did D. H. Lawrence in *Sons and Lovers*, though Thomas, having read Freud (how much one can only speculate), was more self-consciously Freudian than Lawrence, who was writing when Freud's theories were little known in England. (Freud died in London in 1939.) Thomas turned the insights into his inner psyche to artistic advantage. The safe unrest of adolescence was a time when the complexes of childhood erupted with positive results as far as his future career as a poet was concerned. His creative universe was filled with a wealth of imagery drawn from unconscious sources. At the same time, equally powerful forces of repression were at work to make the unrest safe, lending it more or less socially acceptable forms and occasionally reminding its rebellious libido of how maggoty, worm-like and cancerous it was. The conflict is sometimes revealed in Thomas's diction. His simple vocabulary of words that refer to the natural world and the human body, words with strong emotional associations, makes for an over-determination of meaning; each word is made to work at a level of intensity that the restraining ego does not normally allow.

[...] In 'The force ...' the phallic fuse and its ejaculatory flower are symbolically repressed by a root-blasting force which turns the speaker's initial energy against itself. As if this were not punishment enough, the speaker's super-ego repeatedly reminds him of his inability to speak ('And I am dumb to tell'). Referring to the role of the censor in dreams, Freud noted: 'There must be a force here which is seeking to express something and another which is striving to prevent its expression.'[25] Thomas was acutely aware of this conflict, and of the effort required to drag into the light, as if he were his own Freudian psychoanalyst, the rich haul of poetic material from his own unconscious. In 'Ballad of the Long-legged Bait', the poet as seafaring hero rides the boat of ambition and questing desire, his phallic anchor flying high before him like an arrow, his sexual 'bait' (a long-legged girl) bucking in the waves of coition at the end of a phallic rod, luring and hooking all manner of creatures and things from the deep, until 'His decks are drenched with miracles' (CP, 130). Once the voyage is properly under way, the narrative leaves the past perfect tense and enters the eternal present of a demonstrative present tense, the tense of myth, ritual and the id, which as Freud discovered is unconscious of the passage of time and is not subject to the laws of time. Thomas's imagination weaves a complex web of images, whose strands interconnect through sound, cultural meanings, experience and observation, yet each nodal point is determined in the first instance by an unconscious impulse rather than by some haphazard association. A good example of the way his imagination worked is the opening of 'An Adventure from a Work in Progress', where the anchor 'pointed over the corkscrew channels of the sea to the dark holes and caves in the horizon' (CS, 119). The horizon becomes 'the pitted distance' (CS, 119), the vagina-like holes and womb-like caves 'pitied', perhaps, as targets of an aggressive sexuality. The hero 'swam with a seal at his side' (CS, 119). The other meaning of 'seal' immediately surfaces in 'to the boat that *stamped* the water'. A stamp, like a seal, endorses; 'to endorse' means to put on the back, and it rhymes with 'horse', an animal that stamps. The next sentence begins: 'He gripped on the bows *like a mane* ...' (CS, 119). The seal of officialdom is no sooner bred in the dying image of a marine mammal than it too dies in the image of a horse being ridden bare-back. (The inevitable dolphin dives under the waves in the next sentence.)

Images of castration are the symbolic negation of this libidinous energy, taming and repressing it as the 'sly scissors ground in frost / Clack through the thicket of strength' (CP, 76) in 'How shall my animal'. The tailor/scissors motif (deriving, as Michael Neil first showed, from a famous illustration in Strewwelpeter[26] has a clear social meaning. Cut to measure by a 'tailor age' (CP, 19), every potential member of society must (in 'When, like a running grave') wear 'time's jacket or a coat of ice' (CP, 20) for his 'masters'; the 'jacket' is here tailored by Jack Thomas ('Jack Frost' in 'Why east wind chills'), who was a schoolmaster at the school Thomas attended, from which Thomas regularly truanted and where he 'set back the clock faced tailors' (CP, 110). Since the tailor's scissors, as Neil has shown, 'may be identified with the instrument that severs the umbilical cord at birth',[27] and since 'Before I knocked' contains the phrase 'flesh was snipped' (CP, 12), we may deduce that the birth trauma is a primary source for Thomas's castration imagery, for according to Freud birth 'is the prototype of all castration'.[28] And if 'the very frequent phantasy of returning into the mother's womb is a substitute for [the] wish to copulate',[29] bringing its threat of castration by the father (which the displacement mechanism may sometimes replace by another figure), then the association in Thomas of both birth and ejaculatory climaxes with castration and death becomes easier to understand.

The real enemy is time, especially clock time, which cuts us up into quarters. The hero of 'An Adventure' is about to possess the female: 'Time was about to fall . . . and oaks were felled in the acorn' (CS, 120). After he holds her, 'the lopped leg of a bird scratched against rock' (CS, 120), and when he next tries to hug her, 'The mountain in the intervals of his breathing grew many times its size until time fell and cut and burned it down. The peak collapsed . . .' (CS, 122). The 'breathing' here is clearly sexual, which may alert us at this point to the sexual connotations of the word that is born and dies, time which cuts and measures, the built voice, and the vulnerable tongue. Father Time wields his scythe in much of Thomas ('Blunt scythe and water blade . . . Time kills me terribly' [CP, 58]), and the censoriously 'wagging' fingers of a grandfather clock are, if we think about it, sharpened at the pointing end like the scissor-blades held by 'clock faced tailors'

(*CP*, 110). Time and tongue come together in 'When I Woke', with its image of 'a man outside with a billhook', a 'warm-veined double of Time' who is 'Cutting the morning off':

> And his scarving beard from a book,
> Slashed down the last snake as though
> It were a wand or subtle bough,
> Its tongue peeled in the wrap of a leaf.
> (*CP*, 111)

'Time and tide' is a cultural sound-link, but 'time' and 'scythe' may have harvested the 'tithings' (*CP*, 7) of 'I see the boys of summer'. The force that 'drives the flower' is both 'the drive of oil' beneath 'Flower, flower, all all and all' (*CP*, 30) and 'The secret oils that drive the grass' (*CP*, 23) in 'In the beginning'. But if time scythes from the moment of birth, as in the horribly vivid 'second death', the 'harvest / Of hemlock and blades' of the speaker's 'second struggling from the grass' (*CP*, 26), struggling second by second in a cutting birth in 'I dreamed my genesis', then it scythes the driven grass of our heads just as it thinned the hair of D. J. Thomas, who in a family photograph of about 1909, reproduced in Ferris, has it self-consciously combed laterally across his domed head.

Hornick has said that in Thomas 'Jesus is man and the Father is time, death, the repressive forces of society'.[30] Yet Neil, noting Thomas's liking for 'auto-destructive' imagery, missed a possible auto-destructive element in Hoffman's 'red-legged scissor-man' (*CP*, 188n). For if his running scissor-blade legs are red *with his own blood*, he is his own 'running grave' (*CP*, 19). By reducing himself to a female role (cf. the infantile belief that 'instead of a male organ [women] have a wound'[31]), the gelded father becomes an object of compassion, at least as far as the ego is concerned, but the repressed unconscious could make a father with a 'wound' a terrifying image. I suspect that compassion reigned in Thomas for much of the time. But then his father died: and is not death in his poetry associated with castration? In 1934, Jack Thomas was operated on for what his son believed (with premature fears of Jack's death) was throat cancer. The 'wound / In the throat' (*CP*, 113) ('Lie Still, Sleep Becalmed') of the man whose 'raging' voice had helped to mould the poet's own, and later the gentle passing of the father whose curses had been internalised in the poet's super-ego, inspired both compassion and a kind of panic.

Perhaps one could say that the politics of all this is the imposs-ibility of any 'withering away'[32] of the state, since in the politics of patriarchy the state is the father. Nevertheless, envisaging a world without negation and without any controlling authority, and with no people apart from the happy self who is never lonely, an anarchic paradise of play day after day, is what Thomas triumphantly suc-ceeds in doing in the poem 'Fern Hill'. Time, which is personified (and therefore the only 'person' in this libidinous, joyous universe apart from the 'I'), is at first indulgent ('Time let me hail', 'Time let me play'); at the end, 'Time held me green and dying' (*CP*, 134–5). Yet in this amoral and decidedly unsentimental Eden the existential reality of an unrepressed, unashamedly self-centred freedom is memorably and convincingly re-enacted. It is not, for this reason, essentially a nostalgic poem (although it is in the past tense), and this reminds us again that there is nothing in the id that corresponds to the idea of time. Through an imaginative leap into the experience of infancy and childhood, Thomas makes the signifiers themselves mouth what the lips of infancy need and do:

> Now as I was young and easy under the apple boughs
> About the lilting house and happy as the grass was green
> (CP, 134)

The pleasures of the breast are re-enacted; and in the real world, a boy on a swing may subconsciously recall the pleasure of being rocked. In this id-saturated world, time lets both actions happen to-gether in mutual identification. Excitement and ecstasy are aspi-rated: it is 'house and happy', and wishes race 'through the house high hay'. The poem may seem 'as political as a mountain goat' to some, but mid-1945 was not a bad time to celebrate, and in grant-ing the lips a moment (not a ticked 'second') of utopian freedom, Thomas was, in his own way, making a political statement.

From *Dylan Thomas: Craft or Sullen Art*, ed. Alan Bold (London / New York, 1990), pp. 35–65.

NOTES

[Perhaps the most cogent defence of the anti-discursive symbolism of Thomas's poetic style, Stewart Crehan's essay is the piece which has most influenced the editors of this *New Casebook*. Combining elements of

Marxism, linguistics and Freudianism, Crehan notes Thomas's insistence on the autonomy of words, and the arbitrary nature of the link between words ('signifier') and our concepts of things ('signifieds') for the individual subject. This arbitrariness has its roots in the spontaneous pleasure in linguistic play of childhood. Tracing the implications of the adult repression of such pleasurably anarchic and defiant energy, Crehan is able to approach the poetry in a non-moralising manner, outflanking the charge of 'immaturity' so often raised against Thomas. For, as Crehan argues, if Thomas's very style challenges the restraints encoded within language, it must also challenge the way we acquire our identities within familial, social and literary-political structures. Through a detailed analysis of 'The force that through the green fuse', he illustrates the poetry's basically dialectical procedures, which dramatise the conflict within each individual between the various parts of the psyche (the 'id', 'ego' and punitive 'super-ego'). The conflict of images is seen as a kind of psychic 'permanent revolution', a phrase Crehan adopts from Leon Trotsky, and which points to his situation of Thomas's strategies in their historical context of liberal crisis and the fascist and Stalinist freezing of process, dialectic and change. Finally, turning to two middle period poems and a story, Crehan discusses the seascapes which feature so heavily in the work, the manipulation of Freudian motifs and the radical utopian vision of 'Fern Hill'. Eds]

1. Jonathan Raban, *The Society of the Poem* (London, 1971), pp. 70–1.

2. Elder Olson, 'The Universe of the Early Poems', in *Dylan Thomas: A Collection of Essays*, ed. C. B. Cox (New Jersey, 1957), p. 46.

3. Vernon Watkins, 'Mr Dylan Thomas: Innovation and Tradition', *The Times*, 10 November, 1953, p. 11.

4. David Holbrook, *Llareggub Revisited: Dylan Thomas and the State of Modern Poetry* (Cambridge, 1962), pp. 155–61.

5. Dylan Thomas, quoted in Paul Ferris, *Dylan Thomas* (Harmondsworth, 1977), pp. 29–30.

6. Holbrook, *Llareggub Revisited*, p. 128.

7. John Malcolm Brinnin, *Dylan Thomas in America* (London, 1956), p. 26.

8. Catherine Belsey, *Critical Practice* (London, 1980), p. 12.

9. Holbrook, *Llareggub Revisited*, pp. 120, 140.

10. *The Norton Anthology of Poetry*, ed. Margaret Ferguson, Mary Jo Salter and Jon Stallworthy (New York and London, 1996), p. 1399.

11. Donald Davie, *Articulate Energy: An Inquiry into the Syntax of English Poetry* (London, 1955), p. 23.

12. Ibid., p. 126.

13. Anthony Easthope, *Poetry as Discourse* (London, 1983), p. 34.

14. Ibid., p. 35.

15. Russell Davies, 'Fibs of Vision', *Review* (Autumn/Winter 1971–2), 69.

16. Alex Comfort, *Art and Social Responsibility: Lectures on the Ideology of Romanticism* (London, 1946), p. 43.

17. Alan Young, 'Image as Structure: Dylan Thomas and Poetic Meaning', *Critical Quarterly* (Winter 1975), 337.

18. J. Hillis Miller, *Poets of Reality* (Cambridge, MA, 1966), p. 200.

19. Quoted in Hillis Miller, *Poets of Reality*, p. 208.

20. Alan Young, 'Image as Structure', p. 337.

21. Quoted in Henry Treece, *Dylan Thomas: Dog Among the Fairies* (London, 1949), p. 48.

22. Sigmund Freud, 'New Introductory Lectures on Psycho-Analysis', in *Works*, Vol. XXII, ed. James Strachey (London, 1955), pp. 26. ff.

23. Ferris, *Dylan Thomas*, p. 310.

24. Quoted in ibid., p. 28.

25. Freud, *Works*, Vol. XXII, p. 14.

26. Michael Neil, 'Dylan Thomas's "Tailor Age" ', *Notes and Queries* (February 1970), 59–63.

27. Ibid., p. 60.

28. Freud, *Works*, Vol. X, p. 8.

29. Freud, *Works*, Vol. XXII, p. 22.

30. T. Hornick, *The Intricate Image: A Study of Dylan Thomas*, PhD thesis (Columbia, NY, 1958), p. 19.

31. Freud, *Works*, Vol. XVII, p. 78

32. See Frederick Engels, *Socialism: Utopian and Scientific* (Peking, 1975), p. 94.

3

'Daughters of Darkness': Dylan Thomas and the Celebration of the Female

KATIE GRAMICH

> Men say that there are two unrepresentable things: death and the feminine sex. That's because they need femininity to be associated with death; it's the jitters that give them a hard-on! for themselves! They need to be afraid of us. Look at the trembling Perseuses moving backward toward us, clad in apotropes. What lovely backs! Not another minute to lose. Let's get out of here.
>
> Let's hurry: the continent is not impenetrably dark. I've been there often. I was overjoyed one day to run into Jean Genet ... There are some men (all too few) who aren't afraid of femininity.
>
> (Hélène Cixous)[1]

So declares Hélène Cixous in her influential 1976 essay, 'The Laugh of the Medusa'. Cixous mocks patriarchal views of the female body as the 'dark continent', the female as witch or monster, the female as Lack. She celebrates the return of the repressed: 'women return from afar, from always ... from below, from beyond "culture" '. She dramatises a repossession of the female body by women writing ourselves, declaring 'Let the priests tremble, we're going to show them our sexts!'[2]

But the feminist revolution through writing the body is not an exclusively female concern. In her forays into the formerly proscribed dark continent, Cixous encounters a couple of shy Modernist males, namely Jean Genet and James Joyce. These are privileged exceptions, writers who, according to Cixous, have managed to avoid 'glorious phallic monosexuality', who are not afraid of femininity, and have embraced what she terms 'the other bisexuality'. This is not, she emphasises, equivalent to being neuter; rather, it is a subject position which 'doesn't annul differences but stirs them up, pursues them, increases their number'.[3]

Despite the persuasiveness of Cixous's rhetoric, there are obvious problems with her new gospel of *jouissance*. It champions avant-garde, Modernist writers but fundamentally espouses a Romantic aesthetic: 'I, too, overflow; my desires have invented new desires, my body knows unheard-of songs.'[4] The Medusa begins to sound like an X-rated Wordsworth. And, though Cixous challenges what she calls 'the sex police', her new order seems to have its own built-in Amazonian militia. Some women writers don't count, apparently, because they write like men. Excited anticipation may begin to wane a little when one realises that neither George Eliot nor Mary Wollstonecraft is likely to be encountered in the labyrinths of the dark continent. But who else might one find on a Cixousian pilgrimage to female sexuality? Could that be Little Willie Wee lurking in that corner, behind a face of hands? Is Dylan Thomas one of those rare explorers: 'men who aren't afraid of femininity?'

Thomas, like Joyce and Genet, was a Modernist writer quite un-afraid of transgressing literary boundaries. Like them, he was often regarded as obscene by conservative critics and was forced to censor his own work, to which he objected, saying defiantly: 'I'd rather tickle the cock of the English public than lick its arse' (*CL*, 322). The bodily imagery is by no means uncharacteristic. Thomas's fascination with the body and his elevation of it, as will be seen, to a metaphorical majesty is well known and seems to chime with Cixous's resurrection or recuperation of the female body for a feminist purpose. Even the apparent tension between a Modernist practice and a Romantic aesthetic is shared by the two of them. The new bisexuality which Cixous advocates is also per-ceptible in some of Thomas's writings: in the sexual indeterminacy of the foetus in the early poems, in the feminisation of the Christ figure, and in the ambiguous pronouncements about gender con-tinually made in the letters.

It is also possible to argue that Thomas, far from exhibiting femi-nist sympathies, actually flaunted not a few unreconstructed patriar-chal prejudices both in his life and his work. Indeed, there are numerous and embarrassing instances of Thomas's misogyny which one could cite in a counter-argument. It is difficult to see a poem like 'Ballad of the Long-Legged Bait' as other than offensively misogynistic, for example. When asked to gloss it, he told an academic that it was about 'a gigantic fuck' (*CL*, 97). There are also many examples of monstrous, threatening, even castrating female figures in his works, particularly in some of the more lurid Gothic passages of the early stories. Even when there is a clear attempt to elevate and laud the female, it might well be argued that he simply resorts to reductive and stereotypical identification between woman and nature, the source of all fecundity. Like D. H. Lawrence, a writer whom he reluctantly admired and by whom he was undoubtedly influenced, he can be thus viewed both as archpatriarch and as proto-feminist. Both Lawrence and Thomas were interested in the body and sexuality, in the world of nature, realms traditionally associated in patriarchal ideology with the female, rejecting what they saw as the arid rationality and the denial of the body associated with contemporary male writers and thinkers. (As Thomas mordantly remarked: 'the emotional appeal in Auden wouldn't raise a corresponding emotion in a tick' [*CL*, 97]. The image also cleverly suggests the absence of the body in Auden's work, at least according to Thomas, for ticks must have their nourishing flesh.) It is not surprising that these two 'provincial' writers with working-class roots should challenge the hegemony of the male, cerebral, intellectual Oxbridge-London world. Both were dissident outsiders in that clubby, cosy world. Cixous speaks of the writers who inscribe femininity as 'subjects who are breakers of automatisms, . . . peripheral figures that no authority can ever subjugate'.[5] This appears to be an accurate sketch of the iconoclasm of both Lawrence and Thomas.

There is a contradiction, then, a tension between opposing poles, which this essay does not set out to reconcile or 'solve'; in the spirit of Cixous' *écriture feminine*, one 'doesn't annul differences but stirs them up, pursues them, increases their number'. For the moment let us grope our way forward into that dark continent:

> One: I am a Welshman;
> Two: I am a drunkard;
> Three: I am a lover of the human race, especially of women.[6]

Dylan Thomas's declamatory self-definition, given toward the end of his life, is well known. Critics and biographers have dedicated many pages to exploration of his Welshness, his drinking, his alleged love of humanity. They have also explored in sometimes tedious detail the issue of whether he was – in the literal sense – a lover of women. However, the main focus of this essay will be textual (or possibly sextual?) rather than biographical, though we may use this little snippet of bluster as our ball of string to help us on our way.

The self-description, 'a lover of women' could be dismissed as a mere piece of bravado, part of a macho image projected perhaps a little defensively to cover his own perceived inadequacies. It may also be seen as part of a complementary image of the bohemian, the rake, the ruined boy. And yet the words are not simply image-building. Dylan Thomas the poet, the story writer, is a lover of women very often. He uses projections of the female in his works in quite complex and contradictory ways: to explore his own selfhood as a male, to question societal rules and norms, to create alternative images of heroism to pit against a patriarchal society usually viewed by him as sterile and cerebral.

Simone de Beauvoir begins *The Second Sex* in typically ironic mode:

> Woman? Very simple, say the fanciers of simple formulas: she is a womb, an ovary; she is a female – this word is sufficient to define her.[7]

In the early poems, Dylan Thomas appears to be one of de Beauvoir's 'fanciers of simple formulas'. Woman is womb, she is female: her biology defines her. We might justifiably view this as the usual essentialist identification of the female with the flesh, with 'immanence', in de Beauvoir's existentialist terms, rather than with 'transcendence', which is the exclusive realm of the male. However, when one begins to examine the early process poems more closely, the depiction of the female turns out to be more complex than it at first appears as a glance at the first of the *Collected Poems*, 'I see the boys of summer' (a poem in three sections), will illustrate:

> I see the boys of summer in their ruin
> Lay the gold tithings barren,
> Setting no store by harvest, freeze the soils;
> There in their heat the winter floods
> Of frozen loves they fetch their girls,
> And drown the cargoed apples in their tides.
> (*CP*, 7)

Critical readings of the poem tend to emphasise the equilibrium between its positive and negative images; very much like the better known 'The force that through the green fuse', it is suggested, this is a poem which exhibits Thomas's realisation of the fragile balance of the universe, poised between birth and death, growth and decay. Certainly, both poems juggle exuberantly with binary oppositions, such as summer/winter, night/day, desert/garden, barren/harvest. Ultimately, though, this is a poem not of reconciliation but of continued protest. It begins, typically, with masturbation. The boys of summer 'lay the gold tithings [of their semen] barren', wasting the seed that might have been laid in store or harvested. At the same time as there is a strong sense of moral censure of their 'folly', there is also a celebration of their profligate fecundity, described in universal, elemental terms – tides and floods. Their milky fluids are soured and curdled; the female emblem of the moon 'drawing up her silvers' as Gillian Clarke puts it, is rejected as of no import to them in their self-obsessed 'voiding'. The overwhelming feeling is one of sterility.

> I see the summer children in their mothers
> Split up the brawned womb's weathers,
> Divide the night and day with fairy thumbs;
> There in the deep with quartered shades
> Of sun and moon they paint their dams
> As sunlight paints the shelling of their heads.
>
> (CP, 7)

In this, the third stanza of the first section, the vision penetrates even as far as the womb in which these boys were formed: the speaker sees the division of cells by mitosis, doubling ceaselessly, proliferating and yet ironically – through this constant splitting – coalescing to create a single human being. The striking aspect of this foetal scene is the power given to the foetus itself: the womb is merely a receptacle, the mother an animal-like 'dam', within which the child 'paints' its own identity. As Simone de Beauvoir remarks, 'woman's fecundity is regarded as only a passive quality. She is the earth, and man the seed . . .'[8] 'Dam' is also a pun much favoured by the young Dylan Thomas, for the unopened womb functions as a temporary dam, holding back the unborn child and the waters which surround it. It might also be suggestive aurally of damn in the sense of curse, in which case the babes are gloomily concocting their own damnation, even while still in the womb. 'Brawned' womb suggests strength and endurance but little else. Birth is seen as 'sunlight paint[ing] the shelling of their heads', indicative of the sudden irruption into the light from the dark depths of the womb. 'Shelling of their heads' has a hint of violence, too, appropriate to the explosive suddenness of the moment of birth itself. But 'shell' might also contain the picture of an egg being laid, the babies emerging like chicks, with the suggestion of insignificance and sameness which is borne out by the first line of the next stanza, in which they become 'men of nothing'. The prophet-like speaker augurs no change: we are back with images of sterile masturbation, 'seedy shifting', and the 'pulse of summer' remains tantalisingly frozen 'in the ice'.

> But seasons must be challenged or they totter
> Into a chiming quarter
> Where, punctual as death, we ring the stars;
> There, in his night, the black-tongued bells
> The sleepy man of winter pulls,
> Nor blows back moon-and-midnight as she blows.
>
> (CP, 8)

The second section of the poem has an abrupt change of speaker and season. The summer boys are the dark deniers, perhaps attempting to defend themselves but succeeding only in confirming their status as in-veterate masturbators: 'The sleepy man of winter pulls . . . the black-tongued bells'. Their actions are negative ones: 'hold up', 'drop', 'choke', 'comb . . . for a wreath', while the 'planted womb' brings forth only an insubstantial 'man of straw'. The final stanza seems to describe a parodic crucifixion, but as often happens in these early poems the crucifixion is fused with an act of castration, denoting the end of all promise: 'love's damp muscle dries and dies'. The phallus seems to be limp and exhausted in that very season, spring, when it should be ready for anything. But the resurrection is swift: by the last line the boys have re-acquired their 'poles', though surely this proud phallic symbolism is ironic?

> I see you boys of summer in your ruin.
> Man in his maggot's barren.
> And boys are full and foreign in the pouch.
> I am the man your father was.
> We are the sons of flint and pitch.
> O see the poles are kissing as they cross.
>
> (CP, 8)

This final verse offers a final judgement on the ruined boys. The penis is by now a barren maggot – not very impressive, and connoting death. The devastating touch in this last stanza is the admission that the prophet speaker is himself tainted by their guilt: 'I am the man your father was'. The last line is suggestive of homoeroticism: the phallic poles are now kissing each other, while the female, always only hinted at in the poem, is now totally excised from the scene.

The early poems dramatise an attempt to come to terms with masculinity: the boys of summer are unsuccessful in this, taking refuge in 'unnatural' practices which exclude that emblem of the natural, woman. There is no doubt that Thomas includes man and woman in his general pattern of elemental binary oppositions. Yet this crude division of the sexes is a source of anxiety and even anguish in the poems. Several hanker after a state of presexuality or a non-differentiated gender. It has been suggested that the word 'fairy' in 'I see the boys of summer', alluding to the foetus, is suggestive of indeterminacy of sex. The anatomical images of the early poems all tend to dissolve and fragment the human form, while the later poems are concerned to praise individuals conceived as whole human beings. Male and female in the process poems are little more than phallus and womb, raw, elemental organs which lack personality and distinctiveness. The mother is simply a womb, but that is to say that she is also an emblem of the universe itself – the watery globe, the life-giving haven.

The presentation of the female in the early stories is, however, somewhat different. Many of the early prose works, such as 'The Enemies', 'The True Story', 'The Horse's Ha' and 'The School for Witches' present a central female figure with mysterious and dangerous magical powers. Mrs Owen in 'The Enemies' presides over a bubbling pot and gazes into a crystal ball. She is described as 'an uncanny woman loving the dark' (CS, 19) and is indeed repeatedly identified with the darkness. 'The old powers were upon her' (CS, 19–20), the reader is informed, suggesting that Mrs Owen's powers may come from some eternal place of darkness, a female dark continent. Similarly, in 'The Horse's Ha', the undertaker, Montgomery, reads his mother's book of spells and follows her ghoulish recipe, which involves an unappetising mixture of blood and semen. The most extreme of these witch stories is 'The School for Witches', where Gwladys, a doctor's daughter, instructs her seven female apprentices in the rituals of conjuring the devil. The women are grotesque, with beaks and webbed feet, dancing in a Maenadic frenzy of excess. However, in both the latter stories, the sinister witch is contrasted with 'ordinary' women, a homely midwife in 'The School for Witches' and a pair of loving, obedient wives in 'The Horse's Ha'.

In several of the other early stories, women are innocent victims, potential victims, or angelic domestic carers. The pregnant wife in 'The Dress' is beautiful and vulnerable, but the threatened butchery of the madman is mercifully not fulfilled – he simply puts his head meekly in her lap. Rhianon, in 'The Visitor' is sweet and tender, 'like a wind from Tahiti' (CS, 25), smelling of 'clover and milk' (CS, 26). She is 'like a maiden out of the Old Testament' (CS, 27). The much more realistic, suburban story entitled 'The Vest' has a capable, sensible, domestic wife afflicted by a pathological husband who hurts her: the bloody vest seems to suggest at the end that he has finally killed her.

These examples indicate a dualistic conception of the female which is typical of patriarchal views of female nature. Witch versus angel is the classic dichotomy but it is possible to argue that even in these early stories Dylan Thomas is attempting to deconstruct these stereotypes, to challenge the rigid binary oppositions adumbrated. Certainly, women in these stories are figures of fascination and, often, keepers of a mystery. Their power is not so much celebrated as feared. Their vulnerability is depicted with pathos and compassion.

In 'The Orchards', an early autobiographical story, Marlais, the young poet, is visited by recurring dreams of two girls in a burning orchard. The two sisters are opposites, one buxom, the other scarecrow-like; one fair, the other dark. Marlais goes on a fairytale quest to find the girls from his dreams. The girls are objects of desire and keepers of a mystery – they are pointing at the burning trees, like figures in a religious icon, trying to tell him something which he cannot understand. Moreover, the scarecrow sister is Christ-like, her posture echoing the crucifixion, while Marlais partakes of a pseudo-communion of tea, milk, and bread with the other sister. Here we see the beginning of a rapprochement between the dark and the light female. Together, the sisters embody what appears to be a spiritual message – they are the keepers of knowledge. Similarly, in 'The Mouse and the Woman', the male protagonist is unable to decipher the word spelt out by the stars, and this inability is linked to his failure to answer the woman's questions. The woman in this story is the creation of the man: 'She had risen out of the depths of darkness' (CS, 76), 'He had given a woman being' (CS, 77). Again, the female is Christ-like: 'He saw her flesh in the cut bread; her blood, still flowing through the channels of the mysterious body, in the spring water' (CS, 76). The man and woman seem to re-enact the story of Adam and Eve. When he commands her to cover her nakedness, she questions him and he resorts to conventionality: 'It was not good to look upon' (CS, 82). Her questions unanswered, the woman leaves.

Dylan Thomas commented in a letter that 'some people consider the stories dirty and, occasionally, blasphemous – which they probably are' (CL, 235). One of the potentially blasphemous elements of these stories is the repeated suggestion that Christ is female. It is the female characters who understand the mysteries of religion and the universe, while the male characters remain confused and frustrated. Or they take refuge in patriarchal dogma ('It is not good to look upon') which is misogynistic and death-dealing.

There is a marked change in both the poems and stories in the late 1930s, early 1940s. The characteristic vocabulary of the early process poems has virtually disappeared and we find ourselves in a world of fear and tenderness rather than of spasm and impulse. Thomas has been accused by John Bayley of ventriloquising the mother's voice in 'If my head hurt a hair's foot' with 'an embarrassing lack of sensitivity'.[9] This, though, is questionable. There is certainly an idealisation of the mother's selfless role in childbirth but there is also tenderness and an acknowledgement of the mother's subjectivity. Similarly, the mother in 'Vision and Prayer' is noticeably more whole and human; described as 'the splashed mothering maiden / who bore him' (CP, 116), she herself is more vital and animated than the passive womb of the earlier work. This shift in Thomas's work, though, is perhaps best illustrated by the poem 'After the Funeral'.

Auntie Annie in this tender elegy is surely a precise individual. Although she exhibits the maternal and nurturing qualities of some of the allegorised females of the early stories, she is not idealised in the same manner. Rather, she is praised in the bardic sense: elevated through song, but in a way which allows her also to remain the pathetic, put-upon, impoverished Annie of 'The Peaches':

> After the funeral, mule praises, brays,
> Windshake of sailshaped ears, muffle-toed tap

> Tap happily of one peg in the thick
> Grave's foot, blinds down the lids, the teeth in black,
> The spittled eyes, the salt ponds in the sleeves,
> Morning smack of the spade that wakes up sleep,
> Shakes a desolate boy who slits his throat
> In the dark of the coffin and sheds dry leaves.
>
> (*CP*, 73)

The poem begins with fragmentary images of the mourners at the funeral: we hear snatches of their speech, catch glimpses of parts of their bodies – ears, legs, teeth, eyes. The only whole and wholly human beings in this poem are the bardic speaker and Ann herself. The sole true mourner, he speaks for her, assuming an articulacy and a rhetorical grandeur quite alien to the meek and dumb dead woman. As in the earlier 'If My Head Hurt a Hair's Foot', Thomas then takes on a surrogate role, speaking for the woman.

> I stand, for this memorial's sake, alone
> In the snivelling hours with dead, humped Ann
> Whose hooded, fountain heart once fell in puddles
> Round the parched worlds of Wales and drowned each sun.
> But I, Ann's bard on a raised heath, call all
> The seas to service that her wood-tongued virtue
> Babble like a bellbuoy over the hymning heads.
>
> (*CP*, 73)

Some critics, as we have seen, would regard this as presumptuous. On the other hand, one might view this extraordinary ventriloquism as an attempt, however arrogant or inadequate, to make the subaltern speak, with the bardic self as ventriloquist. The speaker recognises and names Ann's self-containment and quietude, but insists nevertheless on noisy celebration. Not content with one voice, he finally endows her with many: all the voices of the natural world, with which she is identified. Her 'threadbare whisper' is translated into a 'monumental argument' (*CP*, 74). The restrictions and frustrations, as well as the pain, of her life are acknowledged, but in the surreal final images the emblems of her closed life (the twitching stuffed fox and the strutting dusty fern) are metamorphosed into emblems of birth and abundant energy. It is therefore possible to view this poem as a proto-feminist text. A woman judged poor and insignificant is elevated to a regal status (since she has her own bard) and this bard questions and challenges the values of a society which ignored and ill-treated such an individual, allowing her no voice, incarcerating her with the dusty fern. One of Thomas's earliest poems was entitled 'The Woman Speaks' and this poem shows that he continued to be fascinated by the often unheard voices of women. Notably, too, it is the voices of the 'daughters of darkness' (*CP*, 152) in the later poem 'In the White Giant's Thigh' which the speaker first hears, heeds, and then transcribes.

In the images of Annie presented in both 'After the Funeral' and 'The Peaches' we see how the suggestion of female martyrdom, indeed the usurpation of Christ's role by the female, continues in a modified form from the earlier stories. Though Annie is, from one point of view 'a little, brown-skinned, toothless, hunch-backed woman with a cracked, sing-song voice' she is also, puzzlingly, called 'Mrs Jesus' (*CS*, 129). This is how the erring Uncle Jim refers to her as, drunk, he takes Dylan home past the hangman's house. Jim mutters, anticipating the scolding he is about to receive, 'I wish he'd have hung Mrs Jesus' (*CS*, 129). Inevitably, the image is suggestive of a mock crucifixion.

The other stories of *Portrait of the Artist as a Young Dog* also contain striking depictions of individual female characters, such as the rival servant girls in 'Patricia, Edith and Arnold', in which female solidarity finally overcomes sexual jealousy. Patricia, seen from the little boy's perspective, is strong, capable, and loving, unlike the worthless and narcissistic suitor, Arnold. In the later stories of the collection, female characters become objects of desire, rather than mother figures. The threatening women in the pub, glimpsed by the frightened boy in 'The Peaches', are encountered more intimately in the later stories, such as 'One Warm Saturday'. The young male protagonist is fumbling and inexperienced, while the women are street-wise, ironic, in charge. Yet these 'loose women' are depicted in an increasingly negative light, particularly in the unfinished *Adventures in the Skin Trade*. Here, the protagonist, Sam Bennet, sees

> these women with the shabby faces and the comedian's tongues, squatting and squabbling over their mother's ruin, might have lurched in from Llanelly on a football night, on the arms of short men with leeks. They . . . were dull as sisters, red-eyed and thick in the head with colds; they would sneeze when you kissed them or Hiccup and say Manners in the dark traps of the hotel bedrooms.
>
> (*CS*, 293–4)

The apparently clichéd reference to gin as 'mother's ruin', when read as part of Thomas's developing depiction of the female, actually becomes indicative of his own shift of attitude. These are the earlier idealised mothers 'in their ruin', become sluts. The disgust at the vulgar women which pervades this passage is also mixed with a self-derogatory distaste for the stereotyped markers of Welshness: 'Llanelly . . . (rugby) football . . . short men . . . leeks'.

In the prose works of the mid-1940s, such as 'A Child's Christmas in Wales' and 'Holiday Memory', Thomas effects a nostalgic return to childhood. This means that women are once again desexualised and reinserted into a comforting domestic space. Female characters tend to be familial – mothers, aunts, and sisters, slightly comic but decidedly unthreatening. It is almost as if, at this stage, Dylan Thomas is deconstructing his own work, unwriting the vindictive opening of *Adventures in the Skin Trade*, which is a savage rejection of the family, where Sam viciously tears up his mother's face and crumples up his sister in their photographs. Thomas is able to enact this deconstruction by reinventing himself as a child, a pre-lapsarian being who can still be cuddled by a mother and spoilt rotten by aunts. It is an escape which many adults would like to act out, which perhaps explains these later broadcasts' continuing wide popularity. In terms of Thomas's development as a writer, though, they seem a peculiar dead-end.

Such an impasse is not encountered in the poetry. The most extreme example of development away from the early work, in terms of the depiction of the female, is 'In the White Giant's Thigh', which is an erotic celebration of female sexuality. Far from being inspired by the phallic glory of the Cerne Abbas giant, alluded to in the title, the poet celebrates the dead women who lie beneath him in the ground. This is a poem not about birth or conception, the main areas of interest in the early poems, but, finally, about sex and copulation for the sheer joy of it. In 1933 Thomas had written a letter to Pamela Hansford Johnson in which he said: 'the hangman still has a lot of work to do, and the anatomical imagery is not yet exhausted. But one day I hope to write something altogether out of the hangman's sphere, something larger, wider, more comprehensible, and less selfcentred' (*CL*, 71). 'In the White Giant's Thigh' is surely one of the poems in which he achieves this ambition:

> Through throats where many rivers meet, the curlews cry,
> Under the conceiving moon, on the high chalk hill,

And there this night I walk in the white giant's thigh
Where barren as boulders women lie longing still

To labour and love though they lay down long ago

Through throats where many rivers meet, the women pray,
Pleading in the waded bay for the seed to flow
Though the names on their weed grown stones are rained away

(CP, 150)

Thomas referred to this as 'a conventionally Romantic poem' but belied this apparent carelessness by working long and hard on it during the summer of 1950, intending it to form part of an ultimately unfinished longer work, to be called *In Country Heaven*. In the scheme of the projected poem, the Earth was to have been destroyed by some act of human madness, and the inhabitants of heaven tell each other through the night what they remember of Earth's beauty. And, Thomas adds, 'the poem becomes, at last, an affirmation of the beautiful and terrible worth of the earth. It grows into a praise of what is and what could be on this lump in the skies.'[10]

The speaker of the poem hears the women's voices in the cry of the curlews and the rush of the river water. It is their desire which overwhelms him as he walks alone on the chalk hill. With certain notable exceptions, such as Lawrence, male poets have not been wont to talk of women's sexual desire and, still more, to celebrate it. More usual is the privileging of male desire and the emphasis is traditionally upon women's coyness or reluctance. Or if not reluctance, then indifference, like the 'adenoidal' secretary of Eliot's *The Waste Land*.

As is commonly noted, there is something Hardyesque in the elegiac tone of the poem's opening, particularly in the reference to the fading names on the gravestones. And the echo of Hardy is surely apt, for Hardy too was a poet who celebrated the female and recognised the restrictions both of femininity and masculinity. The poem then brings the dead women to life, animating their youth and vibrant lovemaking in the breathless, run-on lines: 'gay with anyone / young as they in the after milking moonlight lay' (CP, 151). The women are identified with nature – 'a hedgerow of joys' (CP, 151) – but this potentially essentialist conceit is, of course, literally true. They are a part of the earth; not, Lucy-like, passively 'rolled round in earth's diurnal course / with rocks and stones and trees'[11] but rather clamouring to escape from their graves, to 'clasp'

(*CP*, 151) this rather nice young man and to take him down with them. Their unappeasable sexual appetite and their refusal to stay quietly dead reminds us that this poem belongs to the same period as 'Do Not Go Gentle into that Good Night', with its memorable refrain 'Rage, rage against the dying of the light' (*CP*, 148). This is precisely what the women are doing – naucously, unendingly, they rage and long and pray.

These are country women, like the girl in 'Prospect of the Sea', used to the farmyard, the hayfield, the cowshed, not just the sheltered parlour of stuffed fox and dusty fern. The animal images used in the poem are not demeaning or brutalising in a Caradoc Evans sense, but apt and positive: there is a kinship with these creatures, not a derogation of them. The speaker of the poem does not simply listen, he becomes involved with the crying women, responding to their calls: 'Now curlew cry me down to kiss the mouths of their dust' (*CP*, 152). He descends into their kitchens of dirt and is held hard by them; he then prays to them: 'Teach me the love that is evergreen after the fall leaved / Grave, after Beloved on the grass gulfed cross is scrubbed / Off by the sun' (*CP*, 152). Like Yeats's voyager in 'Sailing to Byzantium', who seeks instruction from the dead sages in the mosaics, so Thomas's young dreamer returns to the dead women, his sages, seeking guidance from them. It is the female who must lead the way forward in the new, post-Apocalyptic world envisioned in the poem 'In Country Heaven'. Her desire and 'evergreen' love must be the new gospel.

One of the most striking aspects of the poem is that although the setting is highly specific – we are in the body of the Cerne Abbas white giant, he of the large club and even larger phallus – it is as if that setting is transcended. We are going, imaginatively, underground, into the realm of the daughters of darkness. Symbolically – and Thomas was ever, by his own admission, a 'Symbol Simon' (*CL*, 136) – we are leaving the realm of the patriarch, the realm of the domination of the phallus, and returning to a matriarchal demesne. The fact that these matriarchs are frustrated ones indicates perhaps that they have been unable to fulfil themselves in a world too obviously bestridden by the giant and his club.

Although the women in Thomas's poem are identified as country girls, their identification with the earth and their designation as 'daughters of darkness' are suggestive of the ancient, chthonic deities of Greek mythology, such as the Furies, daughters of Gaia, the Earth, and of Scotos, darkness. The taming of these terrible goddesses, and their transformation into the Eumenides, the 'Kindly Ones', is splendidly enacted in Aeschylus's *Oresteia* (which Thomas undoubtedly knew). Notoriously, the goddesses are defeated when Apollo argues that the mother is the mere vessel carrying the child, while the true germ of life comes from the father. Clytaemnestra is therefore devalued and the Furies' pursuit of Orestes comes to an end. It is, arguably, a dramatisation of the matriarchy being usurped by a patriarchy which has all the authority of the law behind it, as opposed to the dark, instinctive forces which endow the Furies with their terror. One might argue that Dylan Thomas is here reversing the judgement in that influential court case. The pre-Olympian goddesses are here reinstated, their venerability underlined by the fact that they lie beneath (beyond, before) the ancient carving of the Cerne Abbas giant.

The poem ends with an image of the bonfire; clearly this suggests the continuing fire of the daughters' passion, but it may also be read as the funeral pyre of the old patriarchal order. On Guy Fawkes night, the stuffed figure of the guy is burnt ritualistically; here, it stands for the old patriarch, whose rule may now be at an end.

Read in this way, 'In the White Giant's Thigh' may be seen to anticipate some of the prevailing ideas of French feminism. Feminist thought has moved away from the rejection and repudiation of the female body as the site of oppression (as one finds, depressingly, in the works of, say, de Beauvoir and Sylvia Plath) towards a celebration of the female body as superior and even miraculous. A recent book by Natalie Angier entitled *Female Geography*, for example, anatomises the female body in a powerful amalgam of poetic and scientific discourse, and more or less presents the female as the new *Übermensch*. Such texts build upon the writings of Cixous and, especially, those of Luce Irigaray, who states:

> Female sexuality has always been theorised within masculine parameters ... Woman and her pleasure are not mentioned in this conception of the sexual relationship. Her fate is one of 'lack', 'atrophy' (of her genitals), and 'penis envy', since the penis is the only recognised sex organ of any worth ... [And yet] a woman 'touches herself' constantly without anyone being able to forbid her to do so, for her sex is composed of two lips which embrace continually. Thus, within herself she is already two – but not divisible into ones – who stimulate each other ... [Woman's] pleasure is denied by a civilisation that privileges phallomorphism ... But *woman has sex organs just about everywhere*. She experiences pleasure almost

> everywhere ... one can say that the geography of her pleasure is much more diversified, more multiple in its differences, more complex, more subtle, than is imagined – in an imaginary centred a bit too much on one and the same.[12]

Clearly, Irigarary's claims may be regarded as demonstrated in a rich and subtle manner in Thomas's poem, written some decades before she uttered them.

Dylan Thomas's celebration of the female is thus a prominent feature of his entire work, though the kind of celebration undertaken, as well as the depiction of the female, modulates considerably. I speak of the female, rather than the feminine, because Dylan Thomas conspicuously avoids praising the social construction which we label femininity. When his female characters display noticeably feminine traits, as the three girls in the story 'Extraordinary Little Cough' do, for instance, they tend to be mocked or viewed with contempt. For all Jean's affected and flirtatious behaviour, even the naïve narrator of the story is able to confess 'Although I knew I loved her, I didn't like anything she said or did' (*CS*, 177).

If femininity is rejected, what is meant exactly by the claim that Dylan Thomas celebrates the female? In feminist discourse, 'female' usually denotes the biological, rather than the societal and, certainly, in the early process poems, Thomas exhibits a fascination with the biological sex which is female. But, even here, the preoccupation goes beyond the biological. Thomas is interested in gender, over and above sex, as the aforementioned commentary on the sexually undifferentiated nature of the embryo and the sexual ambiguity of the Christ figure has suggested. Thomas is concerned with the gender roles prescribed by society and with the way in which individuals accept, negotiate or evade those roles. Femininity for Thomas is a too-willing acceptance of societal constrictions on the female. His impatience with this is seen again in his early correspondence with Pamela Hansford Johnson: invariably it is when his correspondent is writing 'girlishly' in his view that he chastises her. He sees her femininity as responsible for her producing weak, pretty, respectable, 'nice' verse. And this at a time, of course, when he was dedicating himself enthusiastically to the excessively nasty and the Grand Guignol.

But that Thomas recognised a particular power in the female, a power prior to femininity, is indubitable. He revelled in depicting powerful women: witches in his early stories and streetwise pub women in the later ones, the elemental mother in the early poems and the chthonic energies of the later 'daughters of darkness'. It is tempting to suggest that Thomas found the female so attractive partly because he found his own masculinity something of a burden. In a 1934 letter to Glyn Jones, Thomas thanks Jones for praising Thomas's poem entitled 'The Woman Speaks', which had recently been published in the *Adelphi* magazine. Thomas writes: 'The woman speaks but the young *man* writes, and your doubt as to my sex was quite complimentary, proving (or was it simply my uncommon name?) that I do not employ too masculine a pen' (*CL*, 96). It is interesting to note that Thomas should regard having a 'masculine' pen as something negative, despite his censure at the time of Pamela Hansford Johnson's 'too feminine' pen. To Johnson, moreover, he had also written, under the heading '*Hints for Recognition*: Sex: male, I think' (*CL*, 67). He earlier describes himself in a deliberately androgynous way: 'I am a little person with much untidy hair' (*CL*, 22). Naturally enough, he feels obliged to condemn homosexuality in his letters to Hansford Johnson in quite a crass way, presumably to reassure her that he is willing and game. Nevertheless, biographers have established that he had homosexual encounters in London with Oswell Blakeston and Max Chapman. The flirtatious letters to Blakeston also reveal that the blustering homophobia played out elsewhere is a protective front. Phallic anxieties are reflected in the work, for example, in the very obviously named 'Little Willie Wee' in *Under Milk Wood*, whose presumably modest endowment is preferred by Polly Garter to Tom, 'strong as a bear and two yards long' (*UMW*, 41). Such brash masculinity, like timid femininity, is a conditioned role. As Anthony Easthope points out: 'Masculinity tries to stay invisible by passing itself off as normal and universal . . . [But] . . . the forms and images of contemporary popular culture lay on a man the burden of having to be one sex all the way through. So his struggle to be masculine is the struggle to cope with his own femininity.'[13] The letters suggest that Thomas is willing to act out the brash masculine role occasionally, and to act it with rumbustious relish ('I am a lover of the human race, especially of women!') but that he also felt bored and restricted by it. Thomas's celebration of the female might therefore be seen as a critical commentary on masculinity and its impoverishment. As Hélène Cixous comments: 'man has been handed that grotesque and scarcely enviable destiny (just imagine!) of being reduced to a single idol with clay balls.'[14] Thus, Polly Garter, that caricature of female power and fecundity in *Under Milk Wood*, is a longing sketch of what Thomas regarded as the unrestricted female's liberty and expansiveness, which males, by virtue of their sex, could never achieve.

Though there are marked differences between Thomas's early and late styles, one common factor is the dissatisfaction expressed in the works with binary oppositions. Even in the early Gothic stories where women are variously presented as evil, powerful witches or innocent victims, there is a sense of uneasiness with this duality and attempts are made to blur the boundaries. In 'The Orchards', for example, the two female figures are actually sisters and their opposing attitudes appear to be fused together by the end of the story. The movement towards the denial of dualities could be apprehended as part of Thomas's project to express kinship with everything. Yet reconciliation is not easily achieved, if it is achievable at all. From early on Thomas expressed his opposition to what R. S. Thomas has named as 'the tyranny of the either-or'.[15] In a letter to Pamela Hansford Johnson Thomas spoke of the opposition between D. H. Lawrence, advocating the life of the body, and Aldous Huxley, advocating the life of the intellect. He refuses to choose either (though it is clear that his sympathies lie more with Lawrence than with Huxley). Perhaps in the title of the early poem, 'My World is Pyramid', Thomas is suggesting a geometrical figure as his emblem, one opposed to duality. One senses continually that the poems grope towards a third possibility, which perhaps exists out there 'in the androgynous dark' (*CP*, 92).

Thomas's depiction of the female seems to follow a circular movement, from the elemental to the particular and back to the elemental. But the final position is very different from that at the outset: in the later poems there is more of an identification with the female figures, whereas the mother's womb in the early poems is the mysterious elsewhere whence the male speaker has come – even if desired, it remains Other. It is also interesting to note the transition from the womb as the locus of the poetic drama to the grave. Both are places of transition, border-crossings where transformations occur.

In a letter to Henry Treece, commenting on the latter's critical book on Thomas's own work, Thomas makes the following comment:

> In your Introduction you say that I do not, like other poets of (my) age, lean over gates, 'seeking kinship with daffodils and sheep' . . .

actually, 'seeking kinship', with everything, daffodils, sheep, shoe-
horns, saints, bees, and uncles is exactly what I *do* do.

(CL, 310–11)

He might have added 'women' to his list, for it seems that Dylan
Thomas's work moves progressively from a classic demonstration
of Woman as Other to an exploration of human kinship and a dissolution of traditional gender boundaries.

NOTES

[Katie Gramich's essay is the first full engagement of feminist theory with
Thomas's work. It asks whether it is possible to look at Dylan Thomas as the
kind of modernist writer privileged by Hélène Cixous, and hence as one, to
some extent at least, who is not 'afraid of femininity'. Wary of the limitations
of Cixous' lurking Romanticism as well as of Thomas's apparent misogyny,
Gramich nevertheless refuses to judge the work on the basis of moralising accounts of the life. Subverting any 'phallic monosexuality', Gramich discovers
a struggle to come to terms with masculinity in the early poetry and prose
which generates and permits to flourish a range of subject positions and
sexual identities. (Like Jeni Williams [essay 9], she also sees in the turn to
childhood themes a nostalgic desexualising of women through their rein-
scription in domestic settings.) In the later poetry she finds a frank celebration of female sexuality and – referring to other feminist theorists and writers
– she notes that, despite his occasional brash masculinity, Thomas challenges
conventional gender constructions, moving from either-or polarities in which
Woman is Other towards an androgynous dissolution of gender boundaries.
Eds]

1. Hélène Cixous, 'The Laugh of the Medusa', in *New French Feminisms*,
   ed. Elaine Marks and Isabelle de Courtivron (Hemel Hempstead,
   1981), pp. 255–6.

2. Ibid., pp. 247, 255.

3. Ibid., p. 254.

4. Ibid., p. 246.

5. Ibid., p. 253.

6. John Ackerman, *A Dylan Thomas Companion: Life, Poetry and Prose*
   (Basingstoke, 1991), p. 4. Ackerman quotes Geoffrey Moore in *Dylan
   Thomas: The Legend and the Poet*, ed. E. W. Tedlock (London, 1960),
   p. 251.

7. Simone de Beauvoir, *The Second Sex*, translated by H. M. Parshley
   (London, 1988), p. 35.

8. Ibid., p. 176.

9. John Bayley, 'Chains and the Poet', in *Dylan Thomas: New Critical Essays*, ed. Walford Davies (London, 1972), p. 68.

10. Dylan Thomas, quoted in Ackermann, *A Dylan Thomas Companion*, p. 146.

11. William Wordsworth, *The Poems*, Vol. 1, ed. John O. Hayden (Harmondsworth, 1982), p. 364.

12. Luce Irigaray, 'This Sex Which Is Not One', in *New French Feminisms*, pp. 99–103.

13. Anthony Easthope, *What a Man's Gotta Do: The Masculine Myth in Popular Culture* (New York and London, 1992), pp. 1, 6.

14. Hélène Cixous, 'The Laugh of the Medusa', p. 254.

15. R. S. Thomas, *Cymru or Wales?* (Landysul, 1992), p. 1.

4

'Birth and copulation and death': Gothic Modernism and Surrealism in the Poetry of Dylan Thomas

CHRIS WIGGINTON

In one of the more bizarre asides in 'The Function of Criticism', an essay which has come to look increasingly radical the more the notion of a unitary modernism is revised, T. S. Eliot observed that 'the possessors of the inner voice ride ten in a compartment to a football match at Swansea, listening to the inner voice which breathes the eternal message of vanity, fear and lust. It is a voice to which, for convenience, we may give a name: and the name I suggest is Whiggery.'[1] The claim is evidence of Eliot's rightward progression in the 1920s, a coincidental seizing on the birthplace of Dylan Thomas as a location for irredeemable provincialism. For Eliot, having Vetch Field rather than Little Gidding as a destination is a sure sign of the plebeian 'inner voice'; Swansea equalling Dissent, industry, philistinism and possibly also internal British difference, a would-be insider's put-down to distract from Eliot's self-fashioning as Anglican, classicist and monarchist. Yet the slur cuts both ways, and can equally be said to furnish a starting-point for a consideration of Thomas's poetry and its relationship to modernist precursors like Eliot himself. While Thomas was, in several ways, the closest of his generation to *The Waste Land* and Eliot's essays on the Metaphysicals and Renaissance dramatists, his work also acts as a form of punishment for high modernist condescension, embodying as it does the fear expressed in *Sweeney Agonistes* that life is no more than 'birth and copulation and death'.[2]

Born in 1914, Dylan Thomas came of age as a poet in the early 1930s, a period of economic turmoil, social radicalism and the supersession of High Modernism by new literary styles. W. H. Auden's *Poems* (1930), the *New Signatures* (1932) and *New Country* (1933) anthologies edited by Michael Roberts, and collections by poets represented in them – William Empson, Cecil Day Lewis, William Plomer, Stephen Spender – rapidly established a non-experimental, discursive, politically left poetic norm.[3] This response to modernism has been summed up by Spender:

> What we had . . . in common was in part Auden's influence, in part also not so much our relationship to one another as to what had gone before us. The writing of the 1920s had been characterised variously by despair, cynicism, self-conscious aestheticism, and by the prevalence of French influences. Although it was perhaps symptomatic of the political post-war era, it was consciously anti-political . . . Perhaps, after all, the qualities which distinguished us from the writers of the previous decade lay not in ourselves, but in the events to which we reacted. These were unemployment, economic crisis, nascent fascism, approaching war . . .[4]

In this account, Spender's definition of the political is relatively narrow and sociologistic, the notion of politics as purely superstructural revealed in his switch from the internal and subjectivist ('despair') to the external and determinist ('lay not in ourselves'). Today this would appear a curious distortion; how could Ezra Pound, Wyndham Lewis, D. H. Lawrence, 'the writing of the 1920s' seem 'consciously anti-political'? That said, it is a shift endorsed more recently by historians of modernism. Thus Bradbury and McFarlane argue that after 1930 'certain elements of modernism seem to be reallocated, as history increasingly came back in for intellectuals, as, with the loss of purpose and social cohesion, and the accelerating pace of technological change, *modernity was a visible scene open to simple report*'[5] (my emphasis). To Dylan Thomas, however, precociously aware as he was of metropolitan literary developments, qualities like visibility, openness and simplicity were anathema which he rejected for a closed and complex writing in which formal conservatism was estranged from itself by its modernist content, and modernist form undermined by an organicist pseudo-coherence.

At the time, then, that the *New Country* poets were turning a diagnostic gaze upon society, Thomas was deliberately opposing what he saw as their presumptive hyper-rationality. Despite the differences in approach, though, the *New Country* writers were generally impressed by *18 Poems* (1934). One reason for this was an intellectual climate heavily influenced by Freudianism and surrealism. Freud, of course, was central to the decade's poetic of demystification; as Robin Skelton has claimed, Freud was read politically, as a champion of individualism and freedom and an honorary socialist, and any psychoanalytic exposé of human nature was regarded, *per se*, as revolutionary.[6] Thus, in 1936 Cecil Day-Lewis could mark the difference between Thomas, Barker, Gascoyne and Clifford Dyment on the one hand, and the *New Country* poets on the other, but place both groups within broadly Freudian parameters; in an echo of the politics of Popular Frontism which began in 1934–35, the younger poets were treated as literary allies against a common enemy.[7] If Auden was the gallant lieutenant leading the main body of troops over the top, Thomas was the salt-of-the-earth NCO in charge of a more plebeian team of sappers who were detonating their mines under the ruling class; the id teaming up with the ego to strike against the tyrannical (and increasingly fascist) bourgeois superego.

Given their social agendas, the *New Country* poets were incapable of grasping that Thomas's resistance to their own abstraction and discursiveness was a major part of his point and they relegated the poetry he wrote to an ancillary, subaltern status, a complement to, rather than a critique of, their own. Early reviews show that, despite impressing, Thomas was seen as a hit-or-miss writer, and also that his work was increasingly seen as surrealist. Louis MacNeice, for example, referred to the 'surrealist principles' and 'nonsense images' of Thomas's work.[8] To Stephen Spender it was 'just poetic stuff with no beginning nor end, shape, or intelligent or intelligible control' (*CL*, 297). Thomas argued, though, that his poems were not automatic writing and therefore not surrealist; the ignorance pleaded in a letter of 1934 is typical:

> But who is this Gascoigne? I saw a geometrical effort of his in one *New Verse*, and also a poem in which he boasted of the ocarina in his belly. Is he much subtler or more absurd than I imagine? It is his sheer incompetence that strikes me more than anything else.
>
> (*CL*, 105)

This kind of response – to protest painstaking craftsmanship – was understandable. Yet both the denial and its narrow definition of surrealism have been accepted too uncritically; Thomas was, after all, an avid reader of the avant-garde periodical *transition*. Surrealism, whose project, according to Walter Benjamin, was 'to win the energies of intoxication for the revolution',[9] was in fact a complex set of artistic practices which went far beyond voluntarism or associationism, as a glance at the variety of surrealist visual art – say, Salvador Dali's hallucinatory realism and the collage of Max Ernst's *La Semaine de Bonté* – reveals. (The claim that surrealism, in Freudian terms, simply *inverts* passive realism is true up to a point, but overlooks the linkage between the movement and political activism, most strikingly illustrated by André Breton's alignment of radical surrealism to Trotsky's Fourth International.) More importantly, to the extent that surrealism had affinities with the Metaphysicals' violent yoking together of heterogeneous images (the conceit as a distant cousin of Lautréamont's chance encounter between an umbrella and a sewing machine on an operating table) there was a link between surrealist practice and the climate created earlier by Eliot and Herbert Grierson. Thomas, an avid reader of Donne, exploited such similarities to forge a semi-surrealised Metaphysical mode, a form of Gothic, from a marginalised and belated Welsh modernism. In this – as with Freudianism – he was pragmatic and ambivalent rather than systematic. 'Altarwise by owl-light', most frequently adduced as proof of surrealism, reproduces its effects. Sonnet V reads,

> And from the windy West came two-gunned Gabriel,
> From Jesu's sleeve trumped up the king of spots,
> The sheath-decked jacks, queen with a shuffled heart;
> Said the fake gentleman in a suit of spades,
> Black-tongued and tipsy from salvation's bottle,
> Rose my Byzantine Adam in the night;
> For loss of blood I fell on Ishmael's plain,
> Under the milky mushrooms slew my hunger,
> A climbing sea from Asia had me down
> And Jonah's Moby snatched me by the hair;
> Cross-stroked salt Adam to the frozen angel
> Pin-legged on pole-hills with a black medusa
> By waste seas where the white bear quoted Virgil
> And sirens singing from our lady's sea-straw.
>
> (CP, 60)

The poem can, of course, be read as furnishing a visual confirmation of surrealist-type images: the pin-legged frozen angel on pole-hills could fit into any of Dali's landscapes, as could the classically inclined bear into a painting of René Magritte's, while a gun-slinging Gabriel and what might be read as a card-sharping Jesus are suitably iconoclastic for a surrealist collage. Furthermore, parts of the sonnet are historically representative of the 1920s and 1930s when two of the most powerful legitimating discourses were religion and cinema. So that what is at work is a dialectic between the mythology of the Wild West, a modern extension of the Romantic notion of the frontier of the imagination, and the author-ised version of the Bible. Caught somewhere in the middle of all of this is Captain Ahab, a man in pursuit of a false purity, driven by the perverse religiosity of the puritan principle. Equally, however, there is a calculated appeal here to a sense of the surrealist absurd. Thomas, in other words, guys and mimics the attributes of a metro-politan style where it can be made to coincide with his own tactics of estrangement. And in both embracing and rejecting surrealism he created a provincial simulacrum of surrealism, or what might be called (for want of a better word) *surregionalism*.

The miscegenation of modes and genres in Thomas's work can also, if indirectly, be seen in the way claims for identifiably Welsh elements in his early poetry have been continuously thwarted by its lack of obvious markers of nationality, despite ingenious attempts to detect the influence of *cynghanedd* or Welsh speech rhythms presumed to result from *métèque* status.[10] Although a more oblique influence may be detected in his ability to take an outsider's advan-tage of the English language, it can scarcely be distinguished from the kinds of linguistic subversion which mark many poets, regard-less of origin, and particularly those who write, as Thomas did, in transitional periods. What is more significant is his shifting relation-ship towards fixed identities perceived as constraints. Thomas's am-bivalence towards nationality was expressed not so much in outright denials as in the tongue-in-cheek styling of himself as the 'Rimbaud of Cwmdonkin Drive' (*CL*, 487), a *voyant* who felt lost without 'the aspidistra, the provincial drive, the morning café [and] the evening pub' (*CL*, 222) of suburbia. His poetic identity, or rather *process*, is precisely this mediation between the bardic and the banal, the balance of *hywl*-inflated rhetoric and literary *lèse majesté*. Tony Conran has deemed Thomas's national identity 'largely a negative thing – he is not English';[11] but this itself is a one-sided assessment. In the Machereyan sense the 'negative thing' is also an absence that speaks, and what it speaks of is an initially enabling isolation, a source of self-belief, a calculated philistinism and a defensive humour.[12]

But if consideration of Thomas's status forces us to modify our view of the way in which national 'identity' operates, what precisely was his relationship to Welsh modernism? As Gareth Thomas has pointed out, in Thomas's time 'no Anglo-Welsh literary tradition that was in any way comparable to the Anglo-Irish had yet been established'.[13] The Anglo-Irish/Anglo-Welsh comparison is devastating, of course, precisely because Welsh modernism was patchy and disparate even by comparison with the English variety. If modernism in Britain was largely imported – think of James, Conrad, Pound, Eliot and Joyce – it was heavily Irish-influenced. Predictably, the Welsh variety has been seen solely in terms of its input to the definition of British (i.e. English) modernism, in the shape of David Jones. Although its anomalousness and belatedness are arguably a sign of writing which deals with the condition of Welshness, concentration on Jones's High Modernism (endorsed by Eliot and Faber publication) has led critics away from Welsh modernism.

Crucial to an appreciation of Thomas's Welsh modernist context is the work of Caradoc Evans. Evans, who Frank Kermode has termed a palaeo-modernist (that is, a writer modernist in content but not in form), was author of the pioneering short story collection *My People* (1915), described as the Welsh equivalent of James Joyce's *Dubliners*. The stories of this collection combine anecdotal structure with savage, grotesque realism in its attack on rural Welsh Nonconformism, hypocrisy, greed and cruelty, and made Evans 'the most reviled man in his country'.[14] There is no doubt that Thomas, who visited Evans in 1936, saw him as a literary hero (*CL*, 172). But Evans is also a literary forerunner for Thomas in the sense that his tales reverberate with the discourses of Nonconformism; their language is 'simple, often majestic, and suggestive also of parable and myth',[15] while mocking those who use it for blatantly repressive ends. As in Thomas's poetry, religion's musical and rhetorical resources – part of its radical tradition – were exploited, even as the social forms it had capitulated to were critiqued.

Yet as well as belonging to a later generation, very different forces intersected in Thomas than in Evans; his upbringing was freethinking, his surroundings suburban and his literary and political contexts more radical and cosmopolitan (this requires some qualification, of course; rejecting organised religion, Thomas seems to have opted for a form of Lawrentianism, a faith in the interrelatedness of all things which became more religiose during the 1940s). Again, it would be wrong to see this as a simple split, this time along urban-rural lines. Swansea lies at the westernmost point of English-speaking South Wales, its frontier, liminal situation reinforced by the fact that it also represented the class divide which Thomas's parents had crossed in order to achieve middle-class respectability. In the 1920s the Welsh-speaking farming communities of Carmarthenshire still lay within easy reach of Thomas's home; Swansea was a mainly (but not totally) English-speaking town hemmed around to the north and west by its Welsh-speaking hinterland. Historical change was less ambiguous and inflected the treatment of Welsh identity as repression and ambiguity. Not only did the effects of World War 1 post-date *My People*, so too did the economic crisis which gripped Wales from the early 1920s. This can be put another way by noting that Thomas's move to London in 1934 was that of an entire Welsh generation. And if Wales was more closely tied to England than any other of the UK's component parts, it was because its economy – lopsided to serve imperial rather than domestic needs – had produced what Gwyn A. Williams has called an 'offshore working class',[16] with its middle-class appendages. It was thus especially vulnerable to the decline of British power; recession bit more deeply and earlier in Wales than anywhere else in Britain.

The Depression pushed the already high Welsh unemployment level up to 32 per cent, a figure around which it lingered until the end of the 1930s. The demographic effects were devastating; over half a million people left Wales in the 1930s, most of them from the South. Though it was one of the more advanced areas of the South Walian economy, 'even Swansea with its poets and musicians . . . fell into a pall of neglect and depression, a collapse of social capital and a dismal legacy in bad housing, ill-health, poor environment'.[17] Thomas's own (dis)location ensured both relative personal comfort and an inescapable awareness of suffering; his political response was a socialism as intense but more diffuse and durable than those of the more overtly Left poets. The general disaster of the times sharpened the differences between a generation of radicalised Anglo-Welsh writers and Welsh language writers, whose nationalism and rural values were often reinforced by ethnic-linguistic exclusivism, or even flirtations with fascism.[18] As Tony Conran claims, 1930s Anglo-Welsh writers had nowhere to go but London; 'They either stayed in Wales and festered in isolation, or they offered themselves as international or colonial recruits to the London intelligentsia. Nationalism was hardly an option for most of them.'[19]

This is an important point given recent attempts to interpret modernism in nationalist terms. Robert Crawford's *Devolving English Literature*, for example, argues that modernism should be read as a provincial revolution against a complacent anglocentric literary establishment, and this can clearly be applied in some measure to Thomas. Crawford is certainly on firm ground when he opposes what he calls 'cursory' accounts of modernism which stress its 'cosmopolitanism and internationalism to present it as a facet of "high" metropolitan culture'. Yet the resultant claim that the provincial/demotic on the one hand and cosmopolitanism on the other 'are not opposites; they complement one another'[20] is too neat a reversal, a too-easy overcoming of very real and material differences of class, gender and so on within the nation and modernism as a literary trend. Crawford overlooks the role of bourgeois nationalist culture in submerging the kinds of internal national differences which produce hybrid, mixed, boundary writings (for his argument to work, the desire to integrate within the London literary and social mainstream on the part of writers like Thomas and Eliot also has to be seen in purely personal terms as an error of judgement).[21] To view modernism chiefly as an outgrowth of a wholly positive nationalist self-assertion, then, is to depoliticise both nationalism and modernism; celebration of national difference erases internal difference and ignores nationalism's reactionary potential. Crawford cannot account for the juxtaposition of 'international' *and* 'colonial', and ultimately settles for the kind of cultural identity politics sketched above, according to which Thomas can only be interpreted as either 'genuinely' Welsh or an inauthentic showman.

What this suggests is that it is the acceptance of the existing terms of the debate about Thomas – authentic or inauthentic, success or failure – which is the truly impermissible critical move. In other words, when Paul Ferris, for example, registers 'fears' that Thomas's poems 'are thick with the affectations of poetry', this is a problem not so much for Thomas's poems as for a narrow and conventional conception of poetry, and modernist poetry in particular.[22] *All* poetry – in its intertextual, parasitic, hybrid practice – is 'thick with the affectations of poetry', and this is not altered by presenting subjective moralising (who defines 'affectation', and on what grounds?) as universally agreed judgements. Modernism itself can be read as literary parody, and it is precisely what constitutes 'affectation' – or what the Russian Formalists would have called 'the literary' – which demands attention in Thomas's work. In this connection an area which immediately suggests itself is the use of grotesque style and the Gothic, elements which can be linked to Thomas's displaced, hybrid location and which have traditionally been seen in more purely Freudian and surrealist guise. Traditionally associated with mixing and impropriety, grotesque style and the Gothic have affinities with Evans's black humour and brutal sexuality as well as with larger literary trends. The grotesque played a central role in Welsh modernism, as Tony Conran has argued:

> Modernism in Wales is most at home with the grotesque. It is there that modernism characteristically shows itself, in Saunders Lewis as much as in Caradoc Evans and Dylan Thomas. The nightmare of monstrosity underlies the middle-class rejection of the *buchedd*, the sense of being suffocated by its hypocrisy and narrowness.[23]

It is in the short stories written before *Portrait of the Artist as a Young Dog* (1940), that the Gothic and grotesque aspects in Thomas are flaunted most extensively. Many of the stories – some collected in *The Map of Love* (1939) – centre on the imaginary Jarvis valley. Jarvis is Caradoc Evans's Manteg at one remove, gothicised under the pressures of social crisis and literary displacement, and it provides the setting for a collection of Welsh rural stereotypes; thus, its weather is always lowering, its landscapes charged with apocalyptic threat and repressed sexual energy, its scattered dwellings inhabited by children, murderers, gardeners and vivisectionists, haunted by the Holy Six and other religious fanatics, by witches, visionaries, lunatics, decayed gentry. But despite the critical solemnities pronounced over them, the stories have more than a hint of *Cold Comfort Farm* about them, referring as they do to the town of Llarregub ('bugger all' when read backwards), and containing such characters as Sam Rib, Dai Twice and old Vole. This location, then, is a version rather than a copy of Evans's, travestying even as it draws on its bleak realism. What applies to the prose applies, yet more variously, to the poetry. Both *18 Poems* and *Twenty-Five Poems* (1936) trail their Nonconformist, Gothic-inflected properties, and are crammed with – to list a sample – ghosts, vampires, cadavers, references to Struwwelpeter, tombs, sores, flies, cataracts, carcasses, cancers, cypresses, hanged men, mandrakes, gallows, crosses, worms and maggots. Both books exude a charnel atmosphere of decay and mortality and their libertarian strivings are inextricably linked to the darker aspects they purport to reject, with the first poem of the first collection exploring the idea that the 'boys of summer' are 'in their ruin', always in the process of themselves becoming 'the dark deniers' (*CP*, 7, 8).

From this it is clear that, far from being 'universal'[24] in its portrayal of adolescent crises of identity, Thomas's extraordinary blend of sex and death is not just of its time and place, but also very lower middle-class and *male*. The early poems chart not the achievement of stable identity but a realisation of its impossibility – in both national and personal terms – figured in part through gender. In pushing back to pre-natal origins, the speakers of the poems are attempting to reach the point at which they can escape the anxieties of sexual maturity facing Thomas himself. Thus, in 'Before I knocked', the speaker is without specific gender, 'brother to Mnetha's daughter / and sister to the fathering worm', existing 'in a molten form' (*CP*, 11). Nevertheless, this is no prelapsarian or ahistorical vision; even before birth, suffering cannot be escaped:

> My throat knew thirst before the structure
> Of skin and vein around the well
> Where words and water make a mixture
> Unfailing till the blood runs foul;
> My heart knew love, my belly hunger;
> I smelt the maggot in my stool.
>
> > (*CP*, 12)

But if there is a gesture towards the elimination of anxiety, there is also a petit-bourgeois bravado, a desire to exorcise uneasiness by dramatising it. As elsewhere in Thomas's poetry, then, the unborn child is identified with, even as he rebels against, paternal and meta-physical authority. He is Christ – 'You who bow down at cross and altar / Remember me and pity Him / Who ... doublecrossed my mother's womb' (*CP*, 12) – and Christ is the representative of the father, of the phallocentric authority of the Symbolic Order and the promise of plenitude. But he is also the betrayed son ('double-crossed'), both masculine and feminine, what Thomas called the 'castrated Saviour' (*CL*, 54) of official religion, and the attempt to escape anxiety by imagining an ungendered past generates new anxiety in the actuality of the father-dominated present. The anxiety, it might be argued, *is* the poetry; Christ is Logos, the word, the poet-as-hero charting his narcissistic, onanistic sexual experience in 'My hero bares his nerves', wherein masturbation and writing both figure as an unnerving absence and as a disquieting plenitude:

> And these poor nerves so wired to the skull
> Ache on the lovelorn paper
> I hug to love with my unruly scrawl
> That utters all love hunger
> And tells the page the empty ill.
>
> (*CP*, 14)

Writing, the means of achieving paternal sanction for the son and thus the way to sexual experience, breaks down, leaving the speaker trapped in a cycle of identity formation through self-abuse:

> He holds the wire from this box of nerves
> Praising the mortal error
> Of birth and death, the two sad knaves of thieves,
> And the hunger's emperor;
> He pulls the chain, the cistern moves.
>
> (*CP*, 14)

Either form of self-authentication disrupts itself (and it is noticeable that the poem begins in the first and ends in the third person). The paper – both writing paper and tissue paper – is 'lovelorn' because it bears the evidence of an absent presence, the unruly scrawl of ink/semen telling the narrator of the deferral of real voice or love as opposed to his auto-affection. In his discussion of Rousseau's *Confessions* in *Of Grammatology*, Jacques Derrida comments on the dangers of this process in terms of the 'supplement', that addition which would complete self-presence but which instead reveals its incompletion and lack: '[a] terrifying menace, . . . The supplement has not only the power of *procuring* an absent presence through its image; procuring it for us through the proxy [*procuration*] of the sign, it holds it at a distance and masters it. For this presence is at the same time desired and feared.'[25] Because of its assumption of authority, Thomas's 'baring' of this 'nerve' clearly threatened a more understated, 'English' self-presence, as revealed by a critical language which charged him, on occasion, with sexual immaturity and 'unmanliness'. Typical of this kind of attack is Robert Graves's claim that 'Thomas was nothing more than a Welsh demagogic masturbator who failed to pay his bills.'[26] Interestingly, Graves mirrors here the notorious assaults on Keats's poetry a century before; just as Keats's 'shabby genteel' class origins, for Byron, were linked to masturbatory immaturity in his poetry ('Johnny piss-a-bed Keats'), so Thomas's class and national identity, and through them his poetry, are impugned by Graves.[27]

The value of Gothic to Thomas, then, stemmed from its generic capability for organising disparate stylistic and thematic elements – parodic appropriation, belated modernism, social radicalism, sexual uncertainty and the plenitude/lack of writing – within the outrageous constructedness which is its hallmark. Precisely the excess of Gothic enables it to perform this kind of function; as Fred Botting has pointed out, Gothic is the 'signification of a writing of excess'[28] which shadows the progress of modernity and Enlightenment with a dark counter-narrative. In this way it also fulfilled Thomas's career need to subvert *New Country* hyper-rationality and dogmatism (although not necessarily in a merely irrational or ahistorical manner; as Stewart Crehan notes, the 'rich polysemy and fluidity'[29] of the early poetry – thematic as well as linguistic – can be seen as an attempt to keep alive the dialectic which had been frozen by dictatorship in the 1930s). The Gothic – like Thomas's work – operates with hybrid states and forms, insisting on the inescapability of the biological bases of existence. In it, as in the poetry generally, 'ambivalence and uncertainty obscure single meaning',[30] while the anxiety over boundary transgression it feeds off was, at the geopolitical level, in line with the 1930s *zeitgeist*. In alluding to a Gothic model – *Frankenstein* – to describe his practice at this time, Thomas implicitly defended such an oblique approach: 'So many modern poets take the living flesh as their object, and, by their clever dissecting, turn it into a carcass. I prefer to take the dead flesh, and, by any positivity of faith that is in me, build up a living flesh from it' (*CL*, 72–3).

A Gothic thematics cannot, of course, 'explain' Thomas's early work, but can provide a framework for interpreting a series of Welsh and modernist elements therein. It has been overlooked, I would argue, because of the lack of awareness of those writing about Thomas of recent developments in criticism. The basic evidence, however, is clear enough, and possible Gothic influences – Thomas's 'serious' reading, interest in film and taste in pulp fiction – have been known for years. Thomas's devotion to the work of the horror novelist Arthur Machen, for example, has occasionally been mentioned in critical work but not really considered significant. Machen, the author of what has been described as 'the most decadent book in English',[31] *The Hill of Dreams* (1907), 'took up Darwinian anxieties as the basis for terror',[32] mixing among others Huysmans, Pater, *La Queste del Sante Graal* and Sherlock Holmes. In *The Great God Pan* (1894), to take one example, a doctor operates on a young girl to open her 'inner eye' to the existence of Pan. The resulting visionary power eventually drives her mad, and when the hell-child born after her coupling with the Great God dies, it passes through all the stages of biological species reversion, ending up as primal slime. Parallels with 'The Lemon' and other works by Thomas might be drawn, but the important link lies in the resemblances between Machen's biological and physical emphases and Thomas's concern with cycles of inter-involved growth, biologic recapitulations, and pre-human states of consciousness. It is precisely this kind of influence, of course, which can be used to answer the 'glandular' charge so often levelled against Thomas's work.

This aspect of the work needs to be seen in the light of a powerful modernist influence, besides that of Eliot: D. H. Lawrence. There are many obvious similarities; shared provincial and class outsiderness, Nonconformist background (and personal puritanism) and an emphasis on redemption through the flesh rather than the disembodied intellect. The relationship of both to the dominant metropolitan styles of the day is also similar. Tony Pinkney has argued that Lawence attacked the classicising 'anti-Wagnerian' modernism of Mansfield, Pound, Joyce, Eliot and Lewis in order to forge an alternative Expressionist, northern-Gothic variety.[33] Lawrence's fiction generally – think of *The Rainbow* or *The Plumed Serpent* – rejects the Hellenism running in English culture from Arnold to Hulme and Eliot in which ' "criticism", "consciousness" and "irony" are cardinal virtues',[34] in favour of the creaturely virtues of a more 'native' tradition deriving from Morris and Ruskin. It is this form of modernism which, in the Lincoln Cathedral pages of *The Rainbow*, is shown as incorporating classicism's 'virtues' within its host of small details rather than expelling them. The point is that only Gothic 'deconstructs the rigid model of inside/outside . . . Its outside is its inside; even the sly stone faces that denounce its incompletion are, after all, part of it. The Gothic contains its own "negation", which thereafter ceases to be its negative pure and simple, and is rather granted a local validity within a more generous system which exceeds it.'[35]

Any discussion of Thomas's relationship to modernism must touch at some point on his use of language. This has consistently been seen as *the* distinguishing feature of his work, and he was well aware of its central, even compulsive nature: 'I use everything and anything to make my poems work . . . puns, portmanteau words, paradox, allusion, paronomasia, paragram, catachresis, slang, assonantal rhymes, vowel rhymes, sprung rhythm.'[36] The 1930s poetry displays not just the systematic foregrounding of the 'device' as a vehicle of estrangement, but also a belief that poetry should work 'out of' words, not 'towards them', recalling the Mallarméan dictum that 'Poems are made of words, not ideas'. At its most extreme, this yields attempts at wholly non-referential poems, such as those whose antecedents lie among the Russian *zaum* poets, the Dadaists, and the Gertrude Stein of *Tender Buttons*. One point of such exercises, of course, is to prove that no writing can completely escape meaning-construction at the hands of a sufficiently determined (or self-deluded) reader. Only two of Thomas's poems – 'How Soon the Servant Sun' and 'Now' – go so far, and they show the parodic aspect of his modernism, foreshadowing in their extremism the shift away from it in the poetry of the 1940s. Yet even when not testing limits, Thomas is utterly modernist in his insistence on the materiality of language and in the autonomy he grants to words. It was in this connection that he insisted he be read *literally*: his objection to Edith Sitwell's well-intentioned explication of the first sonnet of 'Altarwise by owl-light' was that 'She doesn't take the literal meaning: that a world-devouring ghost-creature bit out the horror of tomorrow from a gentleman's loins . . . This poem is a particular incident in a particular adventure, not a general, elliptical deprecation of this "horrible, crazy, speedy life" ' (*CL*, 301).

It is worth saying a little here about the implications of modernist practice for Thomas's style, since his 'everything and anything', in its relationship to the constraints of the poetry's conservative form, represents an internalised, imploded, even mimic modernism. The plethora of devices *replicate* the effect of modernist techniques such as collage, creating modernist textual instability and epistemological uncertainty. The parodic element which helps constitute modernist writing is foregrounded in this poetry. Thus, rhyme schemes and stanza patterns are deployed whose elaborate ingenuity is in excess of any mimetic or structural requirement.[37] Syntax is sabotaged, such that 'normal' grammar becomes at least as hard to construe as modernist fragmentariness, usually through the deferral of main verbs by subordinate, but apparently independent, clauses. Of the poem which opens 'Hold hard, these ancient minutes in the cuckoo's month, / Under the lank, fourth folly on Glamorgan's hill, / As the green blooms ride upward, to the drive of time' (*CP*, 44), Walford Davies claims that,

> In these lines we are bound to hear *Hold hard these ancient minutes* as a main clause, even though the commas show that the real main clause is 'Hold hard . . . to the drive of time'. And before we've grasped as much, we will also have heard (as a complete syntactic unit, despite the comma) *As the green blooms ride upward to the drive of time* . . . Similar ghost-effects of syntax occur too often in Thomas to be mere accidents. He seems bent on accommodating them.[38]

And this is a straightforward case: in 'When, like a running grave, time tracks you down' there are no less than *thirty-four* subordinate clauses (some as short as a single word) in an opening sentence that stretches for twenty-five lines over five 5-line verses. Not only does this stretch the possibilities of syntax; as with the use of surrealism and Freudianism there is more than a hint of mockery, of an effect analogous to what Mikhail Bakhtin calls the double voice of parody.[39]

Such procedures raise the issue of narrative. Virtually all of Thomas's poems are organised around a powerful narrative drive, a seemingly irresistible unfolding of event. Narrative is vital because it provides both an armature to which the many devices the poem requires can be attached and a pretext for their deployment in the first place. Defending his poetry in 1934 Thomas argued that '. . . all good modern poetry is bound to be obscure. Remember Eliot: "The chief use of the 'meaning' of a poem, in the ordinary sense, may be to satisfy one habit of the reader, to keep his mind diverted and quiet, while the poem does its work upon him" ' (*CL*, 97). Meaning, as Thomas also made clear in 'Answers to an Enquiry', refers to narrative; the echo is of 'Tradition and the Individual Talent', in which Eliot likens the phenomenal text of

the poem to a bone used to distract a guard-dog by a burglar before he goes about his business, the lived materiality of the poem – as in *The Waste Land* – acting as a 'cover' for, and authentication of, the operations of the ghostly discourse of the mythologies framing it. The narrative of *The Waste Land* is famously discontinuous, yet its very discontinuity produces a metanarrative, aided and abetted by Eliot's knowing annotations. In Thomas's poetry, on the contrary, the local narrative of the poem appears to offer immediate coherence, unity and closure, but is frequently empty, or banal, in the usual sense. That is, the discursive meaning-content is usually straightforward, invariably associated to the interrelatedness of the human and cosmic, the inextricability of processes of decay and growth. When Thomas wrote of the New Country poets that he could 'see the sensitive picking of words, but none of the strong inevitable pulling that makes a poem an event, a happening, an action perhaps, not a still-life or an experience *put down*, placed, regulated' (*CL*, 278) he went only part of the way to explaining the difference between his work and theirs. More to the point is the claim that the drive towards unification (of body, spirit, cosmos, etc.) leads directly to a language-use in which the materiality and autonomy of the signifier is a given. Thomas grants images almost the same degree of 'literalness' and autonomy, such that poems are not only *not* sustained by external reference, but that they seem to be generated by the self-evolving dynamic of images, in narratives whose linguistic events frequently exceed any abstractable sense. Thomas's description of his writing process alludes to this:

> I let, perhaps, an image be 'made' emotionally in me and then apply to it what intellectual and critical force I possess – let it breed another, let that image contradict the first, make of the third image bred out of the other two together, a fourth contradictory image, and let them all, within my own imposed formal limits, conflict.
>
> (*CL*, 281)

This kind of poem is entirely, or almost entirely, interiorised, moving solely amongst irreducibly literal images that 'nevertheless seem to have the kind of air of significance about them that tempts us (unhelpfully) to unpack the poem like a suitcase'.[40] One image 'breed[s] another' in a piece like 'Where once the waters of your face', in which the initial mention of 'waters' is elaborated in a series of *implicit* metaphors; that is, the vehicle (the figurative part of the metaphor) – 'mermen', 'channels', 'wet fruits', 'corals' and so on – is not related back to its tenor (what is actually being referred to) – sexual desire, psychic depths, the amniotic 'waters' of the embryo (*CP*, 14, 15). This is a narrative that 'just never *had* a real-world equivalent that could stand as referent [i.e. as tenor] in the first place'.[41] Narrative advances, but the poem has been turned inside out; or, to use a different image, it is as if we are viewing the back of a tapestry. Paradoxically, the high degree of control the poems display is offset by the arbitrary power of individual words and images on their development.

There is a social dimension to this. In Saussurean terms the stress on verbal autonomy weakens the links between signifiers and their socially-agreed signifieds, raising linguistic arbitrariness above ostensible message content. According to Saussure, all meanings attached to signifiers are arbitrary, since meaning is generated not by homologies between words and things but through the system of differential relationships between words themselves. To enable social discourse to occur, however, the bonds between signifier and signified are habitually agreed to be stable. Yet as Saussure points out, for the individual subject the bond never ceases to be an arbitrary one. The putative stability of social meanings inevitably becomes naturalised, and it is this fossilisation of the signifier–signified bond which Thomas's writing subverts, attacking the repression of our pre-moral delight in words. Put a different way, this could be taken to indicate the operation of the semiotic in Thomas's work, that infantile, pre-gendered, inchoate energy which, according to Julia Kristeva, is repressed by our induction into the symbolic order of social injunctions which marshal signifiers with their signifieds.[42] As Crehan argues, a poem like 'From love's first fever' is about the ways in which, through the process of language acquisition, we are interpellated as human subjects, accepting an inherited system of agreed linguistic meanings.[43] Again, the radical implications of Thomas's poetic practice have been overlooked by critics who seek (or fail) to find a social dimension to the poetry precisely because they look for evidence only at the level of overt 'reference' or 'allusion'.

As he used up the poems from his adolescent notebooks, pushing certain aspects of his work to their logical conclusion in *Twenty-Five Poems*, Thomas's poetry began to signal a shift away from modernism in *The Map of Love*. Thomas – partly due to personal circumstances, partly due to the marginalisation of experimental writing and partly due to the new crisis of impending world war – was trying to write more accessibly by the late 1930s. In this he was not alone, of course; T. S. Eliot, Igor Stravinsky and Béla Bartok, for example, were all part of a general movement away from radical High Modernism at the end of the 1930s and beginning of the 1940s. Whereas the modernist credentials of these artists are fully established, however, Thomas's are not, as criticism of his work has, for the most part, concentrated only on the work which appeared after *The Map of Love*. The fudging of issues that has led directly to a continued misrepresentation of Thomas as solely a 'Regional Romantic' is no longer acceptable, I would argue, and it is high time that one of the century's most discussed poets ceased to be one of its most critically misinterpreted and neglected.

NOTES

[Chris Wigginton's essay, like John Goodby's (essay 10), stems from the research on and interest in Thomas which led to the 1998 Dylan Thomas Conference and the chapter on Thomas and the modernist lyric in *The Locations of Modernism*, edited by Alex Davis and Lee Jenkins (Cambridge, 2000). Contemporary theory is to be embraced, not feared, Wigginton insists, as it has much to offer an understanding of Thomas's work. While earlier critics tended to underplay the modernist inheritance because of his later rural and 'Welsh' qualities, in this essay Wigginton argues that we have to read Thomas primarily as an inheritor of the modernist problematic at a time of formal retrenchment in British poetry. Looking specifically at the poetry most influenced by modernism – that of the first three collections: *18 Poems* (1934), *Twenty-five Poems* (1936) and *The Map of Love* (1939) – Wigginton notes the density of poetic devices and patterning by which Thomas mimicked something of the spatial dislocations of High Modernist poetry within formally conservative verse structures. Further, in emphasising the liminal and hybrid qualities of Thomas's early work, its negotiations of Welshness through a gothicised, even grotesque, modernism, he is able to read its radical and disruptive qualities in the context of the mainstream *New Country* reaction against experimentalism and the social crisis of the 1930s. In this way Wigginton offers the possibility of reading the Welsh dimension of Thomas's work dwelt on by Walford Davies and James A. Davies together with more theoretically nuanced considerations of modernist language-use, gender, and the political implications of Thomas's practice discussed by Stewart Crehan, Katie Gramich and Stan Smith in this volume. Eds]

1. T. S. Eliot, *Selected Essays* (London, 1932), p. 27. Terry Eagleton has glossed Eliot's 'Whiggism' in an English context as 'protestantism, liberalism, Romanticism, humanism' in *Criticism and Ideology* (London, 1986), p. 147. Welsh Dissent, socialism and 'celtic' emotionalism can be taken to represent extreme versions of these categories.

2. T. S. Eliot, *The Complete Poems and Plays* (London, 1969), p. 122. See also John Bayley 'Dylan Thomas', in *Dylan Thomas: A Collection of Critical Essays*, ed. C. B. Cox (New Jersey, 1966), p. 165.

3. The term *New Country* is hereafter used to refer to the house style of the Auden-influenced 1930s poets.

4. Stephen Spender, *World Within World* (London, 1953), p. 119.

5. *Modernism: 1890–1930*, ed. Malcolm Bradbury and James McFarlane (Harmondsworth, 1976), pp. 51–2.

6. *Poetry of the Thirties*, ed. Robin Skelton (Harmondsworth, 1964), pp. 30–1.

7. Ibid., p. 31.

8. Louis MacNeice, *Modern Poetry: A Personal Essay* (London, 1938), pp. 159–60.

9. Walter Benjamin, *One-Way Street and Other Writings* (London, 1998), p. 236.

10. See Walford Davies's essay below, pp. 107–9. See also John Ackerman, 'The Welsh Background', in *Dylan Thomas: A Collection of Critical Essays*, ed. C. B. Cox (New Jersey, 1966), pp. 25–44. For a spirited counter-argument, see Roland Mathias, 'Lord Cutglass, Twenty Years After', in *Poetry Dimension 2*, ed. Dannie Abse (London, 1974), p. 84.

11. Tony Conran, *Frontiers in Anglo-Welsh Poetry* (Cardiff, 1997), p. 113.

12. A Macherean criticism sets 'out to deliver the text from its own silences, by coaxing it into giving up its true, latent or hidden meaning', quoted in Tony Bennett, *Formalism and Marxism* (London, 1979), p. 107. For Macherey, the gaps, omissions and lapses of a text, its 'unsaid', are as important as that which is 'said'; they reveal its 'real' meaning, rather than its 'intended one'. See Pierre Macherey, *A Theory of Literary Production*, trans. G. Wall (London, 1978).

13. Gareth Thomas, 'A Freak User of Words', in *Dylan Thomas: Craft or Sullen Art*, ed. Alan Bold (London, 1990), p. 66.

14. Caradoc Evans, *My People*, ed. John Harris (Bridgend, 1997), back cover.

15. Ibid., p. 10.

16. Gwyn A. Williams, *When Was Wales?* (Harmondsworth, 1991), p. 253.

17. Ibid.

18. Ibid., pp. 280–6.

19. Conran, *Frontiers in Anglo-Welsh Poetry*, p. 111.

20. Robert Crawford, *Devolving English Literature* (Oxford, 1992), pp. 218–19.

21. Again, recent work on Irish writing provides something of a corrective; a similar critique of Crawford is made by Peter McDonald, who notes the 'useful warning' sounded in his book, but also the contradictions involved in desiring that a new identity-discourse of nationalism arise from the old one (of Englishness concealed by 'Britishness'): 'A complacent Englishness is no more subverted by (say) a complacent Scottishness than it is by the strident assertion of Irish identity; it is much more likely, in fact, to be reinforced by such pre-programmed systems of declaration.' McDonald, *Mistaken Identities: Poetry and Northern Ireland* (Oxford, 1997), pp. 193–4.

22. Paul Ferris, *Dylan Thomas* (Harmondsworth, 1978), p. 53. A similar point is made by John Haffenden in his review of the *Collected Letters*. See Michael Hulse, 'Dylan Thomas and the Individual Talent: A Dialogue', in *Dylan Thomas*, ed. Bold, p. 121.

23. Conran, *Frontiers in Anglo-Welsh Poetry*, p. 113.

24. Walford Davies, *Dylan Thomas* (Cardiff, 1990), p. 21.

25. Jacques Derrida, *Of Grammatology*, trans. Gayatri Chakravorty Spivak (Baltimore, MD, 1976), pp. 154–5.

26. Quoted by Stewart Crehan, 'The Lips of Time', *Dylan Thomas*, ed. Bold, p. 92.

27. Marjorie Levinson maintains that it was precisely those 'sensual' and improper aspects of Keats's style – his very 'badness' and excess – which were foregrounded in his most significant poetry; see her *Keats's Life of Allegory* (Oxford, 1988). This is a typical outsider strategy which has its similarities with Thomas's own poetic practice of the 1930s.

28. Fred Botting, *Gothic* (London, 1996), p. 3.

29. See Stewart Crehan's essay above, p. 56.

30. Botting, *Gothic*, p. 3.

31. David Punter, *The Literature of Terror: A History of Gothic Fictions* (London, 1980), p. 263.

32. Ibid.

33. Tony Pinkney, *D. H. Lawrence* (London, 1990). See especially ch. 2, 'Northernness and Modernism'.

34. Ibid., p. 73.

35. Ibid.

36. Dylan Thomas, 'Poetic Manifesto', in *Early Prose Writings*, ed. Walford Davies (London, 1971), p. 158.

37. 'I, in my intricate image', for example, is in three sections of six 6-line stanzas (72 lines), each of which contains four end-rhyme variations on 'l' or 'ls', with the two other lines linked by a different rhyme. 'I see the boys of summer' follows an 11-7-10-8-8-10 syllabic pattern through nine stanzas with only one lapse.

38. See Walford Davies, *Dylan Thomas: A Study Guide* (Milton Keynes, 1986), p. 105.

39. Mikhail Bahktin, *Problems of Dostoevsky's Poetics*, ed. and trans. C. Emerson (Minneapolis, 1984), p. 199.

40. See Walford Davies's essay below, p. 118.

41. Ibid., p. 114.

42. See Julia Kristeva, *The Powers of Horror* (New York, 1982).

43. 'Interpellation' is the term coined by Louis Althusser to refer to the process by which the ideologies which permeate society 'call up' or 'recruit' human subjects. See 'Ideology and Ideological State Apparatuses', in *Lenin and Philosophy and Other Essays*, trans. B. Brewster (London, 1971).

5

The Poetry of Dylan Thomas: Welsh Contexts, Narrative and the Language of Modernism

WALFORD DAVIES

'I never thought that localities meant so much, nor the genius of places, nor anything like that' (*CL*, 197) Thomas wrote in a letter of 1935 to the closest of his early Swansea friends, the composer Daniel Jones. This letter elegised the fantasticating games, mainly with words, that the two had played on regular evenings in his friend's home, 'Warmley'. Attaching conveniently to that name were also comfortable thoughts about so much of this early world. The first place-within-a-place that any fuller account of Thomas's life would discover is suburbia. The poet's home for the first twenty years of his life was a semi-detached provincial villa, 5 Cwmdonkin Drive, in Swansea. Its modesty did not inhibit a sense of cosiness. But it was a cosiness that, at the time, Thomas was capable of dramatising in letters as a smugness characteristic of the immediate society that formed his context. This wasn't a smugness seen in relation to Swansea's poorer industrial districts or its 10,000 registered unemployed and 2000 families subjected to the 'Means Test'. It reflected, rather, the imaginative frustrations of being, as he put it, 'at home with the *bourgeoisie*' (*CS*, 187). Later he could see that the shaping influence of such a milieu was permanent: from the scenic outdoors of Cornwall in 1936 he wrote that 'I stand for, if anything, the aspidistra, the provincial drive, the morning café, the evening pub' (*CL*, 222). And even then, an early poem such as 'I have longed to move away' already showed that he was half in love with the easeful death represented by suburbia. But at the time it must also have helped to drive him to search for other certainties. He did long to move away.

And before literal escape proved possible, imaginative escape into the privacies of his Notebook poems presented itself. Such a connection (by reaction) between inner and outer worlds might not be brought to mind by the early work of a different kind of poet. But the curious intensities of Thomas's early poems suggest almost an urge to decreate the social world that lay most immediately around him. The earliest Notebook poems (if we ignore what was always an unorthodox way with language) are often *thematically* conventional. But the Notebooks gradually work through such themes as relate (often satirically and bitterly) to an outer world, until they start exploring the strangely unpeopled world of the organic, 'process' poems.[1] Obviously, flight from provincial suburbia won't explain, certainly not on its own, the material strangeness of the poems with which Thomas first made his name. But reference to that context is more fruitful than merely psycho-analytical explanations built on the assumption that Thomas was from the outset a psychologically damaged human being. At least it does not hopelessly confuse man and poems to claim that the latter, in their search for elemental themes and especially in the quality of sexual assertiveness that they show, may have been shaped partly in reaction to the tidy puritanical world around him. It also keeps alive and relevant that part of his 'psychology' that we *are* qualified to identify – his independent, irreverent, 'young dog' personality, so evident in his autobiographical short stories. This factor does not diminish the seriousness of the early poems. But it usefully reminds us that in the kind of provincial obscurity in which he wrote or drafted or initiated, before the age of twenty, nearly a half of the poems that now comprise his final *Collected Poems*, the physical intensity of his themes must have been exactly what enabled him to imagine ultimate recognition and escape.

[His] unorthodox way with language may also evoke the Welsh context in a more specific linguistic sense. Thomas's father relayed strong influences into the poet's life. But it is also worth noting something that he did not pass on. That was the Welsh language itself. The father's Welsh was equal to his perfect English, which means that it was in effect his first language. He even taught Welsh in evening classes, and tended to criticise his wife's 'Swansea Welsh'. So both parents were Welsh-speaking. But D. J. Thomas's concern for 'getting on' through education – in which process, in the early decades of this century, the first abandoned ballast tended to be the Welsh language – led him to decide consciously not to raise his son as a Welsh-speaker. The name Dylan, lifted from the Welsh mediaeval classic the *Mabinogi*, would have to suffice. Thus Thomas's only language was English, beautifully enunciated in what he later called his 'cut-glass accent', the result of elocution lessons paid for by his father. But the rural, Welsh-speaking origins from which both parents came (in the old county of Carmarthenshire) could not be completely sealed off. Thomas's regular schoolboy holidays from his earliest years at his maternal aunt's farm, Fernhill, were amongst people whose own daily language was Welsh. Later, Thomas's wife was to say that he had 'the groove of direct hereditary descent in the land of his birth'.[2] She also tended to speak of his 'vegetable background'.[3] More important, along with such roots there went, in both Swansea and Carmarthenshire, a direct living awareness of another language left behind.

The significance of this, though difficult to prove or gauge, is at least likely to be more real than the view of him when being introduced at his first public reading in America – as having come 'out of the druidical mists of Wales'.[4] Yet it isn't a simple case, as is sometimes assumed, of a Welsh-speaker involuntarily reflecting in his English linguistic patterns determined by the Welsh language. By the same token, direct knowledge of the intricate rules of the prosody and internal rhyming patterns of the Welsh poetic tradition is also something that cannot in this case be claimed. Thomas was at least capable of claiming that 'I dreamed my genesis' was 'more or less based on Welsh rhythms' (*CL*, 117). As it happens, the rhythmic oddness of that poem is the result of its regular count of the number of syllables per line. Though this *is* a factor in classic Welsh metres, it does not produce, in any of the many poems that Thomas structures syllabically, any specifically 'Welsh' rhythms. In any case, 'rhythms' are determined more by the internal rules of the actual language used (its syntax, for example) than by externally imposed structures of form. A similar caveat applies to structures other than syllabic ones. Thomas rhymed 'Before I knocked' on 23 words ending in *er*; he patterned 'I, in my intricate image' on

72 words ending in *l* sounds; and the 102 lines of 'Author's Prologue' rhyme the first with the last line, the second with the 101st line, and so on inwards until the exact centre of the poem is a rhyming couplet. Thomas claimed that techniques of this kind 'may be a waste of time for the reader, but not for the poet'.[5] They are obviously very external techniques. At most, such heavy industry provides only an analogy for the meticulous craftsmanship associated with the Welsh poetic tradition, however much it may suggest a particular *kind* of respect for the craft of verse. Thomas certainly had friends who could (and did) tell him as much about the Welsh tradition as he wanted to know. A blurred awareness of alternative models is not in doubt. But to link 'alternative' possibilities to any *detailed* model provided by Welsh literature is not only inaccurate: it obscures possibly deeper aspects of the 'Welshness' of his position and linguistic methods.

We might in any case be looking for the wrong thing in searching for specifically 'Welsh' effects. 'Un-English' effects would be a different matter. If we allow our yardstick to be simply a very generalised norm, it is at least clear that Thomas showed an above-average readiness to subvert it. There are moments when an un-Englishness is reflected by individual words which, from the point of view of strict grammar, are not correctly used. Note the use of 'stringed' instead of *strung* in 'When once the twilight locks' (*CP*, 9), for example, and in 'How shall my animal' we see the image of the poet's mouth as 'The invoked, shrouding veil at the cap of the face' (*CP*, 75). The mouth would properly be *invoking* rather than 'invoked'. Although not thinking of Thomas, F. W. Bateson once commented on a phenomenon that would seem relevant to Thomas's case: 'The important difference between the native English writer and the *métèque* (the writer with a non-English linguistic, racial or political background) is the latter's lack of respect for the finer points of English idiom and grammar. This allows [him] to attempt effects of style, sometimes successfully, that the English writer would feel to be a perverse defiance of the genius of the language.'[6]

The fluency and idiomatic confidence of Thomas's letters and prose works show that eccentric effects in the poetry are not accidentally faltered into. There is, rather, something in his disposition towards the language that makes him welcome (or at least causes him not to resist) the off-centre impression that such effects create. Evidence of his linguistic opportunism is copiously there, however, even in the letters. These often reveal the kind of objective, alert wonder that a friend remembers Thomas showing when he discovered on a restaurant menu that the word 'live' spelt 'evil' backwards.[7] This hypersensitivity to accidental meanings created in the flash-points between words is what produces the punning energy of the poems. And we can reasonably speculate that it arises from what is still a certain sense of externality to the English language, a refusal to leave it alone, to take it for granted. An analogy with James Joyce suggests itself: a strong sense of provincial, cultural, even religious, 'otherness' leads to the writer taking revenge as it were (even for the most mixed of motives) on the imperial, standardising norms of the English language itself.

But one could imagine a darker interpretation of the phenomenon, one that is at least worth mentioning, wherein Thomas's poetry represents a kind of no man's land between two languages – one dead, the other powerless to be born. Or at least powerless to be born into any kind of natural ease. This would explain not only why he appears so *radically* different from any other poet of the 1930s, but also why he found poetry more and more difficult to write. (What is the significance, for example, of the fact that 'Poem on his birthday' was partly constructed from word-lists drawn from Roget's *Thesaurus*?) It would also explain why his later career depended more on oral performance of poems already accomplished than on the production of new ones – in readings that some would regard as willed and mechanical, as if the product of some struggle between the Welsh and English ('cut-glass') voices. All this might then be taken to explain the 'regressive' impulse in so much of the poetry, not just towards an idealised childhood (from his late twenties) but towards pre-childhood states at a much earlier age. A poetry of adulthood (the theory would run) was peculiarly difficult since, culturally, it could not be a Welsh adulthood. Consequently he found less and less to write about that was not connected with the fact that he was not a child and wouldn't live for ever.

Such a view runs at least two risks. First, the danger of sounding plausible on the failures and deficiencies but without (from the same negative base) being able to account for the obvious successes and merits. Secondly, the danger of patronisation, of attributing to a theory of linguistic damage effects whose wider context includes also the new adventurousness that accompanied poetic Modernism. This is a context to which we shall return. Its relevance, however, will be to larger aspects of style than just the verbal inventiveness that we've noted so far. In the meantime, the negative view outlined above usefully reminds us how descriptively thin is the standard explanation 'provincial' on which we tend to fall back in labelling writers whose roots lie outside the centre. Real cultural tensions are likely to be there, however difficult they may be to describe, tensions all the more likely to be intensified when an alternative language is also involved. What is also brought home is the way Thomas's poetry has been, and still is, appropriated by more politically powerful cultures, so that only abstract idealising accounts of it become possible.

Nevertheless, it is in the sharpening of a certain external opportunism that the context of a different culture, centring also on a different language, is most obviously manifest. It is clear that a good deal of Anglo-Welsh literature in the relevant part of this century, even in the form of the novel, and in the hands of Welsh and non-Welsh speakers alike, showed a relish for what is, in terms of linguistic and stylistic effects, high-definition performance. The phenomenon has analogies also in the spheres of broadcasting and acting styles in the same period and in the case of personalities from the same kind of background as Thomas. Though it is a spin-off from genuine cultural difference, we don't have to pursue explanations back to deep atavistic roots. What is relevant is the Welshman's impulse to draw on the differences that help him gain visibility and identity in an essentially centralised Britain.

That identity comes from a language that is more the expression of the poet's almost physical feel of his own selfhood than it is a 'comment on' experience or a 'description of' its ostensible subject. It is as if the poet is most genuinely himself when at a remove from a style that conveys opinions, mediates traditional emotions, or manifests self-possession. This presumably explains why Thomas's early themes are essentially few: his song is in any case ultimately of *himself*. Though in a sense this remained true of the whole career, [John]Bayley finds what he calls the 'trapped effectiveness'[8] of the best early poems more impressive than what he sees as the more open, plangent commentaries of the later ones. The early poetry, then, closes the traditional gap between poet and poem.

It also closes the usual gap between word and thing. Often, the words don't seem referentially to *indicate* things as much as *become* things themselves. To some degree, I feel it is easy to over-emphasise this aspect. A phrase like 'brambles in the wringing brains' (*CP*, 12) certainly makes us feel the sensation *in* the words. But there is much less of this purely mimetic effect in Thomas than in, say, Hopkins.

However, another example from Thomas may suggest why we always feel that there is more of it there:

> The bagpipe-breasted ladies in the deadweed
> Blew out the blood gauze through the wound of manwax.
>
> (*CP*, 61)

Isn't the 'thinginess' of these words the result of our not quite knowing in the first place what the things are that they communicate? Isn't it the strangeness of the referents that gives such apparently autonomous life to the words? It is as if the poet who evacuated his poems of the social world around him, and who seems most characteristic when he reveals his own sensibility rather than when he articulates ideas or opinions, is also attracted by material which, because of its strangeness, makes thing and word appear to become one.

The strangeness of his material also bears on the question of syntax. We have already seen that Thomas's syntax can be difficult. But the critic Donald Davie has gone further, and claimed that what we often get in Thomas is 'pseudo-syntax', a play of empty forms.[9] Davie quotes from the seventh of the 'Altarwise' sonnets, as follows:

> Time, milk, and magic, from the world beginning.
> Time is the tune my ladies lend their heartbreak,
> From bald pavilions and the house of bread
> Time tracks the sound of shape on man and cloud,
> On rose and icicle the ringing handprint.
>
> (*CP*, 61)

Davie comments on that penultimate line: 'The verb "tracks" is completely void of meaning. What appears to be narrative ("Time", the agent, transfers energy through "tracks" to the object, "sound") is in fact an endless series of copulas: "Time is tracking which is sound which is shape . . ." and so on.'[10] Alastair Fowler countered: 'One is irritated into replying. "The verb 'tracks' is *not* devoid of meaning: prove that it is".'[11] But Davie's point is at least wider than just our difficulty in working out the syntax. His argument is that Thomas's sentences only appear to drive on through their verbs; that, although 'formally correct, his syntax cannot mime, as it offers to do, a movement of the mind'.[12] Clearly, Thomas's style would not be a good one in which to write the minutes of a committee meeting! But surely the strangeness of a poem's materials or events is bound to have some bearing on the genuine expressiveness or otherwise of its syntactic forms. We could argue that the logic of the events and the logic of grammar are being suspended for something like the same motive.

Let us explore the point further by noting first of all that Davie has wrongly punctuated the first line of his quotation from the 'Altarwise' sonnet above. Davie ends that first line with a comma whereas Thomas in fact ended it with a full-stop. Therefore that line syntactically belongs to what has gone before, not to what Davie quotes here! Yet the interesting thing is that one can see how easy it would be to make that misquotation. That first line does indeed appear to lead fairly happily into what follows. And it does so precisely because of the repetitive, appositional nature of Thomas's syntax. The line already has some kind of ghost-relationship to what follows. Davie himself notes the characteristic stylistic effect of what he calls 'simultaneity and identification', but doesn't like it; it abandons, he says, the 'intelligible structure of the conscious mind'.[13] Yet simultaneity and identification are the *theme* as well as the style of these sonnets. Of course, style in poetry doesn't always have physically to mime meaning. If it did so, it would be too much a case of killing one bird with two stones! But it should at least be noted that in the specific line whose main verb Davie finds 'completely void of meaning', 'Time tracks the sound of shape on man and cloud' (*CP*, 61), what is being mimed is already a strange and difficult abstract idea – that of the simultaneity of time and space. 'Time tracks the sound of shape on man and cloud' is Thomas's way of expressing what Time is: Time is imaginable only in terms of the sound and shape of *things* – things that are not abstract, and that move ('cloud'), fade ('rose'), and melt ('icicle'). Time 'tracks' these things both in the sense of creating the sad music of their mortality (the 'sound' or significance of their shapes) as on a *sound-track*, and also in the sense of *tracking them down*. The reality of abstract Time is simultaneous and identical with the physical things it destroys. Ironically, Davie seems close to the truth even in the dismissive parody he offers: 'Time is tracking which is sound which is shape'.[14] Our concern at present is the nature of the syntax, rather than the ramifications of meaning. But the way in which the two are always interrelated in Thomas is at the heart of our experience of reading his densest poems. Donald Davie would also argue that Thomas's syntax and rhythm do not create enough ventilation around the images to ease the act of reading (as opposed to the act of explicative commentary). And there is a good deal of truth in this. But it is surely not the same thing as saying that 'tracks' is 'completely void of meaning'.

Again, the whole enterprise argues a certain 'external' feel for the opportunities of the language. And this impression remains in the effect of the whole. On the question of syntax, not even a reading-aloud could bridge the syntactic delays and tangential phrases of the densest early poems in a way that would give them idiomatic naturalness. (A good example on which to test the truth of this would be 'I, in my intricate image'.) Though this is not true of all early poems to the same degree, its logic and significance are general. Despite their obvious musicality, the early poems, from the point of view of what sense demands, are designed first of all as if for solid existence on the page. The poems are heavy with trapped possibilities, at one remove from what the spoken voice could release. It may be significant that Thomas's own later readings did not include many of the early poems and, apart from the first 'Altarwise' sonnet, none of the densest ones. What made the later poems more suited to public readings was exactly the degree of 'dilution' he had managed to achieve in them, in syntax as well as image. Yet the logic of the whole career still came from the very poems that needed such dilution. And it is paradoxical that what is most deeply revelatory of the man himself is, in those early poems, inextricably tied in with strange narratives and irreducible images and syntax. This suggests again his situation as one writing from outside the English centre. From the beginning, his eye was on London publication, but in mediating his themes indirectly in this way, Thomas seems to have felt free to bear an actual reading audience only vaguely in mind. It is as if the Welshman was preserving his sense of his own identity as man and poet by sub-verting the cultural expectations normally associated with the English tradition.

We should remember that the prime exemplars of poetic Modernism (Pound, Eliot, the later Yeats) were themselves not English. Their freedom to change the nature of poetic expression came from something like the same cultural independence. Thomas would not have been interested in all of the theory or rationalisa-tion that went along with poetic Modernism, and the seedy urban-ism or allusive metropolitanism we associate with its leading products are at a distinct remove from Thomas's themes of organic process. Indeed, some of the techniques and forms central to the shaping of Modernist poetry (brief Imagist-type lyrics and impressionistic free-verse patterns) were the very things left abandoned in the early Notebooks when Thomas discovered his own characteristic voice. Yet, even having turned to more private themes and to heavily-designed stanzaic forms, he may well have consciously hung on to, and intensified, what any young poet would have perceived as the main object-lesson of Modernism: concreteness of presentation. Thomas is Modernist in his acceptance of the final barrier that Modernism itself in this sense had placed against any return to Victorian discursiveness or Georgian descriptiveness. And of course another Modernist trait that he absorbed was the conscious foregrounding of language as language, language itself as theme, within poems.

Yet if we take the two key aspects of Modernist poetry to be Imagism and Symbolism, Thomas's aims were clearly less modest than the former and probably less ambitious than the latter. So a typical Imagist poem did little more than present a series of clear pictures. Thomas would clearly not be satisfied with the small compass that such an enterprise allows, and he satirised wickedly the unadventurousness of poems in this tradition. But the [Imagist] taboo on commentary as such is not unrelated to his own methods. The difference is that, in his case, a strong *narrative* emphasis links, and takes us through, the images. His images are also themselves energetic actors, locations or events in that narrative (not simply 'things' mediated or mediated upon) and come from strange landscapes.

When we turn to Symbolism, it is again from the point of view mainly of contrast, though there are some connections which will help us focus further what Thomas does in his own way. For all that Thomas called himself 'the Rimbaud of Cwmdonkin Drive'(CL, 487), his knowledge of the *Symboliste* poetry of late nineteenth-century France was at best negligible. His fondness for synaesthesically mixing the senses may have come from Rimbaud, via translation, but is in itself no stranger than many other effects in his work. It is in any case the legacy of *Symboliste* method in Yeats or Eliot that probably counted. Two of its main features seem worth evoking.

First, the *musical* implications of the Symbolist ideal of living in a world of words. Paul Valéry had claimed that what the poet did to ordinary language was to 'musicalise' it. This meant not just

poetry's usual capitalisation on the sounds of words, but a determined attempt thereby to deny that the most important function of
language comes from its referential or denotative power. Thus as-
piring to the condition of music, Symbolist poetry sought to express
states of feeling directly, allowing language to negotiate referentially
with the world as little as possible. One can see why this should
remind us of Thomas, the poet most often accused of writing musi-
cally without sense. And even a friendly critic can see that Thomas
promotes, sustains, and elaborates the musical potential of his
words. But non-referentially? Surely Thomas's narratives are busily
descriptive of *things*, however strange. And a further consideration
is the question of the rhythmic impression of the whole. *Symboliste*-
influenced poems, like so many by the early Yeats, match their ethe-
real language with moody, hesitant, hovering rhythms. But the only
mature poem with anything like a world-weary *Symboliste* music is
'We lying by seasand'. Its opening, characteristic of the whole,
shows the *Symboliste* trick of promoting an etherial effect by
muting the tangibility of things and rhythms:

> We lying by seasand, watching yellow
> And the grave sea, mock who deride
> Who follow the red rivers, hollow
> Alcove of words out of cicada shade,
> For in this yellow grave of sand and sea
> A calling for colour calls with the wind
> That's grave and gay as grave and sea
> Sleeping on either hand.
>
> (*CP*, 70)

This, surely, isn't characteristic Thomas. But certain other poten-
tials in Symbolist Modernism (there only in miniature in Imagism)
might have been influential. Such influence might not be a case of
copied models, but an awareness of new kinds of structural
freedom. One Symbolist effect, sanctioned pre-eminently by Eliot's
example, was the effect of discontinuity. Since this has often, in
Thomas's case, been laid at the door of Surrealism, we should consider that accusation first before returning to the kind of discontinuity that a poet such as Eliot employed.

Obviously, much in early Thomas smacks of Surrealism and there
can be no doubt that a certain kind of image took some of its
flavour from such writing. But Surrealism proper is not defined by

kinds of imagery. Its hallucinatory effect comes from the odd *relationship* of images, unselected and irrationally juxtaposed. David Gascoyne, a Surrealist poet and contemporary of Thomas, defined such poetry as 'a perpetual flow of irrational thought in the form of images'.[15] Like the Surrealists, Thomas thought of himself as drawing on subconscious material. But whereas the Surrealists allowed no room for the selection, control, and development of images, Thomas again seems busy with those very activities, and with everything carefully subjected to the aesthetic demands of poetic form. Take the opening verse of 'When, like a running grave':

> When, like a running grave, time tracks you down,
> Your calm and cuddled is a scythe of hairs,
> Love in her gear is slowly through the house,
> Up naked stairs, a turtle in a hearse,
> Hauled to the dome
>
> (*CP*, 19)

A 'running grave', a 'scythe of hairs', a 'turtle in a hearse' seem, on their own, suitably Surrealistic. But even in this obscurest of poems we feel that the connections are being made for us, and the images consciously developed. It is a poem argued (or rather a narrative enacted) completely through images, so it is almost impossible to paraphrase, but the images are certainly not left in only a one-off juxtaposition to each other. Thus we later see (via an image of a cinder track) why Thomas wanted to say 'time *tracks* you down'. Again, it is clear later that a 'running' grave was in any case meant (like a running sore) to suggest infection and disease. The 'scythe of hairs', on reflection, is that which scythes hairs. The verb 'is' in the third line is consciously made to have the ghost-effect of a complete positive action ('*is* slowly through the house') before we realise that it is in fact a subsidiary verb in a passive action ('is . . . Hauled'). 'Hearse' makes 'gear' mechanical, but 'tailor' later also makes it an image of clothes (as in *night-gear*); and in the meantime the idea of clothes has made the stairs 'naked'. The wit in describing uncarpeted stairs as 'naked' is also that which puts the slowest animal ('turtle') in the slowest vehicle ('hearse'). One feels that there might be no end to the ingenuity, and all this is certainly no defence of the poem's ultimate obscurity. But not only is Thomas's comment about letting one image 'breed' another, even while allowing them to contradict, a fair description; it describes a method that has by no means surrendered 'intellectual and critical forces' to automatic writing.

It is not Eliot's techniques of discontinuity as such that make him more relevant than Surrealism here. It is, rather, the fact that this particular aspect of Symbolist method helped promote a view of poems as autonomous or irreducible semantic worlds. This view in Thomas will bring us back ultimately to what he meant by saying that his early poems were to be read 'literally'. What would it be like, within a poem, to move *only* amongst irreducibly literal images that nevertheless seem to have the kind of air of significance about them that tempts us (unhelpfully) to unpack the poem like a suitcase? Such a poem would surely parallel even more Dylan Thomas's kind of obscurity if it also – like Yeats's 'Byzantium' for example – completely inhabited an already strange landscape.

That possibility of a *complete* poem being irreducible (of being Symbolist rather than symbolical) is something we encounter particularly in Eliot's earlier verse. The world of such a poem need not be a strange one. *The Waste Land*, for example, presents us in the main with recognisable social or geographic scenes. The strong emphasis on at least *narrative* continuity in Thomas sets him at a great remove from such a phenomenon as is represented by *The Waste Land*. But the degree of discontinuity need not be as extreme as that, even in Eliot. Indeed, that degree of discontinuity is made both necessary and effective only by the special needs of writing a *long* poem in the Symbolist mode. Eliot's shorter earlier poems, however, also make surprising leaps or rapid, unexplained transitions that are designed to prevent them from 'adding up' in conveniently tidy ways. Thus the Jamesean social materials of 'Prufrock' tempt us to reduce that poem back into some descriptive narrative of an orthodox realistic kind: as if what Eliot had done was imagine such a narrative, and then write it out more challengingly by omitting the connections, or blurring the realism. But if we do such unpacking, the narrative we are left with (though it *is* partly evoked) cannot account at all for the particular resonance of the poem itself, and would locate the poem more firmly in a merely realistic world than it appears to want. Such difficulties are raised even more strikingly by other Eliot poems such as 'A Cooking Egg' and 'Mr Eliot's Sunday Morning Service'. Donald Davie has persuasively argued that the strange coexistence in those poems, of objects not normally thought of as being associated, can only be understood if we accept that Symbolist poems are not cryptic versions of realistic narratives.[16]

Such writing must have brought about a sea-change in what younger poets perceived as allowable possibilities, and Thomas would seem, more than any poet of his generation, to have seized on Modernism's sanctioning, not only of the discontinuity of disparate images, but also of the irreducibility that comes from a relentless concreteness of presentation. And if we now return to what Thomas meant by saying that his poems were to be read 'literally', we can see a wide variety in the implications of that term. Let us first of all consider the irreducible literalness of individual images. It seems clear, doesn't it, that when Thomas says 'The ball I threw while playing in the park / Has not yet reached the ground' (*CP*, 52) we would be foolish to want the park or the permanently suspended ball to 'represent' other things. The unstated logic of the poem allows us to negotiate the symbol (as with Yeats's chestnut-tree and dancer) without unpacking it. We can talk of its meaning certainly, but would be foolish to think that the items in the symbol stand for other things. Even when the items evoke a less familiar landscape, the same air of irreducible literalness applies. So we would also be wrong to hold back literal assent even from such lines as 'Above the waste allotments the dawn halts' (*CP*, 24). As we have seen in that particular poem, the 'dawn' is already a metaphor of a traditional kind: it is the 'dawn' or 'light' of consciousness; it *does* stand for something else. Here, surely, we get our bearings from recognising that there is indeed some measure of point-for-point equivalence. And this is fine – as long as we recognise also that the aim of the poem ('Light breaks where no sun shines') is to make us delight in the independent literal life that the metaphor has been allowed to achieve. The point is that we don't feel we want to translate the lines back to other referents; we have come to read even recognisable metaphors as if they were *themselves* 'literal'.

Determining the difficulty raised by all this is the degree to which the opening of a poem reveals the ostensible area in which it is working. Despite its strong and original phrasing, the opening 'Before I knocked and flesh let enter, With liquid hands tapped on the womb' (*CP*, 11), reveals its subject as prenatal life quite directly. The outer circumference of the poem, as it were, is established – and there is a sense in which all the particularising images that follow are indeed metaphors, and known to be so, because we don't lose sight of that outer circumference. But it is another thing when a poem starts by thus denoting its area of reference but then develops *only within* the independent logic of its original metaphors. Different again is the case of the poem 'The spire cranes' which *starts*, and continues, only with metaphor. The irony is that the majority of Thomas's early poems allow us, in these different ways, to speak, if we must, of ordinary metaphor. It is when such metaphors become the very foreground of the poem, as it were, that the term seems inadequate; or (to change our own metaphor!) when the poem seems to have been turned inside-out; that is to say, when the normally inward secret comparisons that we think of metaphor as being become the main outward life of the poem. In such cases, the 'real' referents in the actual world seem almost like 'other' things to which this 'literal' narrative is compared.

But it is yet another thing when Thomas writes out a narrative that has just never *had* a real-world equivalent that could stand as referent in the first place. They don't have what we've called an outer circumference or outer reference, like pre-natal life or the process of birth. Yet isn't language without reference, by definition, nonsense? Yes, it is. But we must remember that it is *narrative* without reference that we are talking about. In the last poems mentioned it is the *events* described that have no equivalents in the real world. Yet, it follows that their individual words or images don't need defending against the charge of being non-referential or of being only spuriously literal. The realities they refer to (realities like 'the atlas-eater with a jaw for news' [*CP*, 58]) are clearly *there*, but there within the autonomous logic of what are already strange (not just discontinuous) narratives. When Eliot was asked what the line 'Lady, three white leopards sat under a juniper tree'[17] meant, all he could do in reply was repeat the line. There, it is the abruptness of the reference, its discontinuity with what surrounds it, rather than any logical impossibility in itself, that prompts the difficulty. Thomas had to explain stranger images. His explanation of the phrase 'the country-handed grave' (*CP*, 48) asked us to imagine a grave with a country for each hand (*CL*, 300–1). With such materials, there is a sense in which a poem's 'meaning', in Thomas's case as well, has to flower from spaces. But they are not spaces caused by gaps in the narrative, and not just spaces in between quickly changing images. They are the spaces left by the narratives not having any equivalents in the realistic world. Narratives of this kind *can* only be read literally. And they don't have to be in a 'Jabberwocky' language honourably to demand it.

Despite differences, we feel that what such poems share in is still essentially the central enterprise of Modernism. Even though the Modernist-Symbolist ideal developed from the increased subjectivism of Romanticism, no Romantic poet had made poems live to such a degree in imaginatively autonomous worlds. In hanging on to a continuous narrative line, Thomas was less ambitious than, say, Eliot in the structural method by which poems could be cut off from the logic of the world, even though his materials, in themselves, came from much stranger territories. But even while he claimed that 'narrative is essential' he saw it as a means whereby the ordinary expectations of the reader could be accommodated while the poem worked, otherwise, in less obviously logical ways. And, however paradoxical, it is significant that the authority Thomas quoted for this strategic function of narrative could still be Eliot himself. 'Narrative, in its widest sense,' he said, 'satisfies what Eliot, talking of "meaning", calls "one habit of the reader". Let the narrative take that one logical habit of the reader along with its movement, and the essence of the poem will do its work on him.'[18]

From Walford Davies, *Dylan Thomas* (Milton Keynes, 1986), pp. 94–123.

NOTES

[Walford Davies's book first appeared at a time when Thomas's critical fortunes were at their lowest ebb, in the 1980s. In some ways a guide to close reading, Davies's text consists of 'discussion' sections, based on questions directly addressed to the reader, linked by contextualising passages. The final chapter, extracted here, turns from the analysis of individual poems and interpretative issues to a more general summary of the contexts of Thomas's poetry. Without discounting the importance of biography, Davies dismisses reductively Freudian readings of Thomas as 'a psychologically damaged human being' to consider his national, linguistic, social and political milieux. Of particular significance for Davies is Thomas's Welshness, but he traces the subversiveness of his 'eccentric' use of English to his position in a linguistic 'no man's land' rather than to bardic or subliminal Welsh language influences. This enables a nuanced opposition to the 'provincial' label by which Thomas's work had previously been appropriated to produce 'abstract idealising accounts'. At the same time, however, he stresses the 'external opportunism' and performative element which Welsh origins nurtured, and which led Thomas to resist the ratiocinative discursivity of his English contemporaries in favour of a poetry of 'irreducible' image and 'sexual assertiveness' (qualities which meant that his work later fell foul of the Movement's emphasis on syntax as opposed to imagistic density). In doing so, he gestures – without recourse to critical theory as such – towards the issues of gender, liminality, postcolonialism and hybridity which more recent critics have found to be central to Thomas's writing. Eds]

1. 'Process', organic, emotional, physical, sexual, etc., is perhaps the commonest theme in Thomas's early, notebook-derived poetry, identified as such in the title of 'A process in the weather of the heart' (*CP*, 10–11), for example. As a critical term, it was first systematically applied to these poems by Ralph Maud in his study *Entrances to Dylan Thomas's Poetry* (London, 1963).

2. Caitlin Thomas, *Not Quite Posthumous Letters to My Daughter* (London, 1963), p. 27.

3. Caitlin Thomas, *Leftover Life to Kill* (London, 1957), p. 35.

4. John Malcolm Brinnin's phrase. Quoted in Paul Ferris, *Dylan Thomas* (London, 1977), p. 232.

5. Reported by Aneurin Talfan Davies. Quoted in ibid., p. 119.

6. F. W. Bateson, *English Poetry: A Critical Introduction* (London, 1966), p. 67.

7. See Alastair Reid, in *Dylan Thomas: The Legend and the Poet*, ed. E. W. Tedlock (London, 1960), p. 53.

8. John Bayley, 'Chains and the Poet', in *Dylan Thomas: New Critical Essays*, ed. Walford Davies (London, 1972), p. 70.

9. Donald Davie, *Articulate Energy: An Inquiry into the Syntax of English Poetry* (London, 1976), p. 126.

10. Ibid.

11. Alastair Fowler, review of *Articulate Energy* in *Essays in Criticism* (January 1958), 83.

12. Davie, *Articulate Energy*, p. 126.

13. Ibid., p. 129.

14. Ibid., p. 126.

15. Quoted in Henry Treece, *Dylan Thomas: A Dog Among the Fairies* (London, 1949), p. 23.

16. In *Eliot in Perspective*, ed. Graham Martin (London, 1970), pp. 74–9.

17. T. S. Eliot, 'Ash Wednesday', in *T. S. Eliot: Selected Poems* (London, 1986), p. 85.

18. 'Answers to an Enquiry', reprinted in *Early Prose Writings*, ed. Walford Davies (London, 1971), p. 149.

6

'Death is all metaphor': Dylan Thomas's Radical Morbidity

IVAN PHILLIPS

A half-decent elegy will always take on something of the character
of the elegised, acting as a partial or distorting mirror of what
has been lost. This is never more evident than in a poet's elegy
for another poet and George Barker's 'At the Wake of
Dylan Thomas' – surely a definitive example of a *half*-decent
elegy – is thick with honorific Dylanisms: rhythms sprung high
on alliteration ('The word that wore the ring of his married
breath'), clichés tweaked ('the one undoubting Thomas') and
rhymes halved ('amoeba / labour') or quartered ('infants /
onslaughts').[1] At the same time there is an adherence to the self-
conscious proprieties of elegy, most notably in the poem's
ritualistic, formalised balancing of life against death and in its representation of linguistic dearth through a barely restrained surplus
of language:

> Silence is what we hear in the roaring shell.
> The first sea whence we rose and to which we shall
> Go down when all the words and the heroes
>
> Striking their lyres and attitudes in the middle
> Of that burning sea which was a cradle,
> Go down under the silence of that sea.[2]

Barker's attempt to memorialise the 'corpse of curls' goes some way towards proving his contention that 'simply by dying we add to the manic chorus'.

Similar patterns of convention and conversion can be traced, however, in Louis MacNeice's less lyrically over-ripe elegy for Thomas in Canto XX of *Autumn Sequel*:

> If a birth
> Extends a family circle and glasses fill
>
> Confirming its uniqueness and the worth
> Of life, I think a death too does the same,
> Confirming and extending[3]

Here Thomas enters the poem as a physical rather than stylistic absence, MacNeice awaiting the poet's arrival at his own boozy wake: 'it is absurd / He should not join us here'. Nevertheless, there is the same sense of formal consolation and of language silenced inside language, of elegist and elegised co-existing at an interface between art and life, life and death. In Barker's case this is a fantasy of exchange ('The I undead and the dead who was my friend // Change places'), in MacNeice's an expectation of bar-room reunion ('late or soon, / He will come jaunting in'). In both it represents a matching of genre to subject matter which is all the more striking because it seems to highlight the singular nature of Thomas's own work and attendant mythologies.

Writing to Pamela Hansford Johnson at the end of 1933, Thomas described his poetry as 'death-struck', and asserted his belief in 'the writing of poetry from the flesh, and, generally, from the dead flesh' (*CL*, 72). Two years earlier – shortly before his seventeenth birthday – he had scripted his own epitaph, blaming the mother 'Who gave me life and then the grave' and declaring: 'I am man's reply to every question, / His aim and destination' (the idea of Thomas as a poet of corporeal and morbid obsessions, a subject amenable to Freudian analysis, was well worn at the time of his death). As early as 1933 he was tongue-in-cheekily enquiring of Trevor Hughes: 'Are you playing Freud to me as I tell you that, like Havelock Ellis, I bore holes in the floor to piss through, or cut a pigeon's throat as I copulate?' (*CL*, 162). Nevertheless, a year later he answered a solid 'Yes' to *New Verse*'s question 'Have you been influenced by Freud?' (*CL*, 311n.) and the incipient sense of death as not only an inevitability but also an *aim* is worth reconsidering, particularly if its approximation of Freud's notion of the 'death urge' – death as the ego's ultimate escape from contradiction and frustration – is read alongside an awareness of Thomas's role as celebrity necromancer, a 'Dionysian' (Barker's term) archetype for the mass media age. What might be revealed is a strangely Gothic dissidence, a recasting of the elegy as protest poem. In order to assess the peculiarly death-driven vitality of his writing, I will focus on a period – a problematic one for Dylanites – in which the historical pressures of that century came to a head, intensifying his sense of his poetry (expressed in a letter to Henry Treece of May 1938) as 'an enquiry and a terror of fearful expectation, a discovery and facing of fear' (*CL*, 297).

It has always been easy to caricature Thomas, particularly the Thomas of the war years. This is because – seeing the war, in Constantine Fitzgibbon's words, 'as a personal affront'[4] – he gave too many hostages to fortune. His letters of the time are jittery with comments that hang somewhere between craven cynicism and childish defiance. 'What are you doing for your country?' he asked Treece as early as July 1939. 'I'm letting mine rot' (*CL*, 390). And ten days into hostilities he was telling Glyn Jones: 'I want to get something out of the war, & put very little in (certainly not my one & only body)' (*CL*, 408). At the end of that cataclysmic September he announced to Bert Trick that 'the demon Hitlerism can go up its own bottom. I refuse to help it with a bayonet' (*CL*, 417).

Time enough to rot? The brazen 'aim and destination' of less than a decade earlier seems a long way from these intimate, instant, anxiously comical paeans to individual survival. It is small wonder that Thomas's attitude to the war has so often found a convenient shorthand in his comparison of a stumbling squirrel to the Anschluss. But far from indicating apathy and retreat, that notorious remark – returned to its context – is actually a reaction *against* Treece's reading of his work as attempting to transcend history:

> You are right when you suggest that I think a squirrel stumbling at least of equal importance as Hitler's invasions, murder in Spain, the Garbo–Stokowski romance, royalty, Horlicks, lynchlaw, pit disasters, Joe Louis, wicked capitalists, saintly communists, democracy, the Ashes, the Church of England, birthcontrol, Yeats's voice, the machines of the world I tick and revolve in, pub-baby-weather-government-football-youthandage-speed-lipstick, all small tyrannies, means tests, the fascist anger, the daily, momentary lightnings, eruptions, farts, dampsquibs, barrelorgans, tinwhistles, howitzers, tiny

death-rattles, volcanic whimpers of the world I eat, drink, love, work, hate and delight in – but I *am* aware of these things as well.
(*CL*, 310)

This is a skittishly inclusive checklist, which refuses quietism and insists on a necessarily outlaw but nevertheless historically engaged status for poetry. Significantly, Thomas reiterates what Treece had already singled out as the 'social awareness' of his 'little finger-poem' (*CL*, 310), 'The hand that signed the paper'. Some critics have seen this work, written in August 1933, as a specific response to Hitler's rise to power in Germany but it seems more likely that it was written out of a general sensitivity to the build-up of pressure within European politics. As such, it is possible to see it as an extension of Thomas's morbid poetic into the arena of political prediction – not a pseudo-mystical prophecy of Apocalypse but a percipient gesture towards Guernica, the Blitz, Dresden and Hiroshima:

> The mighty hand leads to a sloping shoulder,
> The finger joints are cramped with chalk;
> A goose's quill has put an end to murder
> That put an end to talk.
>
> (*CP*, 51)

Blakean tyrant, monstrous statesman, terrible poet, cruel pedagogue: in a petrified topos of language, Thomas merges private psychology with public event and achieves a terrifying personification of historical process, a brute equation of language and power: 'Great is the hand that holds dominion over / Man by a scribbled name' (*CP*, 52). This drama of silenced voices and brutalising text – orality versus the formal word – casts a forward shadow across both the operations of Hitler's Minister of Enlightenment and Propaganda and the subsequent stages of Thomas's own career.

The bombing of Guernica in 1936 – 'The hand that signed the paper felled a city' – set a grim precedent for the targeting of civilian settlements and meant that, for those living through the Second World War, there was always going to be a fine line between quotidian existence and the violent encroachments of war. If Wilfred Owen and his peers had felt a need to educate those back at home about the realities of life and death in the trenches, no such moral imperative existed for the conscripts of the Second World War: they knew only too well the dangers faced by those they left behind. This vital shift in the topography of warfare meant that, in a sense, every poet was a war poet. It also meant that, where the poets of the Great War had been forced to bruise their decorous Georgianism into startling documentary, those of the later conflict, whether combatant or civilian, were able to write their ready-stressed individual styles straight across the scar-tissue between peace and war. That itchy transitional line is famously ironised in the instruction-manual calm of Henry Reed's 'Lessons of the War' but its true and disturbing crossover is demonstrated elsewhere. In Keith Douglas's war writing, for example, where the translation of everyday life into merciless battlescape enacts a strange cool horror of juxtaposition that is entirely contiguous with his civilian work. Similarly, Alun Lewis's poetry pulls back again and again into an understated hinterland between home and training camp, home and war-zone, and the bony graveyard symbolism of Sidney Keyes adapts naturally to the atmospherics of wartime, what he termed its 'fields of wreckage and white marble'.[5]

The most seamless transition, though, is to be found in Thomas's work. There a formal and thematic mix of the familiar and the alien, the intimate and the public, the rooted and the rootless, has been fundamental from the outset, refracted through a style that is at once blatant and cryptic. And if the alienations of Douglas, Lewis and Keyes express a sense of the wartime experience as a kind of grisly tourism – we might think of Douglas's decapitated corpse with its chocolate and traveller's keepsake in 'Cairo Jag', or the elements of fascinated, vulnerable travelogue in Lewis's 'Holi' and 'Karanje Village', or Keyes's extended meditations on the no-man's-land between life and death, his Baedekers of the underworld, 'The Foreign Gate' and 'The Wilderness' – then Thomas's own restless itinerance during the early years of the war, shuttling between South Wales, London and the Wiltshire village of Marshfield, marks him as a kind of inner émigré, a non-combatant traveller in the realm of sirens, black-outs and searchlights. The war slowed his creative torrent to an agonised but brilliant trickle. At the same time it complicated the terms on which his earlier work could be read, suggesting the latent historical heat that his sexualised, death-obsessed solipsisms had always contained.

What is unique to Thomas's war poetry, then – reading the concerns of the 1930s poetry into the hostilities of 1939–1945 – is its exploration of the radical equilibrium that exists between death and sex, the way in which they 'exchange their energies and excite each other'[6] in a perpetual cyclical motion that is a long way from the stalling antagonisms of Freud. For Thomas, as for some contemporary critical theorists, sex and death are 'nuances' of life, not events or oppositions within it, and they operate as signs of continuity, transgressive of the disjunctive individualism of modern existence; that is, his body of work (the phrase has never been more appropriate) seems to move in morbidly erotic circles around itself, coiling back and spiralling forward through a densely rhythmical and reiterative range of images and themes. Falling halfway between *18 Poems* and *Under Milk Wood*, the war years – which simultaneously emphasised and erased an individualism which, in Thomas's work, centred so heavily on the sex and death drives – might be read as the still, intense heart of this circling web, rather than a period of awkward withdrawal. Since they were also years of marital turbulence, young parenthood, creative unease and financial fluctuation, they can also be seen as a period in which the somewhat monumental and static, if complex equations of festivity and loss in the early poems were thrown into fruitful confusion, blurring more than ever the poetic line between domesticity and history.

'On the Marriage of a Virgin' is an interesting case in point, seeming to imagine sexual awakening not only as a sunrise – 'this day's sun leapt up the sky out of her thighs' – but as a kind of air raid: 'For a man sleeps where the fire leapt down' (*CP*, 105). This poem, finished in the aftermath of the London Blitz in 1941, was started in the year of Thomas's first visit to the capital, 1933, and developed through numerous revisions a succession of images – 'a navy of doves', 'unending lightning', 'the vibrations of the sun', 'the avalanche / Of the golden ghost' – that seem to link the poet's characteristic psycho-sexual concerns to the external features of war (*CP*, 105).

The longer, more complex 'Into her lying down head' offers further evidence of this tendency to address historical circumstances through intimate expression and a ready-made style. Sending the poem to Vernon Watkins in June 1940, Thomas suggested the title 'Modern Love', and his allusion to George Meredith's nineteenth-century sonnet sequence on the decline of a marriage serves to underwrite his own extended meditation on marital storm and stress (*CL*, 455). At the same time, however, the poem's imagery effects an often seamless conjunction of private and public anxieties, sexual jealousy and wartime vulnerability combining even in the terse opening couplet: 'Into her lying down head / His enemies entered bed'. The threatening sense of encroachment – the equation of lover and spy, lover and aggressor – is picked up again in a reference to 'The colossal intimacies of silent / Once seen strangers or shades on a stair' (*CP*, 94). The home is invaded by a sinister figure who wields a 'dark blade' and – depicted as the reaper, as a seductive rapist, as a terrifying war-machine – has 'scythes' for arms. Identifying marital infidelity with martial violence, Thomas refers to the 'Trespasser and broken bride', to 'All blood-signed assailings and vanished marriages' and – effectively predicting the Blitz – to 'the burning England'(*CP*, 94–5). In the closing section of the poem the figure of the wife – 'O she lies alone and still, / Innocent between two wars' – becomes a figure both for the home or land violated by 'the second comers, the severers, the enemies from the deep / Forgotten dark' and for a personal style caught on the threshold of history (*CP*, 96). (Feminist exception might be taken to this too-easy appropriation of the woman as a symbolic home but it should be noted that this is part of a wider tendency within the poetry and plastic arts of the 1940s to express individual vulnerability through topography, to absorb the human body – whether male or female – into a damaged landscape. Loss of individual identity, physical fragility, and hostility of environment are the themes of the era, here reflected in the formal decadence of metrical sprawl, jagged lineation, scattered rhyme.)

In 'Into her lying down head' the turbulent political atmosphere provides the subtext of an ostensibly domestic poem. The same melting together of sexual and historical concerns is evident in 'Deaths and Entrances', described in a letter to Watkins in the summer of 1940 as 'my poem about invasion' and first published in *Horizon* in January 1941 (*CL*, 464). Building from the central and repeated 'incendiary eve' – the Luftwaffe as formal refrain – the poem develops the themes and imagery of the earlier work: there is the same paranoid sense of espionage and trespass – with references to enemies, 'the watched dark' and 'lips and keys, / Locking, unlocking' – and the same sense of love lost or betrayed in a broken, deadly landscape, a landscape of 'raining blood', 'thunderclapping eyes', 'flying breath', 'thunderbolts'(*CP*, 98). So fluid and self-contained is the movement of the poem (and this is true of much of Thomas's work) that it is difficult to extract representative phrases or passages with any cogency, but another of that summer's letters to Watkins might be suggestive at this point. In it he responds to news of the bombing of South Wales by penning a brief and incred-

ulous map from memory – Gower, Pennard, Pwlldu, Union Street:
'This is all too near' – and then goes on to describe a recent raid on
London:

> I had to go to London last week to see about a BBC job, & left at the
> beginning of the big Saturday raid. The Hyde Park guns were
> booming. Guns on the top of Selfridges. A 'plane brought down in
> Tottenham Court Road. White-faced taxis still trembling through the
> streets, though, & buses going . . . Are you frightened these nights?
> When I wake up out of burning birdman dreams – they were frying
> aviators one night in a huge frying pan: it sounds whimsical now, it
> was appalling then – and hear the sound of bombs and gunfire only a
> little away, I'm so relieved I could laugh or cry.
>
> (*CL*, 463)

As with the list of names from Thomas's childhood landscape, there
is an excitable, almost fetishistic quality to this account of desolation. War becomes not only a terror but also a heady disruption of
culturally fraught signs (Hyde Park, Selfridges, the BBC, the
black (but now 'white-faced' London taxis), an intensifier and
potential eraser of memory and language. And consider that
strangely equivocal word 'relieved'. When physical threat is
translated into imaginative encroachment, however, it is restored to
unambiguous nightmare, a petrification rather than a shake-up of
sign-systems:

> What *is* so frightening, I think, is the idea of greyclothed, grey-faced,
> blackarmletted troops marching, one morning, without a sound up a
> village street. Boots on the cobbles, of course, but no Heil-shouting,
> grenading, goose-stepping. Just silence. That's what Goebbels has
> done for me.
>
> (*CL*, 463)

In the noiseless march of jackboots up a cobbled village street invasion is equated with inarticulacy, with linguistic dispossession, the
silence of death becoming the silence that succeeds language and
free expression. It should be remembered here that *Under Milk
Wood* has its origins in the war years, conceived by Thomas as an
enclave of healthy eccentricity which votes to cut itself off from a
'sane' world that had gone genuinely incoherent and crazy. The
streets of Llareggub are cobblestoned. Returning to 'Deaths and
Entrances', we might read into its intricate pattern of codes, trans-

gressions, gaps and confusions a formalised erosion of articulation and meaning. This culminates in the final stanza's willed, almost sacramental silence:

> One who called deepest down shall hold his peace
>> That cannot sink or cease
>> Endlessly to his wound
> In many married London's estranging grief.
>> (CP, 98)

The inviolable, nearly unquotable self-suffiency of the poem might be seen, in this respect, as both a continuation of an individual romantic style and an act of historical defiance.

As its counterbalanced title suggests, 'Deaths and Entrances' is a noisy poem which edges towards silence. It shows Thomas, a poet of prolific boisterousness, tempering his verbosity through a sharpened concern for the nature of poetic responsibility, a concern which informs all the best poetry of the Second World War (Douglas's 'How to Kill', for instance). In Thomas's work the heightened sense of tact, control and restraint is most clearly seen in a handful of poems that forms the core of his war writing. 'On A Wedding Anniversary', another poem of marital strife, is also a compact dramatisation of war's obliterating effect – literal and emotional – on personal relationships:

> Too late in the wrong rain
> They come together whom their love parted:
> The windows pour into their heart
> And the doors burn in their brain.
>> (CP, 103)

A sketch in four tight quatrains, this is comparable to Lewis's deceptively simple elegy 'Raider's Dawn' – where a woman's necklace survives on a bomb-damaged chair – but it also summons up the haunting symbolism of Keyes, the brutal fusions of Douglas.

Messier but equally fascinating is 'Among those Killed in the Dawn Raid was a Man Aged a Hundred', a poem which jams the delicate lyrical mechanism of the sonnet with rubble. The journalistic title, stark as a banner headline, leads into four of the most stripped and direct lines that Thomas ever wrote:

> When the morning was waking over the war
> He put on his clothes and stepped out and he died,

The locks yawned loose and a blast blew them wide,
He dropped where he loved on the burst pavement stone.
                                                    (*CP*, 112)

Once again the merging of human body and exploded landscape is
both literary and literal, a matching of Thomas's surrealist manner
to the violent facts of war: 'he stopped a sun / And the craters of his
eyes grew springshoots and fire'. In the closing lines, however,
Thomas seems to suffer an attack of artistic nerves:

O keep his bones away from that common cart,
The morning is flying on the wings of his age
And a hundred storks perch on the sun's right hand.
                                                    (*CP*, 112)

The uncertainty here – a clichéd symbolism softening the previously
hard edge of the poem – is the dead end to an otherwise fine piece
of writing. It is, to adapt Beckett's famous phrase, a stain on the
bombed silence. Unsurprisingly it was followed by the dormancy
predicted in 'Deaths and Entrances'; in the three years between
'Among Those Killed in the Dawn Raid' and 'Ceremony After A
Fire Raid' Thomas wrote no poetry at all.

Thomas's mid-war hiatus literalised the theme of withdrawal
developed in Lewis's work and ensured the avoidance of 'immense
bullshitting' demanded by Douglas.[7] Its roots were partly practical,
of course, with Thomas's time being devoured by the demands of
family and work (for the BBC and Strand Films) and the tempta-
tions of Fitzrovia, but it can also be seen as a period of slow poetic
incubation. The result was a subtle but striking shift in the nature
of his war verse, a movement away from the traditions of public
elegy and lament, with their mournfully patriotic undertones, and
towards a more cryptic, unsettling mode of address. So it is that, in
'Ceremony after a Fire Raid' and 'A Refusal to Mourn the Death,
by Fire, of a Child in London' Thomas eschews what Neil
Corcoran has referred to as 'the expected, usable rhetoric of
indignation'.[8]

In the light of this, it is worth reminding ourselves that, like
everything else, death is mediated by history, and that its role and
function are mediated differently in different societies. According
to Jean Baudrillard, in modern 'ideologised' societies of the post-
Enlightenment West the original discrimination was against the
dead. Collective rituals maintaining difference and 'communication'

between living and dead (the pre-sixteenth-century Dance of Death, for instance) were absorbed into exclusive power ceremonies overseen by Church and State. The dead, in other words, were excluded from life. In this account, death becomes a social line of demarcation beyond which the dead exist in a radical utopia, outside the reach of a capital motive which has subsumed the Church–State nexus into its agency of control:

> Historically, we know that sacerdotal power is based on a monopoly over death and exclusive control over relations with the dead. The dead are the first restricted area . . . Power is established on death's borders. It will subsequently be sustained by further separations (the soul and the body, the male and the female, good and evil, etc.) that have infinite ramifications, but the principal separation is between life and death. When the French say that power 'holds the bar', it is no metaphor: it is the bar between life and death, the tollgate and border control between the two banks.[9]

The power of the modern State inheres in its ability to define and control the capital exchange value of individual human lives. For this reason, death – which cannot be assimilated easily to the smooth functioning of society – assumes a subversive potential that is greater than that of more containable antisocial conditions such as insanity, criminality, nonconformity: 'Strictly speaking, we no longer know what to do with [the dead], since, today, it is not normal to be dead, and this is new. To be dead is an unthinkable anomaly; nothing else is as unthinkable as this. Death is a delinquency, and an incurable deviancy.'[10] It is, in a literal sense, beyond good and evil. In State terms this makes it the public enemy *par excellence*, a revolutionary untouchable. Various evasive mechanisms now click into subtle action (the dead are dressed as living dolls), generating 'the secret idea' that 'life is natural and death is against nature'. In the existential double-bind that this produces – a 'natural' death is everyone's 'duty', but it is also an impossibility – 'Everyone is dispossessed of their death'.[11] An obsessional collective avoidance of death-risk ensues, in balance with a fascination for accident, illness and catastrophe. Conversely, there is a related fascination for modes of 'artificial' or 'willed' death – dangerous sports, violent criminality, self-abuse, martyrdom – a form of transgressive playfulness that is linked to the extreme act of suicide. One *commits* suicide: the phrasing is significant: it is a crime and a pledge. Cheating the all-pervasive political economy of an individual 'parcel of capital', suicide can be seen as 'the form of subversion itself'.[12]

War – and modern war in particular – complicates matters, although Baudrillard himself underplays this. In his terms the war dead have a basic capital exchange value which maintains rather than subverts the dominant ideology-system, transmitted in tallies which convert human reality into cold statistic. His compelling radicalisation of the death urge, then, takes no account of the Hitlerian shadow in retrospect. The Second World War poets, on the other hand, both combatant and non-combatant, anatomise it in prospect and up close. Their work seems to discover a more finely layered formula, one which effectively fuses the rather crudely eschatological registers, as quantified anonymity is human- ised in poetry into the recognition of individual willed death, justified self-sacrifice and at least a tacit recognition of suicide. Out of this tangled and fatal mathematics, the war poem is able to disturb patterns of piety and signal dissent. Into the space, that is, where the selflessness of such writers coincides with their gloomier obsessions, they project the figure of the criminal and the martyr. Lewis, Douglas and Keyes exist on the damaged iconic margins of collective memory, writers whose chill and unsentimental self- elegies imply both martyrdom to a just cause and dissent from the smug consensus of a rational liberal humanism. Thomas is, of course, a somewhat different case. Because he stayed at home, because he dodged and squirmed and protested, opting for – or lapsing towards – slow self-destruction rather than frontline fatal- ity, he attains a more dissolute version of the suicidal ideal, in some ways a more obviously defiant one. Yet because his poetry is shaped by an instinctive grasp of the power network that envelops the idea and the fact of death, it is – on its own terms at least – as heroic as that of the soldier-poets. (It is also as vulnerable to the degradations of posterity, since where the combatants seem to have sacrificed themselves first to the war-effort and then to the conde- scension of critical neglect, Thomas has offered himself up for posthumous ridicule and disdain, becoming at the melodramatic moment of his death a gilt-edged media commodity, an ineffectual angel with wings of clay. If we stick to the poetry, however, we might still feel the insurgent kick that preceded the bleak farce and recognise the potential defiance of elegy.)

The rejection of a moral or propagandist tone in the later war poetry mirrors that in the work of the soldier-poets. The result is work able to shape itself to the pressures of the fascist menace but at the same time resistant to the standards and repressions of the culture out of (or against) which it was written. The unsentimentalised solemnity, the tendency to address wreckage and pain through a vestigial soap-box lyricism, lend his poems the force of revelation. In the shell-shocked apocalypse of 'Ceremony after a Fire Raid' the effect is gruelling and cumulative, a formal triptych being stretched and compressed through furious improvisation. The poem begins in a state of negative synaesthesia, the senses folding in on each other, sucked into a black hole of Ovidian pre-existence: 'Darkness kindled back into beginning / When the caught tongue nodded blind'(CP, 107). In the middle section, a meditation on the charred 'altar of London' conjures the modern moment of the Fall, with incendiaries as as the fruit of the Tree of Knowledge:

> Man and woman undone,
> Beginning crumbled back to darkness
> Bare as the nurseries
> Of the garden of wilderness.
>
> (CP, 108)

Finally, there is rapturous transfiguration, a vision of renewal 'over the sun's hovel and the slum of fire / And the golden pavements laid in requiems':

> Erupt, fountain, and enter to utter for ever
> Glory glory glory
> The sundering ultimate kingdom of genesis' thunder.
>
> (CP, 109)

From primordial silence and darkness to the cacophony of a new dawn; this is the Blitz as creation myth, Thomas as a kind of dissenting lay preacher.

In his most famous and definitive war poem, 'A Refusal to Mourn the Death, by Fire, of a Child in London', a comparable effect is achieved with greater economy of expression, rapture subsiding into secular prayer:

> Deep with the first dead lies London's daughter,
> Robed in the long friends,
> The grains beyond age, the dark veins of her mother,

Secret by the unmourning water
Of the riding Thames.
After the first death, there is no other.

(CP, 86)

The ability to trace patterns of grim musical consolation across
intimations of mortality connects an early piece such as 'And death
shall have no dominion' to the late and remarkable 'Do not go
gentle into that good night', confirming the nodal quality of the war
years in Thomas's poetic career.

Thomas has consistently fallen victim to accusations of self-
indulgence, pretension, excessive plangency, bad taste. But he can
be seen – like Keyes, whose Rilkean poem 'Death Wish' is a close
cousin of Thomas's luxuriant morbidity and whose almost total
erasure from the canon can be attributed to the same prejudices –
as continuing the tradition of English-language war verse that is
typified by William Blake and that found its only First World War
exponent in the civilian D. H. Lawrence. This is a tradition that
sees war as a terrible transubstantiation and elegy as an exercise in
revelation or dissent rather than a Binyon-like affirmation of old
values, old ways. As such it is open to accusations of windy self-
importance, lack of common feeling, even treachery. But the war
poetry written by Thomas, in refusing to mourn, constitutes a
democratic and complex reaction to historical events, one rooted
in restlessly vernacular impulses: it is also a self-display that
constantly threatens to cancel itself out, a music that tends towards
silence. For Keyes, Douglas and Lewis – all killed in the war – the
tragic silence was immediate. For Thomas, living the life of
infamous celebrity until his death in 1953, it was a slower but
no less certain process. In 'In my craft or sullen art', written a
month after the war ended, we see a once-prolific poet haunted by
silence:

Not for the proud man apart
From the raging moon I write
On these spindrift pages
Nor for the towering dead.
(CP, 106)

The key word here is 'spindrift': the paper on which the poet writes
is imagined as sea-spray, as foam (we might think of Keats's self-

penned epitaph: 'Here lies one whose name was writ in water.'[13] Those whom Thomas views as the only audience he now wants mirror the isolation and silence which haunt him, 'the lovers, their arms / Round the griefs of the ages, / Who pay no praise or wages / Nor heed my craft or art' (*CP*, 106).

After this Thomas wrote only one poem in the next four years, and less than ten in the remaining eight years of his life. These included elegies ('Do not go gentle into that good night') elaborate hymns to natural procreation and destruction. ('In the White Giant's Thigh', 'Over Sir John's hill') and a birthday poem to himself, each one, it could be argued, a more elaborately narcissistic coffin-nail than the last. From his Boathouse he could view the Army missile testing range at Pendine Sands, and his last poems are full of the recognition of a final darkness of nuclear war. The suicidal ideal, however dissolute or dissenting, collapses in the face of the threat of total extinction, and the grieving register of the poems is not only for a father, daughter, or even Thomas himself, but for the human race as a whole. Ambiguous to the end, however, the poems are rhythmically and linguistically ebullient enough – especially if taken together with *Under Milk Wood* – to suggest that a good deal of the poet's pre-war vivacity, his expressive death-drive, had survived the silence that followed the bombs and the decomposition that haunts all art.

NOTES

[Ivan Phillips's essay establishes Thomas's poetry of the war years within a broad context, including that of the other war poetry of the time, in order to argue for the historically charged and disruptive nature of what he refers to as Thomas's 'radical morbidity'. Far from seeing the 'decadence' often imputed to the poetry as a liability, Phillips views the poetry as a transformation of conventional elegy into a mode of defiance. His essay is unusual in combining an impressionistic, free-flowing critical aesthetic which owes much to Tom Paulin, with elements of poststructuralism, aiming at eliciting a broadly political reading through close attention to Thomas's style. Recurrent themes of sex and death – frequently seen by Thomas's detractors as puerile and limiting – are considered in terms of an obsessive and cumulatively forceful effort of the dissenting imagination, while the poet's concern for form is recognised as being singularly responsive to the pressures of modernity in general and the War in particular. Although he discusses several of the poems also considered by Steve Vine

(essay 7), Phillips's emphasis is ultimately on the poems as historical mediations rather than linguistic events, and with suicide rather than with
mourning. Eds]

1. George Barker, *Collected Poems*, ed. Robert Fraser (London, 1987),
   pp. 308–11.

2. Ibid., p. 311.

3. Louis MacNeice, *Selected Poems*, ed. Michael Longley (London,
   1988), pp. 122–5.

4. Constantine Fitzgibbon, *The Life of Dylan Thomas* (London, 1965),
   p. 263.

5. The quotation (p. 67) is from 'The Foreign Gate', in Sidney Keyes,
   Collected Poems, ed. Michael Meyer (London, 1945), pp. 66–78. See
   also Keith Douglas, *The Complete Poems*, ed. Desmond Graham,
   intro. Ted Hughes (London, 1988) and Alun Lewis, *Selected Poetry
   and Prose*, ed. Ian Hamilton (London, 1966). For a more general
   overview of the period's poetry, see *Poetry of the Forties*, ed. Robin
   Skelton (Harmondsworth, 1968).

6. Jean Baudrillard, *Symbolic Exchange and Death*, trans. Iain Hamilton
   Grant, intro. Mike Gane (London, 1993), p. 155. This idea is discussed at some length by Baudrillard, who draws on the earlier work
   of Georges Bataille.

7. In a letter to J. C. Hall, 10 August 1943, extracted in Douglas,
   Complete Poems, p. 134.

8. Neil Corcoran, *English Poetry Since 1940* (London and New York,
   1993), p. 46. Corcoran draws on William Empson's reading of
   Thomas in *Argufying*, ed. John Haffenden (London, 1988), pp. 382–6.

9. Baudrillard, *Symbolic Exchange and Death*, p. 130. My own understanding of Baudrillard's theory of death is taken from the chapter
   entitled 'Political Economy and Death', pp. 125–94.

10. Ibid., p. 126.

11. Ibid., p. 181.

12. Ibid., p. 175.

13. See Andrew Motion, *Keats* (London, 1997), p. 564.

7

'Shot from the locks': Poetry, Mourning, *Deaths and Entrances*

STEVE VINE

Dylan Thomas, as a number of critics have noted,[1] took the title of his wartime collection *Deaths and Entrances* (1946) from John Donne's last sermon, 'Death's Duell, or, A Consolation to the Soule, against the dying Life, and living Death of the Body'.[2] In his sermon, Donne figures death as an 'entrance': as the entrance, that is, to mortal life, to the 'dying Life, and living Death of the Body'. Life is an entrance (from the womb) that in fact is *already* a death, an issuing into corrupt mortality that rehearses the earlier 'death' of the womb itself. '[F]or even the *wombe* is a *body of death*', says Donne, '[while] this *issue*, this deliverance *from* that *death*, the death of the *wombe*, is an *entrance*, a delivering over to *another death*, the manifold deathes of this *world*.'[3] Life, for Donne, is a promenade of deaths, a dying life and a living death: an itinerary of deathly entrances and invasive deaths. Instead of death marking the final exit from life as the simple opposite or antithesis of life, death inhabits life; it inheres in it, conditioning life from within. Death is already within life; it has already, like an uninvited other, *made* its entrance.

Thomas's appropriation of Donne's image of death and/as 'entrance' resonates in a number of ways in *Deaths and Entrances*. Walford Davies, for instance, sees the poet's engagement with the contemporary scene of the war as itself an 'entrance' into his work, remarking: 'The ... deaths in the bombing raids on London ... were no longer, as Thomas himself put it, the notional deaths seen only "in the tumultuous world of my own being". The world of historic event had now entered as reality into the poems.'[4] This historical 'entrance' visits death, presumably, upon Thomas's earlier poetic career while at the same time delivering him (to adopt Donne's terms) over to 'another death': the trauma of the war as a violently invasive event, as an unanswerable historical entrance. Davies comments: 'The war was to make central to so many of Thomas's poems at this period the images of the blasting open of private lives. His images for the dispersion of the human body, just as for the breaking of homes and houses, were those of shattered locks and keys.'[5] Thus when, in 'Among those Killed in the Dawn Raid was a Man Aged a Hundred', Thomas writes, 'The locks yawned loose and a blast blew them wide ... all the keys shot from the locks, and rang' (*CP*, 112), the sudden explosion of the old man's body and house is a violent entrance that parallels in a certain way the traumatic irruption of history itself in the body of Thomas's work.

Like other poems in *Deaths and Entrances*, 'Among those Killed' aspires to anti-elegy. Refusing to mourn, it presents its engulfment by an event whose overwhelming force exceeds all the framing and formalising gestures of elegiac commemoration. Audaciously, the text refutes and refuses any gesture of ascribing meaning to loss, and instead discloses the impossibility of attributing significance to the explosive event of the bomb's drop by performing a kind of macabre, self-knowing comedy in the face of its catastrophic eventhood. Mocking the discourse of orthodox meaning and mourning, the text replaces conventional lament with a language of celebration that parodically compounds irony with affirmation: 'The heavenly ambulance drawn by a wound / Assembling waits for the spade's ring on the cage' (*CP*, 112). Impishly repudiating the orthodoxy of the 'heavenly ambulance', the poem flaunts a kind of ironic imagism whose metaphoric potentiality floats free of any attempt to grasp the event of the bomb's descent at the level of representation:

> O keep his bones away from that common cart,
> The morning is flying on the wings of his age
> And a hundred storks perch on the sun's right hand.
>   (*CP*, 112)

In this way, the text explodes linguistic reference into a strange, exorbitant poetic invention, posing its wheeling images *against* the cataclysm of the bomb, not in its mimetic service. Thus brute catastrophe is transformed into ecstatic apostrophe. In this way, the text insists on the radical *difference* rather than congruence between the bomb as event and its linguistic figuration. This difference or gap between the explosive occurrence and its registration in language is, indeed, reinforced by the parodic literalism of the poem's title: taken from a newspaper account of an air-raid death in Hull (see *CP*, 244n.), its blank empiricity is as ironically disjunct from the catastrophe of the happening as is the looping exultation of Thomas's images. That the poem refuses to close the gap between the event and its notation in language, insisting instead on the irreducible gulf between the two, institutes a strange ethics of poetic presentation in Thomas in which, as we will see, the language of poetry is both lacerated and liberated by a traumatic 'entrance': an entrance in which the unassimilable or the unpresentable appears on the inside of poetic figuration, obdurately refusing to be reduced to meaning, mourning or meliorism.

If, in 'Death's Duell', Donne's deaths-as-entrances orchestrate life as the punctual repetition of death, this repetition is overcome by God's liberation of the soul from the body. But Thomas's mortal entrances lack any providential dimension or 'heavenly ambulance' of meaning. '[W]ith *God the Lord are the issues of death*', says Donne; 'he hath the *keys of death*, and hee can let me out at that dore, that is, deliver me from the manifold deaths of this world ... the *every dayes death* and *every houres death*, by that *one death*, the *final dissolution* of body and soule, the end of all.'[6] Life at the level of the body may be, for Donne, a continual series of entrances into more deaths, but God will shoot death's keys from their locks in a final emancipation of the soul from its grave. However, Thomas's deaths-as-entrances refuse all teleological closure or restoration of death to meaning; instead, they rehearse a traumatic alterity that, irrupting inside the texts, powers at the same time as it pulverises the work of poetic articulation.

Death is, indeed, always about to 'enter' Thomas's texts with the force of catastrophe. Thus, in 'The conversation of prayers', a 'child going to bed' and a 'man on the stairs' pray, the child for sleep and the man for the life of a dying woman; but although the woman sleeps and does not die (as if the child's prayer were answered), the child's sleep is dragged 'up the stairs to one who lies dead' (*CP*, 85). In this way, the prayer for sleep is entered by the death that it forestalls, and the language of prayer is shadowed by the occurrence that it seeks to foreclose. Melding the 'quick and the dead' (*CP*, 85) together, the poem forces language (prayer) and event (death) to share the same space, to occupy the same house; entering one another, they haunt, harry and interrupt each other. Moreover, they become what 'A process in the weather of the heart' calls 'two ghosts before the eye' (*CP*, 11); for, mutually inhabiting each other, they live a life that is only half their own.

A general dynamic of incursion or *entrance* could, in fact, be said to define Thomas's conception of the poetic or aesthetic process: a dynamic of incursion in which entrances are deaths and deaths are entrances. Thus, in a letter of 1938, Thomas writes of the images of his poetry as entering and issuing from each other in a perpetual process of death and generation:

> I make one image . . . let it breed another, let that image contradict the first, make, of the third image bred out of the other two together, a fourth contradictory image, and let them all, within my imposed formal limits, conflict. Each image holds within it the seed of its own destruction . . . an image must be born and die in another; and any sequence of my images must be a sequence of creations, recreations, destructions, contradictions.
>
> (*CL*, 281)

Each of Thomas's images, then – born and dying in another – exists in a process of perpetual alteration, of opening up to otherness. Each image, that is to say, is *entered* by another, and frenziedly shot from the locks of its own identity. Indeed, rather than constituted entities, Thomas's images are theatres of conflict, invasion, incursion and interruption. In effect, this means Thomas's poems are themselves rhetorical performances of 'deaths and entrances', swirling dramas of destruction and creation. They are, in a certain way, theatres of war. Thus it is that, in the same letter, Thomas describes his poetic practice as the prosecution of an 'inevitable conflict of images – inevitable, because of the creative, recreative, destructive, and contradictory nature of the motivating centre, the womb of war . . .' (*CL*, 282). Insofar as the 'motivating centre' of Thomas's poetry, then, is the 'womb of war', the issue of his images into existence is the fructification of a traumatic symbolic conflict: a conflict in which poetic signification is produced in tumultuous dissension not resolution, and in which poetry is a dialogue with dissolution not the achievement of symbolic finality.

If Thomas's images, then, are continually opened up by alterity – by the traumatic entrance of the other – the moment of their reali- sation at the level of aesthetic form is necessarily perilous. Certainly, Thomas speaks of his finished poems *as* moments of aes- thetic formalisation and stability; nonetheless, this formalisation is a fleeting moment in a restless, unstable and finally uncontainable temporal process. Thus, in the letter cited above, Thomas presents the finished poem as a moment of arrest whose formal stability is always about to collapse back into the warring flux from which it is born. As a symbolic or verbal structure, that is to say, the poem is ever ready to dissolve back into its own formless or pre-symbolic prehistory. Describing the poem as a struggle towards 'momentary peace', Thomas remarks:

> I do not want a poem of mine to be, nor can it be, a circular piece of experience placed neatly outside the living stream of time from which it came; a poem of mine is, or should be, a watertight section of the stream that is flowing all ways; all warring images within it should be reconciled for that small stop of time . . . [in] each of my earlier poems . . . images were left dangling over the formal limits, and dragged the poem into another; the warring stream ran on over the insecure barriers, the fullstop armistice was pulled & twisted raggedly on into a conflicting series of dots and dashes.
>
> (CL, 282)

Here, Thomas presents the agon of his composition as an attempt to grasp in a fleeting formal 'armistice' the symbolic 'war' of the poetic text. Formal and spatialising in nature, this symbolic armistice momentarily, it seems, arrests the 'warring stream' of time into which the poem's images are thrown. However, the pulveris- ation of the poem's 'formal limits' by the flux of time constantly threatens to undo the enterprise of poetic articulation. For, 'dragged . . . into another', the poem is constitutively in danger of plunging into disintegrative alterity, into a privative otherness; with the result that, shot from its locks, poetic identity issues in death rather than entrance. What is noticeable here, indeed, is that the 'entrance' or 'dragging' of one formal identity into another traumatically reconfigures Thomas's formulation of his poetic practice earlier in the letter (the sense, that is, in which one 'image must be born and die in another'). For, now, death-as-entrance or entrance-as-death is given a troublingly negative twist. Indeed, insofar as it 'dangl[es] over the formal limits', the poem that is 'dragged . . . into another' is submitted not to formal generation but formal death. Poetic entrance becomes poetic death, and a radical derailment of form threatens to plunge articulation into chaos.

This derangement of form or symbolisation is, in fact, uncannily echoed at the level of subjectivity in 'Love in the Asylum' in *Deaths and Entrances*. For, here, the reeling entrance of wild images into the head of a 'girl mad as birds' crazily disorders the 'house not right in the head', so that the house of the head is incapable of keeping its doors or windows locked to the other, and becomes unable to prevent multiple 'entrances' to its pregnable home. There is, that is to say, an invasion or entrance into the girl's head that overpowers identity with alterity, self with other, and thought with thing. Thus the girl, though lying 'Strait in the mazed bed', 'deludes the heaven-proof house with entering clouds' while, walking 'At large as the dead', she 'admits the delusive light through the bouncing wall . . .'. 'Possessed by the skies', she is in effect dispossessed of herself (*CP*, 90). Yet if this amounts to a 'mad' loss of identity, it is a loss that Thomas links explicitly to poetic production itself. Thus the poem ends:

> And taken by light in her arms at long and dear last
> I may without fail
> Suffer the first vision that set fire to the stars.
> (*CP*, 91)

This 'first vision' to which the mad girl submits the speaker suggests a Promethean, poetic, creative spark that makes the dark light and the dead blaze; but it is a visionary light that, possessing and entering the speaker, grasps him at the same time with madness, aberrancy and otherness. The speaker's own head, that is to say, is in danger of reeling and looping like the mad birds and clouds of the girl's mind. The speaker, too, then, is 'possessed' madly by the entrance of the other into his head, so that instead of retaining his self-identity he is submitted to the crazy mobility of the elements and images that fly through the girl's brain. Lost in alterity, the speaker's head has the keys shot from its locks.

That Thomas thus figures poetic 'vision' as the deranging entrance of the other into the self – an entrance that, ambiguously, is both a death and a generation – connects importantly with the traumatic 'entrance' of the war as event in *Deaths and Entrances*.

Consequently, the title poem of the collection deals both with the war's invasion of the metropolis and its invasion of the warring subject, the poet himself. Indeed, 'invasion' is the term that Thomas himself uses to write about 'Deaths and Entrances', describing it in a letter of 1940 as a 'poem about invasion' (*CL*, 464), and reporting that at night he suffers 'nightmares like invasions, all successful' (*CL*, 463). In one sense, the invasion or 'entrance' of the poem – as in 'Among those Killed' – is the catastrophic entrance of an incendiary bomb into London's houses and people, as the 'enemy . . . quivering through locks and cave . . . pull[s] the thunderbolts / To shut the sun' (*CP*, 98). But, in another sense, the poem is about the entrance of the event of the bomb and the war into the very interior of the poet's subjectivity: about death *as* an entrance.

Throughout the poem, the speaker conducts a kind of strange, ghostly dialogue with himself: but it is a dialogue that is *at the same time a dialogue with the other*. For the poet of 'Deaths and Entrances' is invaded *by* the other, by the event, and by the dead. At the largest level, the poet is invaded by history. The second stanza opens:

> On almost the incendiary eve
>   When at your lips and keys,
> Locking, unlocking, the murdered strangers weave,
>   One who is most unknown,
> Your polestar neighbour, sun of another street,
>   Will dive up to his tears.
>
> (*CP*, 98)

Here, the language of the poem mingles and 'weaves' together the speaker with the dead, with the 'murdered strangers' that he writes about. These 'strangers' – the anonymous metropolitan others who are grasped in 'London's estranging grief' (*CP*, 98) – are described as being 'at your lips and keys, / Locking, unlocking', and as 'weaving' in strange patterns the contours of the poet's speech. The poem, though, is scrupulously hesitant about whether it is the poet's 'lips and keys' – that is, his speech and his music (see *CP*, 238–9n.) – that 'weave' the dead into writing and song, or whether it is the dead themselves who 'weave' the poet's utterance:

> He'll bathe his raining blood in the male sea
>   Who strode for your own dead
> And wind his globe out of your water thread

And load the throats of shells
With every cry since light
Flashed first across his thunderclapping eyes.
(*CP*, 98)

In the latter sense, the dead are 'at' the poet's lips and keys like ghosts who invade and harry his labours: they *enter* his house, head and text, shutting and unshutting the poem's symbolic 'locks' with their tumultuous, unquiet presences. The murdered dead, that is, haunt and disrupt the poem's language with their unsymbolisable and unstillable half-life, and 'enter' the interiority of the speaker's text and psyche with the force of trauma, carrying a radical otherness that the poem is unable to convert into meaning. For the dead are in excess of the speaker's grasp, and besiege his symbolic labours with an overwhelming, collective and unanswerable possession or inhabitation. As the last stanza of the poem begins,

On almost the incendiary eve
    Of deaths and entrances,
When near and strange wounded on London's waves
    Have sought your single grave.
(*CP*, 98)

That the capital's wounded, wraith-like citizens here seek out the poet's 'single grave' aligns him strangely with the dead; for the poet himself seems to die into the plural deaths of the metropolis. The poet's 'single' grave, that is, becomes multiple: he becomes plurally inhabited by phalanxes of the dead. A powerful image of the poet's invasion by the victims of the bombs, as well as of the occupation of the poem itself by the event of the war, this crowded inhabitation is, nevertheless, not the only 'entrance' that is dramatised in the text. For, in the last stanza, the poem alarmingly entwines the speaker together with the anonymous bomber pilot who drops incendiary bombs on the city, the 'One enemy, of many, who knows well / Your heart is luminous . . .' (*CP*, 98). As William York Tindall says: 'Having become one with London, this estranged "one" of the "flying breath" becomes one, apparently, with the German flier, a stranger who will drop the bombs. Indeed, the poet seems one with any stranger, down here or up there, yet strange to each.'[7] The poet of 'Deaths and Entrances', then, is multiply identified with the catastrophic event of the war, with its murderers and its dead; for, 'entered' by the thing about which he writes, he relinquishes any distance from the event in favour of an anguished implication in it, renouncing representational mastery for a traumatic enactment of the war's violent incursion into psyche and text. If in other poems in *Deaths and Entrances* the entrance of the other brings 'vision' to the poetic subject (as in 'Love in the Asylum'), in 'Deaths and Entrances' this other takes the form of a historical event whose overwhelming force comes to disable the poet's power to master the event in language. For, in this text, the poet is shot from the locks of his identity, and exploded into the warring others who murder, maim and die about him. The deaths of the poem are entrances into the poet.

The fact that 'Deaths and Entrances' concerns the traumatic entrance of the war into the poetic self has a direct bearing on the issue of the complex relationship between *Deaths and Entrances* and the traditions of poetic elegy. If elegy is dedicated to replacing death with the consolations of meaning, *Deaths and Entrances* refuses the labour of that mourning, even naming one of its major poems after this repudiation, 'A Refusal to Mourn the Death, by Fire, of a Child in London' (*CP*, 85–6) – a poem to which we will return. 'Among those Killed', as we saw, transmutes mourning into ambiguous rhapsody, the elegiac into the ironic; and, as recent commentators on elegy have remarked, this challenge to the conventions of elegy is a characteristic of the modern poem.

But, as Jahan Ramazani notes, even though modern poetry typically subverts the recuperations of elegy – being 'anti-consolatory and anti-encomiastic . . . anti-conventional and sometimes even anti-literary' – it is arguable that 'modern poetry and the elegy should be seen . . . as inextricable'.[8] For the modern poem draws much of its energy from the cultural trauma of mass war, the 'death' of God, the weakening of mourning rites. Ramazani contends that, in their refusal of the 'psychological propensity of the genre [of the elegy] to translate grief into consolation', modern elegists approximate Freud's 'melancholic' variant of normal mourning: that mode of mourning that registers not recovery but a 'fierce resistance to solace'. This means modern elegy becomes an art 'not [of] transcendence or redemption of loss but immersion in it'. By scorning 'recovery and transcendence', Ramazani says, 'modern elegists neither abandon the dead nor heal the living',[9] instead, their mourning resembles the 'open wound' of Freudian melancholy, a wound that 'empt[ies] the ego until it is totally impoverished'.[10] By way of the 'wound' of melancholy, loss enters the subject and empties it: the subject's narcissism is exploded, and no substitutive object or meaning comes to fill the void. The melancholic subject, shot from the locks of its identity (to use Thomas's image), carries within itself a gaping wound that opens on to a lost, dead or absent other: but an other that does not replenish the self, and leaves it perpetually bereft.

In *Deaths and Entrances*, Thomas's poems simultaneously preserve loss by refusing to convert it into meaning, and affirm poetic articulation in the face of loss. In this way, Thomas's poems both broach and break with the 'melancholic' variant of mourning. Thus, in the first stanza of 'Deaths and Entrances', Thomas's speaker – the 'One who called deepest down shall hold his peace', who 'cannot sink or cease / Endlessly to his wound / In many married London's estranging grief' (*CP*, 98) – both holds his 'peace' by refusing to mourn, but also resists sinking 'Endlessly' into the abysmal wound of melancholic withdrawal, into the illimitable mourning of melancholy. In fact Thomas's poems, as we will see, struggle to wrest melancholic withdrawal into jubilant affirmation.

Peter Sacks argues that the elegiac speaker characteristically displays an anxiety about the very use of language, since the elegist's 'reluctant submission to language' involves a relinquishment of the lost object to the substitutive labours of signification – as if to mourn was in some sense to *collude* with loss.[11] As Ramazani says, modern elegists suffer the 'guilty thought that they reap aesthetic profit from loss, that death is the fuel of poetic mourning'.[12] In Thomas's work, this reluctance to convert loss into language involves a refusal of all conventional signifiers of mourning: a repudiation of what 'A Refusal to Mourn' calls mourning's grave 'valley of sackloth'. Meditating on the burning to death of a child in a London air raid, the second stanza of 'A Refusal' insists:

> I shall not murder
> The mankind of her going with a grave truth
> Nor blaspheme down the stations of the breath
> With any further
> Elegy of innocence and youth.
>
> (*CP*, 86)

Here, Thomas's refusal of elegy relates the language of mourning to a 'murderous' dispatching of the dead; for it seems that to mourn the dead girl conventionally (that is, by way of a 'grave truth') is to murder her all over again. In this sense, the language of conventional mourning colludes with the violence that has already obliterated the girl; for, burying her in its specious generality (the 'further / Elegy of innocence and youth'), that language murders the singularity and particularity of the child's death as surely as the bombs reduce her to nothing. To refuse to mourn the girl's death, in this way, is to refuse to convert death into meaning; it is, instead, to preserve death as unrecuperable loss. In the language of Lacanian theory, it is to encounter death as part of the unsymbolisable 'Real'.[13] Indeed, as Ricks Carson notes, death in this poem 'cannot be proscribed or contained',[14] for it exceeds the poem's memorialising gestures even as Thomas struggles in the last stanza towards a perilous remythologisation of the child. In this latter connection, Peter Sacks says that even though 'A Refusal' seems to empty itself of elegy, in the end it turns round to rejoin the genre, for it 'mythologises the child' by evoking 'both a legendary parental figure and an imagined community of the dead that "robes" the daughter in friendship':[15]

> Deep with the first dead lies London's daughter,
> Robed in the long friends,
> The grains beyond age, the dark veins of her mother,
> Secret by the unmourning water
> Of the riding Thames.
> After the first death, there is no other.
>
> (CP, 86)

Sacks says that although the Thames here is 'unmourning', its populated depths recall the classical 'river deities whose daughters were transformed to reeds or laurel', and to this extent the river becomes a figure of 'assuagement' and of 'continuity and ongoing fertility'. In this way, the poem ends in 'traditional fashion'[16] by embracing at last the language of compensatory mourning that earlier it seemed to refuse. Another aspect of the poem's traditional ending, for Sacks, is that its final line, 'After the first death, there is no other', both 'admits and hyperbolically contrives to deny the power of death'.[17] That this final line 'denies' death outlandishly – by incorporating death into a myth of organic continuity – is undeniable, yet Sacks's reading misses the hyperbolism of the contrary reading: the sense in which 'After the first death, there is no other' may mean not 'there is no other death' but 'there is no other *but* death'. In this latter sense, death is admitted absolutely rather than denied utterly; moreover, such an absolute admission or 'entrance' of death suspends all mourning because no symbolic compensation is capable any longer of answering death's engulfing power. On this reading, the Thames is 'unmourning' because no work of mourning can approach death with sufficient symbolic reparation: the rites of mourning, rather, are shot from their locks, death's entrance is unanswerable, loss is absolute. Seen in this way, the last stanza of 'A Refusal' self-knowingly undoes its own mythologising or reparative gestures, for it propounds a rite of mourning even as it renders inoperable the symbolics of mourning as such. Like 'Among those Killed', then, the poem's conclusion disconcertingly installs textual irony within its apparently most jubilant affirmation.

This aspect of 'A Refusal' – whereby elegy's recuperative labour of mourning is both performed and effaced – is writ large in another troubled commemoration in *Deaths and Entrances*, 'Ceremony After a Fire Raid'. Writing to Vernon Watkins in 1944, Thomas remarked that this poem 'really is a Ceremony', with 'the third part of the poem [being] the music at the end' (*CL*, 518). The poem, indeed, both performs and presents the memorialisation of a catastrophic event: a wartime incendiary raid. It narrates a ceremony and *is* a ceremony. Coming 'after' the event of the raid (as emphasised by the title), the poem is thus temporally the event's elegisation: it commemorates and 'grieves' for the event. Yet the ethical dilemma that bedevils 'A Refusal' is dramatised in 'Ceremony', too, with still more urgency. In 'A Refusal' the problem, as we saw, was that the elegiacs of mourning (conventional or otherwise) threatened to erase the event of the girl's death by assimilating it to a language that repeated the murder rather than attested to it. The event, that is, was prevented from imposing *itself* in its unrepresentable (and, to this extent, perhaps unmournable) singularity. In 'Ceremony', that dilemma is rehearsed again, but this time the event pushes the poem into a kind of symbolic crisis – a crisis that, as we will see, can be said to generate an ethical gesture of rhetorical self-undoing in the poem.

Like 'Deaths and Entrances', 'Ceremony', as it opens, collapses the poet into the polis for whom he speaks: the self tumbles into the other, subjectivity into plurality, identity into alterity. The poem begins:

> Myselves
> The grievers
> Grieve

> Among the street burned to tireless death
> A child of a few hours
>
> (*CP*, 107)

Pluralising himself here as 'Myselves', the speaker does not, however, dissolve into a scene of traumatic alterity, as he does in 'Deaths and Entrances'; instead he *commands* that scene by identifying himself hieratically with and as 'The grievers'. He thus begins, like a modernist lyrical priest, to conduct a 'Ceremony', enjoining the grievers to participate in a ritual of poetic mourning invented by himself: a rite of mourning, we might say, that is realised rather than 'refused', writing large the fugitively elegiac mythologisation with which 'A Refusal' ends. In the chain of injunctions opening each stanza in the first section of 'Ceremony' – 'Grieve . . . Begin . . . Sing . . . Forgive . . . Give . . . Cry' (*CP*, 107) – the speaker appears to demand a ceremonialisation of the child's death by the community for which he speaks: as if that gesture of ritualisation might recuperate the trauma of the child's death, staunch the wound it makes in the community, close the *entrance* of death into the social body. However, Thomas's elegy is remarkable for the fact that, although a rite of mourning, it insists on preserving the child's death – specifically, its burned body – *against* the symbolisations through which it figures that body. Thus, in the third stanza, the poem strangely asks for forgiveness – for absolution – *for its own act of ritual mourning*, as if the text ethically acknowledges its own violent and murderous implication in the child's death insofar as it transposes death into symbolic meaning. The stanza runs:

> Forgive
> Us forgive
> Give
> Us your death that myselves the believers
> May hold it in a great flood
> Till the blood shall spurt,
> And the dust shall sing like a bird
> As the grains blow, as your death grows, through our heart.
>
> (*CP*, 107)

If, here, the child is requested to 'Give' the mourners its death so that they may 'hold' it in a redemptive 'flood' (and the image of the saving-and-destroying Biblical deluge is never far from this sanguine sea), this gift involves a blood-spurting *sacrifice* of the child: a sacrifice that restores the community to its own ceremonial meaning as the child's death 'grows' through it, and by means of it. In a real sense, in fact, the growth or burgeoning of the child's death *is this poem*, for the death is magisterially co-opted into the sonority of the poem's performance. To the extent that the poem mourns or grieves the child's death, then, it incorporates that death bloodily in its own ceremony; and in terms of 'A Refusal' it 'murders' the child all over again, sacrificing it to its symbolic 'truth'. But to the extent that 'Ceremony''s figures mark their *own* limit, too, they critically and ethically acknowledge what is left over from or left aside from their grandiloquent symbolisations.

According to Jacques Lacan, writing on *Hamlet*, the work of mourning is called forth by the 'hole in the real' that results from loss: for 'there is nothing of significance that can fill the hole in the real, except the totality of the signifier. The work of mourning is accomplished at the level of the *logos*.'[18] The traumatic 'hole' that appears in the real can only be filled by the signifier, by the radically *symbolic* work of mourning. For Slavoj Žižek, developing Lacan's thinking, the 'Real' is that whose very definition is to *elude the reach* of the symbolic: it is that which is *left over* from any labour of symbolisation, and thereby from any labour of mourning. It is that upon which symbolisation cannot close and with which it cannot fuse. Thus 'the Real is in itself a hole, a gap, an opening in the middle of the symbolic order – it is the lack around which the symbolic order is structured'. Constructed as a 'leftover of symbolisation',[19] the Real obtrudes itself traumatically upon the subject and upon signification with an inertness that resists all attempts to convert it into meaning: the Real is a hole in the symbolic. In 'Ceremony After a Fire Raid', this hole of the Real appears in the child's blackened and 'bereft' body to the extent that that body exceeds in its obdurate materiality the poem's grasp, its work of symbolisation, its labour of mourning. The Real 'enters' unrecuperably; consequently, even though the poem enlists the child's death and body in its ceremony, it also discloses the 'leftover' of its symbolic operations in the 'black husk left' of the child. The fourth stanza runs:

> Crying
> Your dying
> Cry,
> Child beyond cockcrow, by the fire-dwarfed
> Street we chant the flying sea
> In the body bereft.

> Love is the last light spoken. Oh
> Seed of sons in the loin of the black husk left.
>
> (CP, 107)

At one level, this stanza imperiously grasps the child's death in its own figural project, miming the child's last cry in and as the voice of the grievers: 'Crying / Your dying / Cry . . .' The mourners speak for the child, engulfing it in the symbolics of their ceremony. Yet, to the extent that the poem displays its ceremony *as* an engulfment, it strangely keeps the child's body untouched by symbolisation, and as other to rhetorical incorporation. Indeed, while the mourners 'chant the flying sea / In the body bereft' and flood the body with water, they fail to abolish its status as something 'left', 'bereft', left over: something beyond ceremony and 'beyond cockcrow', belonging to the unsymbolisable Real. To 'chant the flying sea' *in* the body is to deluge it with meaning, as it is to see the 'Seed of sons' *in* the 'black husk left': yet the poem is never in any doubt that the flood and seed of the future that it discerns in the 'husk' of the child *is its own*, not the child's. In this way, the poem repeats the gesture of 'Among those Killed' in which a scrupulous distance is maintained between the event (whether bomb or raid) and the representation (whether poem or 'ceremony'). Like 'Among those Killed', indeed, 'Ceremony' does not close on the thing that it figures; rather, it maximises the gap between the event and its figuration. To this extent, the poem maintains an ethical distance between the thing commemorated and its ritual of commemoration, and strives to avoid 'murdering' the child with a 'grave truth' by extravagantly projecting its rhetoric *away* from the child's death, not towards it. Paradoxically, it is in the extravagance of its rhetoric that the poem's ethics reside; for the text sustains the alterity of the child's death by addressing it in a language whose free-wheeling excess leaves that death untouched, 'beyond', left over, a husk, unincorporated. Thus the poem's ending conducts a ceremony that *refuses to mourn* precisely to the extent that it refuses to present the child's death, displacing elegiac representation by hyperbolic invention:

> Into the organpipes and steeples
> Of the luminous cathedrals,
> Into the weathercocks' molten mouths
> Rippling in twelve-winded circles,
> Into the dead clock burning the hour
> Over the urn of sabbaths

Over the whirling ditch of daybreak
Over the sun's hovel and the slum of fire
And the golden pavements laid in requiems,
Into the cauldrons of the statuary,
Into the bread in a wheatfield of flames,
Into the wine burning like brandy,
The masses of the sea
The masses of the infant-bearing sea
Erupt, fountain, and enter to utter for ever
Glory glory glory
The sundering ultimate kingdom of genesis' thunder.
(CP, 108–9)

Here, the poem itself 'erupts' in an outrageous outfacing of death, exultantly affirming a 'sea' that is 'infant-bearing' rather than a 'fire' that is infant-burning. In this way, the poem creates a new 'legend' against the sanctioned 'legend / Of Adam and Eve' (CP, 108) that it doubtingly revisits in its second section. However, this new legend that is constructed so climactically as the poem ends gains no hold over death except through the exorbitance of its rhetorical performance, through its self-glorying poetic inventiveness; for the poem posits itself *against* the thing that it commemorates. Indeed, in the gap between the 'body bereft' of the poem's dead child and its concluding 'infant-bearing sea', in the gap between the poem's symbolic 'death' and symbolic 'entrance', we might say – the gap between the Real and its symbolisation – a tumultuous 'music' (CL, 518) erupts in a ceremony that has less to do with poetic signification than *performance*, less to do with poetic meaning than *event*. Without meaning, without mourning and without elegy, then, 'Ceremony' ends in a groundless affirmation of poetic performativity that, in Thomas's words, is 'an event, a happening, an action perhaps ...' (CL, 278): a happening that suspends 'death' to the extent that, as assay or invention, it allows poetry's *entrance*.

NOTES

[Steve Vine's essay examines Thomas's 1946 collection *Deaths and Entrances* in relation to the themes of mourning and elegy in that volume. Beginning with the imagery of locks and keys which figure in the Blitz poems, Vine argues that Thomas's poetry lies both within and beyond the elegiac modes of twentieth-century poetic language, audaciously replacing conventional lament with what he calls 'a language of celebration that parodically compounds irony with affirmation'. In refusing to mourn, to use the title of the best known of them, these poems heighten already existing strategies from the earlier poetry and explore the 'entrance' of death as a traumatic event into the poetic text. As Vine points out, Thomas is aware of his own implication in war; so that, for example, in the collection's title poem, the speaker shares an occult identity not only with the victims of the air-raid but also with the Luftwaffe bomber pilot. It considers in detail a group of poems from the collection that deal with the complexities and anxieties of symbolising or of 'mourning' death's catastrophic entrances. Drawing on ideas of mourning and of symbolisation in psychoanalysis, the essay suggests that death, as an invasive 'other', inhabits the way that Thomas thinks about the very production of poetry, and that his labour of poetic writing can therefore be understood as a continual performance of 'deaths and entrances'. Eds]

1. See Walford Davies, 'Introduction', in Dylan Thomas, *Deaths and Entrances*, ed. Walford Davies (Gregynog, 1984), p. vii; William York Tindall, *A Reader's Guide to Dylan Thomas* (Syracuse, NY, 1962), p. 206; John Ackerman, *A Dylan Thomas Companion: Life, Poetry and Prose* (London, 1991), p. 106.

2. John Donne, *The Sermons of John Donne*, ed. Evelyn M. Simpson and George R. Potter, vol. X (California, 1962), p. 229.

3. Ibid., p. 233.

4. Davies, *Deaths and Entrances*, pp. x–xi.

5. Ibid., p. vii.

6. Donne, *Sermons*, p. 235.

7. Tindall, *A Reader's Guide to Dylan Thomas*, p. 207.

8. Jahan Ramazani, *Poetry of Mourning: The Modern Elegy from Hardy to Heaney* (Chicago, 1994), pp. 2, 1.

9. Ibid., p. 4.

10. Ibid. Ramazani cites Freud from 'Mourning and Melancholia' (1917), *The Standard Edition of the Complete Psychological Works of Sigmund Freud*, vol. XIV (London, 1957), p. 253.

11. Peter Sacks, *The English Elegy: Studies in the Genre from Spenser to Yeats* (Baltimore, MD, 1985), p. 2. See ch. I for Sacks's view of the relationship between elegy and what Freud calls the 'work of mourning'.

12. Ramazani, *Poetry of Mourning*, p. 6.

13. The Lacanian 'Real' will be discussed later in the present essay.

14. Ricks Carson, 'Thomas's "A Refusal to Mourn the Death, by Fire, of a Child in London" ', *The Explicator*, 54 (1996), 242.

15. Sacks, *The English Elegy*, p. 306.

16. Ibid., pp. 306–7. Ramazani writes similarly: 'in the end Thomas's theological rhetoric belies his rebuff of compensatory mourning, since it evokes an eschatological framework that implicitly redeems the death as martyrdom ("the stations of the breath")', *Poetry of Mourning*, p. 7.

17. Ibid., p. 307.

18. Jacques Lacan, 'Desire and the Interpretation of Desire in *Hamlet*', in *Literature and Psychoanalysis: The Question of Reading: Otherwise*, ed. Shoshana Felman (Baltimore, MD, 1982), p. 38.

19. Slavoj Žižek, *The Sublime Object of Ideology* (London, 1989), p. 170.

8

Questions of Identity: The Movement and 'Fern Hill'

JAMES A. DAVIES

It is conventional wisdom that Thomas's *Collected Poems* was published, in 1952, to great acclaim. This is, of course, true,[1] but it is also true that much of the praise came (in Britain at any rate) from the non-academic literary world. This is one of the last occasions when a serious and difficult poet was championed by representatives of the general reader. More recently, literary status has come to depend more and more on the opinion of the academy. As far as *Collected Poems* was concerned, the opinion of what might be called 'high academia', was invariably unfavourable but not, at that time, generally influential. The main example is that of *Scrutiny*.

From *Portrait of the Artist as a Young Dog* onwards *Scrutiny* had castigated Thomas for being 'the overgrown schoolboy', for 'immaturity of adolescence',[2] for 'playing at games', and for 'clever-boy pranks'.[3] It also attacked Thomas's assumption of 'the mantle of distraught romantic genius',[4] regarding it as 'an excuse to avoid the trouble of precise communication',[5] which led, on occasion, to 'self-indulgent religiosity . . . [and] . . . pseudo-liturgical verbal juggling' and 'a downright disgusting self-righteousness'.[6] One contributor noted grimly that: 'His Welsh nonconformist background effectively sets off this posture in that it encourages the bardic gesture, the Dionysiac vision, the rapture of hell-fire.'[7] Another concluded, unconvincingly: 'without any disrespectful feelings towards the country of the poet's origin – the idea of the Bard counts for not a little'.[8] That idea, *Scrutiny* was quick to assure its readers, had little to do with intelligence.

Scrutiny exerted a powerful influence on Movement[9] thinking and its aesthetic objections to Thomas – his lack of seriousness and intellectual grip, the absence of clarity, his all-pervading self-indulgent emotionalism – are the intrusive sub-text of much Movement response to Thomas's work. To quote Blake Morrison: the Movement prized 'rationalism, realism, empiricism'.[10] John Lehmann described it as well as anyone as having 'a dry anti-romantic flavour, and using the contrast or conflict of a conversational tone and an exacting technical pattern'.[11] In the eyes of some members of the Movement, Thomas's late, purportedly extreme romantic manner therefore made him a necessary enemy.

To say 'some members', however, is to note that the Movement's response to Thomas was not homogeneous. The response of Philip Larkin is a case in point. His relationship with Thomas, never more than slight, began at a reading in Oxford at which Thomas read hilarious parodies of others' poems and two of his own, 'which seem very good',[12] Larkin commented to J. B. Sutton. A year later Larkin was subjecting a visitor 'to a daily battery of jazz & Dylan Thomas – he likes the latter'.[13] Only in letters to Amis does Larkin's attitude change and then not completely: 'I think there is no man in England now who can "stick words into us like pins" [. . .] like he can', he wrote in 1947, and then complained about Thomas's obscurity and 'shocking influence'.[14] Many years later, in another letter to Amis, Larkin writes that he read Thomas's letters, 'with almost supernatural boredom' and praised Amis's parodies of Thomas in *The Old Devils* which recalled 'that wonderful stuff from *That Uncertain Feeling*'.[15] Here, though, is the letter-writer as chameleon, for, elsewhere, in two responses to Thomas's death, the emotional charge is more intense, more sincere. Larkin wrote to Patsy Stone: 'I can't believe D. T. is truly dead. It seems absurd. Three people [the others were T. S. Eliot and W. H. Auden] who've altered the face of poetry & the *youngest* has to die.'[16] Three years later he told Vernon Watkins 'how shocked [he] had been (like everyone else) by Dylan Thomas's death'.[17]

The Movement's ambivalence towards Thomas's work may well have stemmed from the uneasy feeling that poetry of consequence cannot be judged simply in terms of reactionary principles, and that adherence to those principles could not counter Thomas's ability to 'stick words into us like pins'. It might also have owed something to a sense that Thomas had been a victim, that the literary/social world had destroyed the great talent, that the innocent provincial had been corrupted by the great city. Thomas was, in D. J. Enright's marvellous phrase, a 'Bubbles who fell among literary touts'.[18] He fell, of course, with some eagerness.

The view of Thomas as victim of big bad literary London raises questions of origin. Here we might be reminded of *Scrutiny*'s hostility to the Welsh sources of Thomas's faults and its stereotyping of Thomas as the Welsh Nonconformist preacher bard. In his introduction to that seminal Movement document, *Poets of the 1950s*, Enright commends the richness of Thomas's imagination, but then cites its 'deficiency in intellectual conviction' and asserts that 'Welsh rhetoric seems a deadly enemy to all varieties of logic, even the poetic'.[19] Larkin's closest encounters with Welsh poetry were via links with two 'rhapsodic' bards, one of whom (Watkins) hero-worshipped the other (Thomas). One effect of such encounters is the generous selection from Thomas and Watkins in the *Oxford Book of Twentieth-Century English Verse*, which Larkin edited in 1973. But the background to these links appears to be overt prejudice of a kind that now, following the publication of *Selected Letters*, we recognise to be typical of the man, evident in two comments, the first enigmatic, the second roundly abusive. The first is Larkin's account of Watkins, in a letter to J. B. Sutton: 'He is nearly 40 & has just published a book of poems which I don't like an awful lot, but I like him enormously. [. . .] He is also an intimate friend of Dylan Thomas. I hope someday you can meet him. He's Welsh. [. . .]'[20] The second is a remark about R. S. Thomas: 'Our friend Arsewipe Thomas suddenly was led into my room one afternoon last week, and stood without moving or speaking: he seems pretty hard going. Not noticeably Welsh, which is one comfort. [eg. #]'[21]

One reason why we should not be surprised at Larkin's anti-Welsh feeling is his friendship with Kingsley Amis, which also took Larkin to Wales. Amis lectured at the University College of Swansea from 1949 to 1961 and retained strong links with the area. His dislike of Thomas's work was long-standing and of two kinds. First, there are the aesthetic objections proffered by all good

Movement men. These are summed up in Amis's poem 'Against Romanticism':

> To please an ingrown taste for anarchy
> Torrid images circle in the wood . . .
> All senses then are glad to gasp: the eye
> Smeared with garish paints, tickled up with ghosts
> That brandish warnings or an abstract noun.

The poem rejects poetry in which 'Bodies rich with heat wriggle to the touch', and insists, famously, 'Better, of course, if images were plain'.[22] Even more vehement are objections to the man: Thomas as charlatan inspired two of Amis's best known fictional characters. The pretentiously bardic Gareth Probert in *That Uncertain Feeling* (1955) gave Amis the opportunity for viciously amusing parody, both of the poetry and of the Captain Cat sequences in *Under Milk Wood. The Old Devils* (1986) savages Thomas and the Dylan industry through reactions to Bryden, the dead Welsh poet who is now an all-things-to-all-men tourist attraction. All this emerges more directly in Amis's essay 'Thomas the Rhymer', where bardic Thomas is dismissed as worthy of attention only from those who, Amis comments with heavy irony, 'hanker after something sublimer than thinking'.[23]

Thus the Movement's view of Thomas results from a combination of aesthetic disgust based on a misunderstanding of Thomas's work, and on extreme anti-Welsh prejudice. The first is fuelled by the second. The animus strengthens the willingness to stereotype: to be a Welsh poet is to be like Dylan Thomas and this means being rural-lyrical, ecstatic, inspired, bardic, undisciplined, immature.

Dylan Thomas was not wholly responsible for the English view of Welsh writing that prevailed in the early 1950s. To some extent it continued an earlier response to those Welsh writers – such as Caradoc Evans, Glyn Jones, Jack Jones and Richard Llewellyn – who had been taken up by London publishers. But Dylan Thomas was by far the most famous and the only Welsh writer who mounted a serious challenge to an English literary hegemony. The Movement despised Thomas's poetics and had a fundamental hatred of what they perceived to be Thomas's kind of Welshness. The effect was to stereotype and so, to a great extent, dictate the nature of Anglo-Welsh poetic identity, and then – as far as English literature was concerned – to marginalise that stereotype.

Sean Lucy writes, of Anglo-Irish poetry, that 'it is the story of a search; it is part of the quest of the English-speaking Irish for an identity, the reshaping of English to express the Irish experience'.[24] This brings us to the issue of literary or cultural identity which, as with Irish writing, involves questions about the relationship between a literature in English and English literature. Whilst it may be correct to insist that upbringing defines a writer, Stuart Hall is equally persuasive in arguing that cultural identity is not simply or mainly a matter of recovering or sharing a past. Rather, cultural and literary identity is more a matter of *becoming*, of constant *positioning*,[25] here in relation to other larger literatures, and particularly to English literature. [Thus the second part of this essay] is concerned with 'Fern Hill', the apotheosis of confident Anglo-Welsh poetic identity, which is parochial not provincial, to use Patrick Kavanagh's terms,[26] and which effectively pre-empts the criticism of the Movement.

'Fern Hill' is the final poem in *Deaths and Entrances* and the last of that volume's poems to have been written. Two letters, one to David Tennant (*CL*, 565), the other to Edith Sitwell, tell us that it was composed during August 1945 and 'in September, in Carmarthenshire, near the farm where it happened' (*CL*, 583). These dates are important: they place the writing of 'Fern Hill' at a crucial point in history. The war in Europe had ended on 8 May 1945; a left-wing Labour government had been swept to power in Britain, with a large majority, on 26 July. On 6 August the first atom bomb was dropped on Hiroshima; three days later the second bomb destroyed Nagasaki. Japan surrendered on 15 August. Since 1944, Thomas, after a barren and distracted two years, had been writing poetry again. These events instilled in him – as in millions of others – a great sense of freedom, of new beginnings, and doubtless, given his long-professed left-wing sympathies, of welcome social change. His correspondence with Oscar Williams has much on his hopes of moving to work in America. But though literary prospects seemingly had improved, the war's end did not solve his problems. In one sense it made no difference: he wrote to Williams that for a poet, the true war never ended; a poet was only 'at peace with everything except words' (*CL*, 561). More immediately and problematically, the Allied victory ended lucrative and regular work scripting propaganda films for Gryphon.

Despite his leftist sympathies, the arrival of a Labour government was to arouse in him, as Ferris puts it, 'middle-class fears of rampaging socialism' (CL, 560 n.), which meant state interference. Thomas wrote to Williams: 'The rain has stopped, thank Jesus. Have the Socialists-in-power-now stopped it? An incometax form flops through the window. . . . Let's get out, let's get out' (CL, 559–60).

He was also profoundly troubled by the atrocities discovered during the liberation of Europe and by the final acts of the war against Japan. The death camps were much on his mind: Belsen, for example, became a ready figure for disturbance and horror, as when he referred in letters to 'nature serene as Fats Waller in Belsen' (CL, 554) and, less ambiguously, to 'worse-than-Belsen London' (CL, 555) and the 'boiling black Belsen' (CL, 557) of Williams's darker poems. The destruction of Hiroshima and Nagasaki was even more traumatic, causing a further darkening of his apocalyptic vision.

During the late spring of 1945 Thomas, Caitlin and the two children left New Quay, Cardiganshire, where they had lived for a year, to spend the summer with Thomas's parents at Blaen Cwm. In some ways, rather like the end of the war, this was a promising move: Thomas was able to keep an eye on his ageing parents – in particular, on his father, with whom he now had a warm relationship – and, as he told Sitwell, in a place in countryside not far from (and similar to) that which surrounded the eponymous farm, where living expenses were low, and which was far from the dangers of bombing. Like Fernhill, Blaen Cwm was redolent of happy childhood holiday memories and thus was part of his 'never-to-be-buried childhood in heaven or Wales' (CL, 583). It was also a place that, from adolescence, Thomas had always found conducive to the writing of poetry.

Yet once again there was a negative side to these positive developments. The Thomases had been forced to leave their bungalow in New Quay when their landlord reclaimed his property, and Thomas, as usual, was harassed by financial problems. These were exacerbated by being cooped up with ageing and demanding parents, a tense marital situation, and the unaccustomed proximity of the two young children, in dreadful weather and in an isolated, eccentric rural world with whose values – of toil and narrow Nonconformism – he was hardly in sympathy. Understandably, America seemed more and more an attractive option.

'Fern Hill' is a product of such circumstances, of the interstice between different histories, and this is reflected disturbingly in the poem as the speaker explores the possibility of flight from both public and private worlds, a flight which he finally acknowledges to be impossible. One of the central ideas of the poem is of nightly annihilation ('the owls were bearing the farm away' (CP, 134) and the world beginning again the next morning, an idea which is at once a metaphor for a child's carefree eagerness and, more deeply, a reflection of the mentality of the Blitzed Londoner and of the aftermath of Hiroshima (in this regard 'the horses / Flashing into the dark' [CP, 134] may well owe something to recollections of anti-aircraft batteries firing into the night sky). By the final stanza temporary annihilation has become permanent, with the narrator 'take[n]' by time 'Up to the swallow thronged loft by the shadow of my hand' and waking after death 'to the farm forever fled from the childless land' (CP, 135); and while it may be no more than grim prescience that harnesses sterility and flesh reduced to a shadow, Thomas's March 1946 letter to Sitwell noted that he had finished the poem a month after the war's cataclysmic end (CL, 583).

Other reflections in the poem of life at Blaen Cwm are more indirect, more redolent of wish fulfilment. It seems no accident that a poem written in the cramped and squalid country cottage should stress outdoor freedom and social power, or that, given the continuing crises of Thomas's adult life, it should seek to celebrate the carefree and the bliss of ignorance. But once again, as will be seen, such positives encounter difficulties. Moreover, in literary terms, 'Fern Hill' can also be read as an 'interstitial' poem in Homi Bhabha's sense of the word; that is as a poem situated at the interface between one literature and an other.[27] In other words, it is a Welsh poem that, like all Welsh poems in English, is held in a matrix of English literary traditions and associations, to such an extent that it might seem that Thomas deliberately placed his poem – as he did, for example, with the late poems and with 'Prologue' – in relation to influential outside texts or literary movements. Accordingly 'Fern Hill' is a 'traditional' poem in at least two senses, since in embracing English traditions it repudiates, to a large extent, the anti-traditionalist neomodernism of Thomas's earlier work.

Those English traditions include that of the poetry of childhood recollection running from Vaughan (Welsh, but writing within an

English tradition) and Traherne, through Blake and Wordsworth to the present. One of Thomas's favourite poems in that tradition, D. H. Lawrence's 'Ballad of Another Ophelia', was quoted by him in a letter of July 1945 to Oscar Williams during the period when 'Fern Hill' was being meditated. A haunting account of the end of innocence and the destruction of a childhood idyll, with its opening orchard of green apples and concluding 'grey gamer',[28] it seems a direct influence on the poem, which was written soon afterwards. So, too, does Eliot's *East Coker*, which had appeared in 1940 and was republished in 1943 as part of *Four Quartets*; its reminder to Eliot's contemporaries that 'In my end is my beginning'[29] is clearly echoed in 'Fern Hill's 'Time held me green and dying' (*CP*, 135). Similarly, there are links with other English literary traditions. One is that of the country-house poem, glimpsed through the narrator's designation of his childhood self as 'prince', 'lordly', 'huntsman', one 'honoured among foxes and pheasants' (*CP*, 134–5). Another is that of realist rural writing that runs from Wordsworth through John Clare, George Eliot, Anthony Trollope, and Thomas Hardy to Edward Thomas (in, for example, Thomas's 'The Manor Farm' and 'Two Houses').

Yet as was the case with Modernism, Thomas resists being wholly absorbed into any of these traditions. 'Fern Hill' is at once central and marginal to mainstream English literature, simultaneously inside and beyond it. It differs from it in degree, therefore, not kind. It is not fully absorbed into such English traditions because of its Welshness; yet, paradoxically, much of the finest Welsh writing in English is precisely from that petit-bourgeois/suburban milieu deemed to be quintessentially 'English' by those who insist that 'true' Welshness is rural. It is thus both alive to the limitations of realism and sceptical of mysticism or spirituality, a poem which, significantly, deals with a Welsh place with an utterly English name.

All of which suggests that this is a poem out of English-speaking, urban South Wales which mediates the class structure of the specifically Welsh society of its day, one distinguished by its lack of a strong upper-middle class. Partly as a result of this it was a society that valued education, so that a schoolteacher, say, was accorded higher status than in many parts of England. Such a status, in turn, might influence the attitudes of the schoolteacher's son – as Thomas was – particularly when he found himself among his poor rural relations. Hence the poem's edge of superiority and the way in which middle-classness is asserted in Welsh terms, partly in its unusual English usages and in its potentially comic lower-class Welsh vocabulary (the reiterated 'lovely' of verse three, for example, being a characteristic South-Walian intensifier) (*CP*, 134). As elsewhere in Thomas the poem's dominant tenor – what might be described as its rhetorical lyricism – reflects the Bible-based preaching style of Welsh Nonconformism: 'And the sabbath rang slowly / In the pebbles of the holy streams' (*CP*, 134) has markedly un-English connotations for a poem of 1945. Intimations of secular Sabbatarianism, with a dash of pessimism, can be a very Welsh combination.

In this sense, 'Fern Hill' belongs to the English tradition but is also a key text in Welsh writing in English, one which adumbrates some of its standard themes of memory, childhood, and place. Its title and focus on the farm as dwelling-place, for example, are a reminder that, as M. Wynn Thomas has suggested, 'the trope of the house' has a 'centrality to Anglo-Welsh culture'.[30] This trope is one which M. Wynn Thomas sees as a particular feature of Thomas's poem and of Vernon Watkins's contemporary 'Returning to Goleufryn'. Indeed, the critical choice of such poems as touchstones indicates a point about Welsh and/or Anglo-Welsh literary traditions: both houses are transformed, at times rhapsodically, beyond realism into symbolic constructs, mythologised places, yet detached from any sense of the mystical, although the language of either poem can at times recall that of Vaughan, Blake or Wordsworth.

Any interpretation must begin with the recognition that in the first delighted rush of memory, the initial surge of remembered childhood happiness, the poem effects only a momentary escape from the present before its impulses are subverted. 'Fern Hill' is, of course, an adult's view of childhood happiness in rural surroundings, the view of an adult who knows all too well that childhood is fleeting and that time conquers, but accepts that childhood in itself is never altogether reassuring. Certainly, it was mainly a 'young and easy', 'carefree' and 'heedless' (*CP*, 134–5) period; yet the ideas intruded into the poem by its adult awareness include memories of a youthful sense of dislocation, of riding uncontrollably into the powerful (and perhaps sensual) unknown:

> And nightly under the simple stars
> As I rode to sleep the owls were bearing the farm away,
> All the moon long I heard, blessed among stables, the nightjars

Flying with the ricks, and the horses
Flashing into the dark.

(*CP*, 134)

The core of these memories is even more troubling. The boy is
invariably remembered as climbing, playing, running and enjoying
himself, but this only serves to emphasise the poem's uneasy
solipsism: 'I', 'me', and 'my' occur twenty-two times in its 54 lines.
The boy is the sole figure in this childhood landscape; no other
human being, neither friend, relation, nor parent, is mentioned. Nor
is there any reference to childhood games or other communal
activities, or, apart from the hint at helping in 'herdsman', to the
activities of a child's holiday on the farm.

Paradoxically, this solitary world, which seems initially to be a
desirable alternative to careworn life, becomes suggestively and re-
strictively suburban in the farm's name; it is one that would not be
inappropriate for a semi-detached house on Cwmdonkin Drive. The
collocation 'apple towns' (*CP*, 134) is similarly revealing, as is the
fact that the boy seems always to be playing near the house and
yard rather than in the countryside proper. The self-important hier-
archies of the poem – time superior to the golden boy, who as
'prince', 'lord', 'huntsman', and 'herdsman' seems superior to all
else – further echo those of class-conscious Swansea suburbia.
Cwmdonkin's middle-class codes can also be detected in the strange
sexlessness of the boy's country experience: this is the petit-bourgeois, suburban adult's sanitised prelapsarian Eden and not a
muddily realistic farm where a young boy delighted in having
'manure in my shoes and hear[ing] it squelch as I walked, to see a
cow have calves and a bull on top of a cow' (*CS*, 135). Yet if
middle-class assertion is built into the texture of the poem, as the
confidently extended single sentence stanzas that open it proclaim,
there is also more than a hint of suburban uncertainty in the golden
boy plying 'sky blue trades' (*CP*, 135), presumably via the trades-
man's entrance. Above all, a suburban sensibility is reflected in the
presentation of childhood almost wholly in terms of a relationship
with tamed, cultivated nature.

The remembered world – house and farm – is far from a solid
presence, if only because meaning is further destabilised through
ambiguity. For example, 'Easy', in the first line and in the famous
close, suggests an easy-going existence but also carries the potential
connotation of amoral carelessness. Similarly, the meaning of

'green', that ubiquitous Thomas word, slides from natural growth to decay and naïveté. Even the line 'The sky gathered again' (*CP*, 134), part of Thomas's description of a world restoring itself, is darkened by a verb whose signification can range from collecting together to erupting poisonously. The poem's use of musical imagery contributes to this calculated imprecision: the 'lilting house', 'singing as the farm was home', 'the calves' which 'Sang to my horn', 'the tunes from the chimneys ... air / And playing' and time's 'tuneful turning' that limits the 'morning songs' (*CP*, 134–5), are controlled quasi-surrealistic excursions which dramatise the happy fluidity of childhood but resist solidifying paraphrase. Analogously, the attempts of poetic form to shape the past into a strong and confident presence (suggested by the regular stanza form and some patterned repetition) are countered by the somewhat sporadic use of rhyme and assonance, which fails to control the material assertively.

In the poem's last two stanzas the dominance of negatives effects a further shift in language and tone. In the final stanza, despite an initial use of reassuringly traditional spatial terms – the idea of rising out of life into the afterlife – death is conceived of in a wholly secular and discomforting manner as a 'swallow thronged loft' in perpetual night, the moon 'always rising', the dispossessed boy riding into darkness. Little wonder that the poem's lyrical narration is countered by the despairing exclamation, or equally despairing apostrophe, of the last three lines:

> Oh as I was young and easy in the mercy of his means,
>   Time held me green and dying
>   Though I sang in my chains like the sea.
>
> (CP, 135)

At the poem's heart there is rootlessness, uncertainty and a kind of despair, as the past blurs and the present darkens; even happy memory ultimately fails to orientate, order or console. But we should also remind ourselves that the circumstances out of which 'Fern Hill' were written were not wholly bleak and that Thomas's general response to events could be hopeful and often heroic in its humour.

It seems no accident that the most positive accounts of the poem – those by William York Tindall and Walford Davies, for example – are by critics most concerned to realise the poem's place in

English literature. Whereas a consideration of context illuminates the tension between despair and heroic assertion, what can be called a comparative understanding of the poem – that which proceeds from recognising that it belongs to a major literature as well as a minor one – also places it, reassuringly, within two ordering systems. But there can be little doubt that the poem draws its main positive strength, strength in numbers, as it were, from its links with the greater tradition, with *English* literature's version and Eliot's 'ideal order'.[31] To adapt Mikhail Bakhtin: the poem 'has no sovereign internal territory, [it] is wholly and always on the boundary';[32] or, additionally, to apply a term of Lynne Pearce's, the poem exists '*only in relation*'.[33] Its relationship with that glittering and weighty literary past, that past's sense of desirable possibilities, holds the poem 'green' as well as 'dying' as time holds the boy, and counters the impulse towards rootlessness and dislocation.

The poem is profoundly shaped by a historical and literary context that is both English and Welsh. It is 'interstitial' in Homi Bhabha's sense. This is not to say that the poem lies wounded in some desolate no-man's-land. Rather, it exists on what might be called poetical marches, which, like the Welsh Marches, are a place of great beauty and fertility, a site of cultural forces which are often in tension yet which combine and create as much as they compete and cancel out. The poem retains a sense of otherness that requires careful definition, as well as the intertextual presence of a directly available and dominant literature. This availability and dominance results, of course, from a common language, a common education system, intimate and institutional relationships, as well as numerous shared cultural assumptions; and it poses problems for those seeking to assimilate the relationship between Welsh writing in English and mainstream English literature to a colonial or postcolonial paradigm.

From *Appropriations and Impositions: National, Regional and Sexual Identity*, ed. Igor Navrátil and Robert B. Pynsent (Bratislava, 1997), pp. 118–29, and *A Reference Companion to Dylan Thomas* (Westport, CT, 1998), pp. 196–204.

NOTES

[James A. Davies's piece is a blend of extracts from an article published in *Appropriations and Impositions: National, Regional and Sexual Identity*, entitled 'Questions of Identity: Dylan Thomas, the Movement and After', parts of which are incorporated into the chapter on 'Dylan Thomas in England' of his *A Reference Companion to Dylan Thomas*, and sections of the chapter on *Deaths and Entrances* also in his *Reference Companion*. In the first of these, Davies examines the individually mixed, but generally negative responses to Thomas's work of the English 1950s Movement writers who followed him, particularly those of Philip Larkin and Kingsley Amis. He also explores the English reading of Thomas through English stereotypes of Welshness; however, Davies argues that Thomas's work confounds the usual binary polarities in resting within both English and Welsh traditions. In order to demonstrate this, he offers a detailed reading of that most anthologised of Thomas's poems, 'Fern Hill', in its historical, biographical and social contexts, one which – using Homi Bhabha's notion – he locates in the interstitial area, or 'marches', between the two cultures. Eds]

1. Philip Toynbee, for example, described Thomas as 'the greatest living poet'. Review of *Collected Poems 1934–1952*, *Observer*, 9 November 1952, p. 7. Cyril Connolly, in the *Sunday Times*, and Stephen Spender in the *Spectator* were equally adulatory.

2. W. H. Mellors, 'The Bard and the Prep School', *Scrutiny*, 9 (1940), 77.

3. Wolf Mankowitz, review of *Deaths and Entrances*, *Scrutiny*, 14 (1946), 65, 67.

4. Mellors, 'The Bard and the Prep School', 77.

5. R. G. Cox, review of *Henry Treece, Dylan Thomas: Dog Among the Fairies, Scrutiny*, 16 (1949), 249.

6. Robin Mayhead, review of *Collected Poems 1934–1952*, *Scrutiny*, 19 (1952–53), 146.

7. Mellors, 'The Bard and the Prep School', 77.

8. Robin Mayhead, review of *Collected Poems*, 149.

9. The term 'the Movement' is generally used to denote the poetic wing of the realist trend in English writing that emerged in the early 1950s.

10. Blake Morrison, *The Movement: English Poetry and Fiction of the 1950s* (London and New York, 1980), p. 9.

11. Quoted in ibid., p. 43.

12. Philip Larkin, *Selected Letters 1940–1985*, ed. Anthony Thwaite (London and Boston, 1992), p. 28.

13. Ibid., p. 46.

14. Ibid., p. 133.

15. Ibid., p. 758.

16. Ibid., p. 218.

17. Ibid., p. 264.

18. Quoted in Morrison, *The Movement*, p. 146.

19. *Poets of the 1950s*, ed. D. J. Enright (Tokyo, 1955), p. 146.

20. Larkin, *Selected Letters*, p. 55.

21. Ibid., p. 341.

22. *New Lines*, ed. Robert Conquest (London, 1962), p. 45.

23. Kingsley Amis, *What Became of Jane Austen?* (London, 1972), p. 59.

24. Quoted in Susan Bassnett, *Comparative Literature: A Critical Introduction* (Oxford, 1933), pp. 61–2.

25. See Stuart Hall, 'Cultural Identity and Diaspora', in *Colonial Discourses and Post-Colonial Theory*, ed. Patrick Williams and Laura Christman (Hemel Hempstead, 1993), pp. 392–403.

26. 'Parochialism and provincialism are opposites. The provincial has no mind of his own; he does not trust what his eyes see until he has heard what the metropolis – towards which his eyes are turned – has to say on the subject. . . . The parochial mentality in the other hand is never in any doubt about the social and artistic validity of his parish.' *Poetry and Ireland since 1800: A Source Book*, ed. Mark Storey (London, 1988), pp. 205–6.

27. Homi K. Bhabha, *The Location of Culture* (London and New York, 1994), p. 3

28. D. H. Lawrence, *The Complete Poems*, ed. Vivian de Sola Pinto and Warren Roberts (London, 1993), p. 119.

29. T. S. Eliot, *The Complete Poems and Plays of T. S. Eliot* (London, 1975), p. 183.

30. M. Wynn Thomas, ' "Prints of Wales": Contemporary Welsh Poetry in English', in *Poetry in the British Isles: Non-Metropolitan Perspectives*, ed. Hans-Werner Ludwig and Lothar Fietz (Cardiff, 1995), p. 99.

31. T. S. Eliot, 'Tradition and the Individual Talent', in *Selected Prose*, ed. Frank Kermode (London, 1975), p. 93.

32. Mikhail Bakhtin, *Problems of Dostoevsky's Poetics*, trans. and ed. C. Emerson (Minneapolis, 1984), p. 287.

33. Lynne Pearce, *Reading Dialogics* (London, 1994), p. 93.

9

'Oh, for our vanished youth': Avoiding Adulthood in the Later Stories of Dylan Thomas

JENI WILLIAMS

THOMAS AND CHILDREN'S LITERATURE

The 'romantic mythology' encrusting childhood is very much like that used for all racial and gender power-moves: children, 'coloureds', and women are all depicted as naturally carefree, fortunate to be unsuited to the burdens of autonomy and decision-making, and better off protected by those in control.

(James Kincaid)[1]

This tiresome affectation of childishness is particularly marked in the Welsh short stories, and most of all in those . . . translated from the Welsh.

(George Orwell)[2]

Throughout the twentieth century, the treatment of children in the West has vacillated between the protection of angels and the surveillance of demons: attitudes mirrored in the changing institutional values of childcare and educational manuals. James Kincaid relates the emergence of this ambivalent idea of the child, and the children's literature that appeared in its wake, to a paradigm of ideological control, relating both to the Romantic ideas of the 'noble savage', and the 'angel of the house'; unstable concepts which need control in order to prevent slippage into their demonic opposites. This complex mixture of otherness provides a valuable means of addressing the situation of writers, such as Dylan Thomas, excluded from the centre of cultural power. In this context, the figure of the child, like the writer, peripheral to the centres that control power and legislate meaning has a powerful attraction. Orwell's damning review of Welsh fiction seems to recognise this attraction, but his own position at the centre disables him from appreciating its significance.

Betty and William Greenway's discussion of Thomas's later stories as 'children's literature'[3] is thus highly suggestive. Sketching in a historical context for the emergence of children's literature *per se* they agree with Alison Lurie's assessment of successful examples of the genre as 'subversive' and 'child-centred', see Thomas's later stories as answering to this description, and argue persuasively for the influence of Richmal Crompton's William stories.[4] While pointing out that some of Thomas's stories have been packaged for children, they conclude that Thomas's comparative darkness reveals Crompton's sentimentality and marks his stories for an adult audience.[5] This is a substantial contribution to Thomas studies yet it does not go far enough. The fact that Thomas blurs the distinction between adult and children's literature is surely significant. Thomas's protagonists, for example, do not grow up: from the *Alice* books onwards this has been a major theme of children's literature. Indeed Jacqueline Rose sees in the emergence of children's literature a specific attempt to keep children *from* growing up: 'Charles Ludwidge Dodgeson . . . wrote his classic for children on condition that the child remain a little girl, held to him by the act of telling the tale.[6] Read in the light of this comment, the subversive qualities that Lurie and the Greenways detect in 'good' children's literature are contained within – and thus neutralised by – an allowed but peripheral literary space. It is only now, as with post-colonial writing, that this literature is receiving serious academic attention.

When the subversive critique of such writing is compared with that of the other literary form within which child protagonists are found in the nineteenth century – the *Bildungsroman* – the difference becomes clear. In the *Bildungsroman* the child protagonist grows up and, moving from dependency to responsibility, is educated in the ways of the world. The social critique found in this kind of text is both more direct and less subversive than the play and parody found in the literature Lurie praises. But then, the *Bildungsroman* (in which children grow up) is intended to be read by adults, whereas books in which children never leave childhood behind are intended for children. Questions, however, arise over the role and status of texts which deploy a child protagonist for an *adult* audience. By blurring the catagories of innocence and experience, child and adult, such a text destabilises a belief in a trustworthy adult world. Henry James's study of corruption and exploitation in *What Maisie Knew* and Nabokov's famous rewriting of *Alice* in *Lolita* are famous examples. Thomas's blurred categories are equally disruptive but they aim elsewhere. In his *Portrait of the Artist as a Young Dog* the adult world is one from which the narrator flees, variously, confusion and entrapment ('Just Like Little Dogs'), disappointment ('Where Tawe Flows') and mortality ('Who Do you Wish Was With Us?'). Adapting the title of Joyce's *Bildungsroman*, the word he chooses to displace is 'man'. Unlike Joyce's, his character does not 'learn' to be an adult.

Where the Greenways' article focuses on the influence of children's literature in Thomas's work, I am more interested in the politics of identification that come into play when a writer like Thomas, caught between two traditions and inheritor of neither,[7] chooses to use a child protagonist. Kincaid's analysis is valuable because it sets the figure of the child within an ideological structure, but in his focus on the erotics of the situation he refuses to engage with the politics of power and nowhere addresses those of national identity. For all that, his analysis draws attention to the way in which the state of childhood can resemble that of a colonised subject. The 'whimsicality' and 'exaggeration' identified by Linden Peach as one of the 'counterstrategies' of the latter are readily recognisable in the former.[8] Such childish counterstrategies might be particularly attractive to a male writer unconsciously experiencing his subordinated, colonised status in terms of infantilisation and emasculation – and Tony Conran has pointed out how male Anglo-Welsh poets tend to identify with those elements gendered 'feminine' within a materialist society: 'the forces of nature, growth and decay, salvation and frustration'.[9] Excluded from an authoritative sense of self, irresponsible and self-absorbed, such writers may unconsciously refuse the adult world of responsibility and sexuality,[10] turning instead to the world of their Other(s), drawn in narrative terms to the subversions of the Gothic, interested in redrawing or parodying gender positions within their texts, fascinated by the exotic – or the child.[11] Dylan Thomas's writing perfectly illustrates all these characteristics and not only did Thomas trade on the child figure in his texts, he was notorious for his cultivation, even in his life, of those qualities associated with the child.

NARRATIVES OF PLEASURE OR RESPONSIBILITY?

It happened when I was so high and much nicer.
(CS, 347)

It has generally been supposed that Dylan Thomas wrote two distinct kinds of stories. The early ones are defined as bizarre allegories, often brutal and surreal, while the later ones are perceived as autobiographical, dealing with his childhood and adolescence. Critical commentary frequently follows rather than interrogates this model. Peach, for example, writes of 'a general movement away from nightmare into the light of common day', and argues that 'the extent to which men and women appear as fully realised individuals serves almost as a measure of Thomas's developing empirical observation':[12] an observation that implies a movement from a surrealist to a realist model. Leslie Norris takes the same view, claiming that the later stories show Thomas 'growing up': 'he was probably ready to abandon the interior landscape of his adolescent work to create a world more like the one around him' (CS, xii). Here narrative shifts – from surreal to real – are mapped directly onto Thomas's personal development, itself perceived as a growth into maturity, leaving isolated instability for a stable shared perspective.

I would argue however that such readings of Thomas's life, and of his career as a short-story writer, are fundamentally mistaken. In their focus on excess, his later short stories are as selectively 'unreal' as his early ones, while his characters, particularly his women, are far from being 'fully developed individuals'. Preoccupations found in the earlier writings – a predeliction to move outside structures (the mental state of his characters; the physical interiors of the domestic space; a tendency to blur boundaries between what is interior and dream-like and what exterior and meant as 'real') – all continue in a different guise in the later stories. Rather than abandoning the 'interior landscape', Thomas simply relocates it in a new place: the distant, lost and 'nicer' world of his childhood, revisited by the knowing voice of an adult interpreter. This strategy is taken one step further in his last short story, 'A Story', which returns to his lost childhood through the additional filter of the earlier auto-biographical tales.

When the adult world does appear in the short stories it is always presented in terms of the disappointments of a suffocating domesticity. Yet flight from the home – as in *Adventures in the Skin Trade* – does not result in access to authority and agency. In the three chapters of that abandoned novel, the adolescent protagonist seeks only to experience events, not to make things happen but to throw himself into the flux of the exterior world. Yet chaos is fearful and the text concludes, significantly, in a London nightclub, with a hideous vision of the 'foul salt of the earth' (CS, 298) worthy of Swift:

> There were deep green faces, dipped in a sea dye, with painted cockles for mouths and lichenous hair, sealed on the cheeks; red and purple, slate-grey, tide-marked, rat-brown and stickily whitewashed, with violet-inked eyes or lips the colour of Stilton; pink chopped, pink lidded, pink as the belly of a new-born monkey, nicotine yellow with mustard flecked eyes, rust scraping through the bleach, black hairs axle-greased down among the peroxide; squashed fly stubbles, saltcellared necks thick with pepper powder; carrot-heads, yolk-heads, black-heads, heads bald as sweetbreads.
>
> (CS, 298)

This is no 'mature' vision of life but a horror reminiscent of the murderer's vision of the bar in the early tale 'A Vest', a horror emphasised by the sense of entrapment felt by Samuel as he struggles in the grip of Mrs Dacey.

The poignancy of the stories with Welsh rural settings lies in the recognition, shared by both Thomas and his adult readers, that they are securely locked into a place and time that cannot become this one. Standing at the beginning of *Portrait* their security from real pain lies only in the uncomprehending gaze of the child narrator, while the following tales present the modern, Anglicised world of urban constriction, especially in 'Where Tawe Flows' and 'Just Like Little Dogs'. It is interesting, therefore, to discuss two of these later stories, one set in the city and one in the country, one set in adolescence and one in childhood, drawing on and comparing their respective attitudes to the adult world of responsibility and sexuality.

'The Followers' and 'A Story' were published within a year of each other: 'The Followers' in 1952, 'A Story' in 1953. In the former the young boys run away from the window through which they are peering; in the latter the adult world is, itself, one of overgrown children. In neither story does the youthful narrator move into a meaningful relationship with his community, preferring to fantasise instead.

BOYS AND MEN: 'A STORY'

A few cold women stood at their doorways, grimly watching us go. A very small boy waved good-bye, and his mother boxed his ears.

(Dylan Thomas: CS, 351)

Thomas's stories set reality and fantasy in opposition. The narrator of 'A Story' is a man who looks back to a childhood holiday, passed with his uncle and aunt in a country village. It is a place of firmly differentiated gender roles: every year the village men go on an outing – supposedly a trip to Porthcawl but really a sustained pub crawl – and the women stay bitterly at home. In this instance the narrator's aunt goes off to her mother's in protest at the outing, leaving the uncle to take the boy with him. For the narrator this is an opportunity to enter the world of men and the main part of the story consists of amusing descriptions of the exploits of thirty drunken 'old boys' who end up arguing with strangers in their final pub, splashing about in a river and cooking sausage and mash under the moon. As a passive onlooker, the boy provides the voice of the story, retailing bizarre events without comment. The story closes with the closure of his eyes as he falls asleep, nestling on his uncle's waistcoated belly.

'A Story' deliberately moves away from the grown up world of realism, delighting in a playful rejection of common-sense responsibilities, while its significant characters act like overgrown children. It was the only one of Thomas's stories to be read on television, and so its reception by its original audience rested almost as much on the visual and aural presence of the (legendary) author as on the words and images themselves. Leslie Norris points out the extent to which the story was mediated and moulded by the medium in which it appeared: 'I saw Thomas tell this story on the old black and white screen. He filled it with action and colour with his unaided words', words, Norris suggests, that had as powerful an impact on the viewer as that symbol of masculine escapism, John Wayne (*CS* xvi). Norris's analogy is a perceptive one. Far from being a simple, transparent tale of a lost childhood, this narrative seeks in a sophisticated way to control and focus its audience.

In this story a child is introduced to an alien, adult world through the medium of a journey away from, and a movement back to, a home. However, the journey does not lead to a (problematic) exploration of the construction of 'reality' but turns instead to an exploration of fantasy. For a start, both home and destination are unreal: the boy is only a visitor at his uncle's house and the men are only pretending to go to Porthcawl. Instead of returning to the home, or moving into the masculine public world of work, as in the nineteenth-century *Bildungsroman*, Thomas's tale seeks out a chaotic space in which conventional gender identities are undercut with men as overgrown boys at the centre, and women and children displaced to the margins. The fixed co-ordinates of an adult world are undercut: the home is also a workplace and the warmth of the weather allows free movement between interior and exterior spaces. But the story does more than destabilise the domestic interior, it actually reproduces the narrative strategy used in Thomas's early, 'surrealist' stories, one described by James A. Davies as 'invasive difference',[13] a strategy he glosses as an invasion of or intrusion into enclosed spaces. Here the conventionally feminine status of the home is invaded by the snorting presence of the uncle: as 'the steaming hulk of an uncle' eats 'the house grew smaller' (*CS*, 347). Along with the intrusion of masculinity into the domestic sphere comes the natural world – that other element excluded from it:

> the loud check meadow of his waistcoat littered . . . with cigarette ends, peelings, cabbage stalks, birds' bones, gravy; and the forest fire of his hair crackled among the hooked hams from the ceiling.
>
> (*CS*, 347)

Davies develops his concept of 'invasive difference' in relation to *The Map of Love*, a collection of poems and stories written in the late 1930s, and explains it as a response to:

> the most significant activities of those troubled times: the invasions, intrusions, and penetrations carried out by successful fascists,

bewildered refugees, and the mobile unemployed, desperate for work.[14]

This is not a scenario that holds good for 'A Story', written in 1953 at a time of greater political stability. What Davies omits, of course, are the sexual implications of an invasion of private spaces, especially when, as here, those spaces are depicted as feminine. The scenario gains resonance in the light of the attempts in the early 1950s to get the women who had worked during the war back into the home.[15] Invasive difference functions within 'A Story' to undercut the categories which construct the conventional masculine self, blurring the distinctions of home, work and nature; breaking down the distinctions between what is 'masculine' and what 'feminine'. In the process, an image of penetration subverts the symbolic order by defining the masculine in relation to play; the feminine in relation to authority.

'A Story' refigures masculinity by undercutting both the traditionally 'feminine' space of the home, and the women themselves. The aunt is distanced as 'uncle's wife' and almost literally squeezed out of the house by her husband's bulk; while the audience is entertained by a depiction of the aunt's mother as 'one old bald mouse of a hundred and five I won't be wanting to meet in a dark lane' (*CS*, 350). Although the men dislike taking a child with them, 'women were worse than boys' (*CS*, 351).

Although the pattern is a recognisable one in the Welsh communities that provide the basis for this and others of Thomas's stories, his attraction to this pattern cannot be 'explained' as a realist representation. This was not Thomas's everyday reality. Brought up in a middle-class English-speaking home with a dominating father and an over-protective mother, Thomas looked to his Welsh-speaking relations for a mythical exuberance lacking in his own life. (The sadness of 'Fern Hill' testifies to his awareness of the partiality of this vision.) Conran's claim that without a community, the writer is left only with the constructed myth of the self rings as true for this simple tale as for the contortions of more painful poems. Here the painful isolation of the adult world recedes as both writer and reader slide in nostalgic communion into the exotic space of childhood, a childhood glowing in the borrowed haze of an unproblematic 'Welshness'.

Thomas's adoption of a determined misogyny in which the female figures are killjoys and the male ones lovable buffoons should be seen in the context of this narrative desire. For though the structures which define masculine and feminine roles may be familiar in Welsh rural and working-class communities, Thomas exaggerates and exploits these structures in order to awaken a desire for inclusion in his audience or reader. His narrator is rootless, speaks from a fixed and gendered position outside the narrative, appealing to a reader to share this position, to become, in imagination, one of a gang of 'bad boys'.

When the aunt sets the drinking trip against women (and home) – 'If you go on that outing on Saturday, Mr Thomas ... I'm going home to my mother's' (*CS*, 350) – the narrator's commentary 'supports' his uncle and directs his audience to do likewise: 'I would have made my choice at once, but it was almost half a minute before my uncle said ...' The picture is confirmed when the charabanc finally sets off: 'a few cold women stood at their doorways, grimly watching us go. A very small boy waved good-bye, and his mother boxed his ears' (*CS*, 350).

The hostility towards women and a domestic space perceived as constricting is articulated from a position in which the 'masculine' attributes of rationality and order conventionally associated with the middle-class English are rejected – since Thomas was no more English than he was part of the Welsh-speaking community. Likewise the emphasis on orality and horse-play suggests a regression towards what is commonly seen as the child rather than a progression into a world of power and control. The bangers and mash of the final lines of 'A Story' unavoidably summon up the 'alternative' male family of the Boy Scout camping expeditions with jolly songs in the open air under the moon. Divisions are blurred satisfactorily: 'Boys is nasty ... grandfathers is nasty too' (*CS*, 351): Mr Weazley's words are both comic-hostile and true for the group.

Thomas's boy is not the vehicle for creativity and the source of the reader's interest, but is merely taken along for the ride by the group of men: they, and not he, are the figures who really move about and thus create the story. The boy is not given any role apart from that of minding the charabanc while the men drink pub after pub dry – all, like the 'thirty wild, wet, pickled, splashing men' (*CS*, 354) – undifferentiated.

Significantly Thomas avoids the issue of differentiation: his charabanc never arrives at its unreal destination. Its frequent pauses are repeated moments in a journey of pleasure, parodically voiced by Mr Cadwalladwr, whose unerring sense of space and time are linked to the alternative timetable of pleasure of the public houses on their way. His mantra – 'Stop the bus I'm dying of breath' (*CS*, 353), suggests a simultaneous awareness, and denial, of death. It's a dream of companionship which requires the stern supervision of the grown-ups to keep it safe; and in this story all the grown-ups are women. When the treasurer, Mr Benjamin Franklyn, objects to being supervised so that he doesn't run off with the money collected for the outing, the hint of a more daring transgression is given only as a joke in the secure knowledge that it will be quashed by a woman: ' "It's a wonder to me," he said, "he don't follow me into bed at night." "Wife won't let," said Will Sentry' (*CS*, 343). The fearful shadow of sexuality is banished from these overgrown children whose wives have to tell them to 'take [their] boots off before [they] go to bed' (*CS*, 350), while, when a policeman tries to control the boozy crew, the fact that they come from the same place as one of his aunties gives him a personal reference point, removing the threat of discipline and drawing him into their drinking game.

'A Story' is a self-conscious meditation on the process of story-telling. From its opening comment – 'there's no real beginning or end and there's very little in the middle' (*CS*, 347) – it evinces a self-consciousness that allows Thomas to play to the gallery. There is a careless bravado about it in its flow of words and lack of care for plot and characterisation, a crudity in that he is repeating earlier, more fluent, less careless tales. He thus produces what is expected, confirming his image by producing more of the same: it's a closed circle. All the figures are cartoon characters, and the mouse-like aunt scuttles away into corners. Because nothing could go wrong in such a story and no uncomfortable truths could emerge, there is, at its culminating moment, a delight in the denial of truth, in the lie. Enoch Davies, earlier characterised as 'good with his fists' (*CS*, 349), argues with a stranger who claims to have played for Aberavon in 1898:

> 'Liar', said Enoch Davies.
> 'I can show you photos', said the stranger.
> 'Forged', said Enoch Davies.
> 'And I'll show you my cap at home.'
> 'Stolen.'
> 'I've got friends to prove it', the stranger said in a fury.
> 'Bribed', said Enoch Davies.
>
> (*CS*, 354)

Yet despite this apparent confidence, an anxiety about the narra-tor's place in the order of things seems evident in both the rejection of women and the linked problematic concern with home and family, together with a corresponding investment in the oral plea-sures of drinking and eating. The fun of the story is an illusion, an *adult* fantasy of cameraderie. A real child would have been bored by being forgotten and left to mind the charabanc, would have been bewildered – not admiringly amused by – fighting drunken men transforming into 'Beetroot, rhubarb, and puce ... enormous ancient bad boys' (CS, 352).

Those in control can't be trusted, have to be watched – as is evident when the friendly jibes at the 'absconding' Bob jokily equate running off with the money with exploiting children –

> 'Who's been robbing the orphans?'
> 'Who sold his little babby to the gyppoes?'
> 'Trust old Bob, he'll let you down.'
> 'You will have your little joke', said Bob the Fiddle, smiling like a razor, 'but I forgive you, boys.'
>
> (CS, 352)

This, like the story as a whole, would not have seemed amusing if told in the voice of Mr Weazley, for its success rests on the blank, non-judgemental gaze of the child. Thomas speaks as an adult looking back – his child is entirely a cipher, there to lend an air of innocence to the exploits of the real 'children' of the tale – the men – who are amusing only because no serious repercussions can be imagined by the innocence of the child.

In a sense, Thomas is no doubt reversing the familiar patterns of his Swansea suburban childhood, espousing a fantasy world in which fluidity and pleasure are valued over and above rationality and order. But there is a bitterness here too, a complex ambivalence about this community in which (as in earlier autobiographical stories like 'The Peaches') his displaced protagonist is only, and can only be, a visitor. These 'bad boys' are equally locked into fantasy, not part of the modern world with its louring responsibilities. Most importantly, they are not only child-like, they are Welsh. These Welshmen are both desired and denied in his tale: at its centre and yet separated from the reader by the observing eye of the child pro-tagonist. Their conversation is limited to the trip, animosities are as comic among them as their gluttonous drinking, nothing is serious or important. Indeed the tale itself mimics both the structure of their fluid universe (one that repeats itself without 'real beginning or end, and . . . very little in the middle'), and its defiant delight in the gratuitous rejection of facts and figures registered on the final page. Not a single one of these men – for there is little difference between them – could serve as father figures, and even the waistcoat of the boy narrator's uncle is no symbol of patriarchy but a site of dream.

For the adult narrator looking back to a childhood memory these rumbustious bad boys clearly represent the desirable other, a figure, associated with the figure of the writer, who is in opposition to the socio-symbolic order. Thomas famously set aesthetics and politics in total opposition: 'You can't be true to party and poetry – one must suffer. And historically, poetry is the social and economic creed that endures' (*CL*, 185). In this context, Thomas's unreal, unnamed child acts as a conduit for the doubled desire of both author and spectator for something other than the political reality. Although he may move from one place to another and back, apparently indicating a significant role in the plot, in fact he is reduced to a cipher, while the places between which he moves (the wild men within the story; the jovial narrator; the laughing spectator) are characterised by fluidity and imagination. The adult world is itself one of children and the exclusion of women from the tale ensures that there are no sexual complications to spoil its innocence.

THE POINTLESSNESS OF WELSH WRITING

> Nearly always the formula is the same: a pointless little sketch about fundamentally uninteresting people, written in short flat sentences and ending in a vague query . . . There seems to be a sort of cult of pointlessness and indefiniteness, quite possibily covering, in many cases, a mere inability to construct a 'plot'.
>
> (George Orwell)[16]

As the narrative shortcomings detailed in his review of Welsh fiction demonstrate, George Orwell defined valuable writing in terms of its relation to a powerful adult world. Clearly defined, powerful and plot-driven, his favoured writing expresses the kind of 'masculine' authority which rejects indeterminacy as childishness – or, implicitly, effeminacy.[17] Despite his socialist views, he does not understand how to read these texts from the margins. A female Welsh-language writer, Kate Roberts, exposes the hidden prejudices of his critique: 'A Welsh sentence, though difficult in its idiom, is simple and straightforward. Long, complex sentences are not characteristic of Welsh style, although they are used by the young authors of today who are not so acquainted with the Welsh classics as some of us are.'[18] Elsewhere she is cutting about what she sees as the mere technique of 'closing a story with a clever ending'[19] and praises Mansfield, the (significantly female) writer Orwell singles out for disapprobation.

The meticulous patterning of Thomas's intricate verse reveals the vacuousness of equating a lack of plot with a 'childish' inability to write. In terms of style, the long, complex sentences of his stories may not reflect the Welsh prose-style Roberts describes, but then he fits into the category of 'young authors ... not so acquainted with the Welsh classics'. Yet although the convoluted forms of the verse have a correlative in the convoluted plots and shifting registers of the early stories, the later ones do fit the paradigm so scornfully dismissed by Orwell. After all, 'A Story' declares openly that 'there's no real beginning or end and ... very little in the middle', while 'The Followers' could well be described as 'a pointless little sketch about fundamentally uninteresting people ... ending in a vague query'. We are clearly not dealing only with cultural difference. Because he unerringly picks out those characteristics that represent the writer excluded from authority, Orwell's assessment proves unexpectedly useful as a guide to those elements of Thomas's stories which, over and over again, refuse the adult world of powerful and 'interesting' events and people. And, as Conran points out, this is a mark of the writer who feels himself excluded: claiming that the Anglo-Welsh writer is frequently driven into himself by his political and historical circumstances, he suggests that 'you cannot expect to find in the poetry of those who feel that society has deserted them a fitting expression of community life'.[20] In Thomas's stories, the community is a dream of the past, a rural fantasy experienced by a child. Although the urban stories may reflect on the monotony of the town, what they are really protesting against is the fact of growing up: the country companionship of Rhossili sands briefly sketched in 'Extraordinary little Cough' and 'Who Do You Wish Was With Us?' is an illusory escape from the town and is quickly spoilt by the shadows of adult life: sexuality and mortality. Of all the urban stories the most telling in relation to the narrative evasion of the grown-up world is 'The Followers'.

PROBLEMATISING THE MASCULINE GAZE: 'THE FOLLOWERS'

> Why are those two boys looking in at the window?
> (Dylan Thomas: CS, 346)

In 'The Followers', two boys with nothing to do follow a woman home and stand outside her window peering inside. Men outside, looking in, women within, being looked at: the tale simultaneously evokes the stalker/intruder of countless thrillers set in the mean streets of the city, only to cancel it with the protagonists' grumbling innocence. They do not understand the significance of what they do: 'what's the point of following people . . . It never gets you anywhere' (CS, 343). The plot clearly rests on the principle of 'invasive difference' discussed in the previous section, a principle which has strongly sexual undercurrents in this story of adolescence. The story's fascination with secret acts of looking is evident from the opening reference to the two girls in the shop window, carefully undressing a (female) dummy: 'Mind her cami-knicks, Edna' (CS, 334). As in 'A Story', the reader is drawn into an uneasy alliance with the narrative voice and its acts of voyeuristic penetration – we accept, for example, the names that the boys project onto the unknowing women before their (and our) gaze. The thriller narrative is as close to the surface as the 'domestic films' described – and rejected – in the appraising gaze directed on the young woman they have followed home.

In 'A Story' both the separation of innocent childhood from adult experience and its location in another space and time allows for a space of security where unpleasant things stay below the surface and fantasy seems to reign. In Thomas's Swansea tale, these categories are blurred and the boys are both 'too young and too old' (CS, 342). Neither they nor we can enter the 'dank but snug, flickering dark' of the cinema of childhood looking, a fact recognised and parodied in the stylised sentimentality of the narrator's lament – 'Oh, for our vanished youth'. Although they seek the salacious adult world detailed in the *News of the World*, they don't really believe it, and complain dolefully that: 'Nobody murders no one. There isn't any sin anymore, or love, or death, or pearls and divorces and mink-coats or anything, or putting arsenic in the cocoa . . .' (CS, 345).

Many of the comic elements of the tale rest on similar shifts in register. The ghostly voice unexpectedly speaking from the female interior, for example, is comic because it articulates the unspoken question behind the whole story: 'Why are those two boys looking in at the window?' and then, when the boys run away, dissipates an unconscious menace: adult sexuality. The reader laughs *because* the boys' innocence is restored. Poignantly, what they see in the women's kitchen is not an exciting grown-up world but the loss of their own childhood. They are excluded from the cosy interior, wanting food and warmth. The women sit in the glowing light and look at snapshots, telling each other stories about far-off eccentric family members; stories below the surface of the cosy domestic interior which achieve their fascination – as does Thomas himself in 'A Story' – because of their secure separation from the time and place of a present constriction.

This sense of constriction is evident from the opening paragraphs of the story where the wild weather outdoors is set against domestic suffocation: the young men are 'bundled home against the thistly wind' while the older ones scurry back to 'safe, hot, weatherproof hearths, and wives called Mother' (*CS*, 339). There are only two escapes from this monotonous existence: the exotic east where exciting things happen – 'Earthquake. Earthquake in Japan' (*CS*, 339); or pubs like the Marlborough where 'dejected regulars grew grand and muzzy in the corners, inventing their pasts, being rich, important, and loved ... influential nobodies revised the earth' (*CS*, 341). The grown-up world is marked by disappointment and *stories* create excitement, not 'reality'. After all, perhaps 'the *News of the World* is all made-up' (*CS*, 345). Exotic fantasies coalesce in the stories that the boys tell each other about the woman they are following, unfocused fantasies including kimonos, and the sensual pleasures of music, touch and birds. But Leslie's remark demonstrates that they aren't interested in reality, they want to *see* difference: 'Perhaps she'll slit her throat if they don't draw the blinds. I don't care what happens so long as it's interesting' (*CS*, 343).

The story thus plays with lifting the 'blinds' and revealing the unexpected. This being the case it is useful to consider the tale's fascination with vision: the male subject gazing at a female object of desire through a lit window; the reader gazing into the tale, joining the boys to gaze through the window. Predating the cinematic image already discussed, the motif is rooted in the Petrarchan gaze of so much love poetry, whereby the speaker proclaims himself a subject in relation to his beloved object.[21] Cora Kaplan points out that 'the desire to write imaginative poetry and prose was and is a demand for access to and parity within the law and myth-making groups of society'.[22] We are back to the issue with which this essay opened: the cultural construction of both adult and child figures excluded from 'the burdens of autonomy' and the opportunity to legislate meaning. The significance of Thomas's reconsideration of such a potent motif emerges more fully through a brief comparison with the way it is used by key modernist writers who sought to challenge established mores of class, gender and nationality: Lawrence, Woolf and Joyce.

The figure appears most unproblematically in Lawrence's *The Rainbow*[23] when Tom Brangwyn stands in the rain, gazing in through the window at the Polish woman and her daughter, an image of the family to which he will commit himself. It is problematised in Woolf's *To the Lighthouse* in the troubled gaze and art of Lily Briscoe, seeking a new perception of the mother and child image of Mrs Ramsay and James sitting in the window, which means rejecting both Mrs Ramsay's example of femininity and Mr Bankes's adoring masculine vision. Most interestingly, however, it occurs throughout the text most frequently cited as an influence on Thomas's short stories: Joyce's *Dubliners*. In *Dubliners* both subject and object of the gaze shift from story to story, opening with a boy gazing up at the window of his priestly 'father', and whispering the word 'paralysis', moving to the anguished and humiliated gaze of the boy in 'Araby' and thence to the sterile blindness of 'Clay', concluding with Gabriel's imaginative sweep of time and space in 'The Dead'. In each of these examples, the trope suggests an adult order – even if that order is one locked into stasis.[24] In 'The Followers', however, the motif is summoned up only, in line with the evasion of adult order, to be denied. The intensity of this moment is defused by a refusal to take it, and what it symbolises, seriously. In the other cases, changes happen within the solitary subjects as they learn simultaneously about themselves and the order of their world. In 'The Followers' the trope is sent up: there are, for example, two boys – not one – and they mutter to each other in dissatisfaction with the way things are going inside the room. The women are not the passive figures of tradition, not only being too old but having their own secret images (in the album) and their own secret stories (they are speaking but waiting for something to happen). Without meaning the motif is as hollow as anything else in this world and the boys run away, the epiphanic movement into adult consciousness dissipated. All that is left is the desire to tell stories about the past which may well come alive. As in 'A Story', fantasy is preferable to reality. The pattern theorised by Freud, Lacan, Kristeva et al. – a dyadic system (mother/child) triangulated by the intrusion of the principle of the Father to facilitate an awareness of the otherness of culture, which is central to the *Bildungsroman* and equally significant in its absence in the children's story – is quite simply abandoned. In both stories the masculine principle of authority is marked by its absence.

Because the principle of 'reality' – the law of the father – is not only absent but actually rejected by Thomas's protagonists, his late stories are no more 'real' than the surrealist fantasies he wrote as a young man. Thomas's desire for the wild figures of his day-trippers haunts his public persona as a drunken, outrageous Welsh poet, a persona that also attempts to construct its readers in an image of rebellious otherness drawn from a rural world in which – just as the language within which that world operated – he, and they, could only ever be a visitor and voyeur. In 'The Followers' these images of excitement belong to the women on whom the boys are spying. The boys may be growing up but they are not moving towards agency.

One response to the emphasis on childhood and the value of play in Thomas's stories is to dismiss them, with Davies Aberpennar, as products of an 'irresponsible, thumb-to-nose adolescent ... determined not to finish growing up'.[25] Another, of which Louis Simpson's fawning study stands as an example,[26] is to venerate them as products of an inspirational poet of the 'heart' rather than the 'head'. Because both approaches focus on the poet as an individual figure, divorced from his cultural situation, neither is satisfactory. If, on the other hand, the narrative desire for play and fluidity is related to a situation of disempowerment then new readings emerge. This reading also suggests a different way of perceiving Thomas's prose writing, especially its dealings with gender issues. In the rural stories, the emphasis on play and fluidity promotes a masculine role strongly associated with the elements conventionally assigned to the female or the child. This necessitates a reconfiguration of the roles allocated both to actual women (authoritarian figures) and children (passive observers) – drawing on and reinscribing the patterns of a Welshness rendered exotic. This playful quality is possible because of the location of the stories in another earlier time and space when both mortality and sexuality seem in suspension. The young male protagonists of the urban stories, however, enter a lesser world marked by those elements. Because of this childhood is preferable to adulthood in these stories. Despite their desire for an excitement coded 'adult', what the adolescent boys in 'The Followers' are seeking is accessible only in a fantasy located in a place and time where men can continue as children and women take on authority. In this story of growing up, however, that space of fantasy, that escape from the adult world of authority, is returned to the female, a space from which they are excluded and upon which they can only gaze.

NOTES

[Jeni Williams's close reading of Thomas's short stories relates them to children's literature and its adumbration of the themes of responsibility and pleasure. She then develops the issues raised briefly in Katie Gramich's essay (3) in this volume concerning the 'comforting domestic space' into which Thomas seems to re-place female characters in his prose works of the 1940s and after. Williams examines the relationship of the (male) child to adults of both sexes in these works, but views the domestic space controlled by women as one of power rather than of mere cosiness. Challenging the dominant critical narrative which has seen Thomas progressing from surrealism to realism in his prose, she argues rather that he relocates the inner landscapes of the early prose in a revisited childhood, playing fantasy and reality off against each other. In this way, Williams is able to turn Orwell's designation of the 'pointlessness' of Welsh writing against itself, to reveal such fictions as encoding a neo-colonial drama of infantilisation, powerlessness and masculine refusal of responsibility. At the same time, she insists on the elements of asexual misogyny and escapist regression found in the stories, and argues that 'The Followers', in particular, articulates the problematics of the male gaze, in which the act of seeing becomes a presumption of knowledge of the female subject. Eds]

1. James R. Kincaid, *Child-loving: the Erotic Child and Victorian Culture* (New York and London, 1992), p. 64.

2. George Orwell reviewing current fiction in the *New Statesman* (1940); quoted in John Harris, 'Kate Roberts in translation', in *Planet*, 87 (1991), 23.

3. Betty and William Greenway, 'Just Dylan: Dylan Thomas as Subversive Children's Writer', in *Welsh Writing in English*, vol. 5 (1999), pp. 42–50.

4. Ibid., pp. 43–4.

5. Ibid., p. 45. The addition of illustrations to these editions, however, fundamentally changes the reception of the text and codes it as children's literature.

6. Jacqueline Rose, *The Case of Peter Pan or The Impossibility of Children's Literature* (London, 1994), p. 35.

7. See Tony Conran, 'The English Poet in Wales II: Boys of Summer in Their Ruin', in *Anglo-Welsh Review*, 10:26 (1960), 11–21.

8. Linden Peach, *The Prose Writings of Dylan Thomas* (London, 1988), p. 87.

9. Conran, 'The English Poet in Wales II', 14.

10. Rose, *The Case of Peter Pan*, p. 36.

11. See David Punter, *The Literature of Terror*. Vol. I: *The Gothic Tradition* (London, 1996), p. 52; Fred Botting, *Gothic* (London and New York, 1996), p. 23. Also Edward Said's enormously influential *Orientalism* (Harmondsworth, 1985) and Gayatri Chakravorty Spivak, *In Other Worlds* (New York and London, 1988).

12. Peach, *The Prose Writings of Dylan Thomas*, p. 15.

13. James A. Davies, *A Reference Companion to Dylan Thomas* (Westport, CT, 1998), pp. 169–70; p. 180.

14. Ibid., p. 170.

15. See, for example, Jane Lewis, *Women in Britain since 1945: Women, Family, Work and the State in the Postwar Years* (Oxford, 1992); Elisabeth Wilson, *Only Half-way to Paradise: Women in Postwar Britain, 1945–1968* (London and New York, 1980).

16. Orwell, quoted in Harris, 'Kate Roberts in translation', 23.

17. I adapt Edward Larrissy's discussion of the implicit gender of favoured modes of writing in *Reading Twentieth Century Poetry: the Language and Gender of Objects* (Oxford, 1990).

18. Roberts, quoted in Harris, 'Kate Roberts in translation', 28–9.

19. Quoted in *The World of Kate Roberts: Selected Short Stories, 1925–1981*, trans. Joseph Clancy (Philadelphia, 1991), p. xii.

20. Conran, 'The English Poet in Wales II', 14.

21. Petrarch has been seen as the 'first' humanist, with critics suggesting that, whilst self-abasing, his idealisation of Laura allows for a thoroughly autonomous portrait of the poet. See Gary Waller, *English Poetry of the Sixteenth Century* (London, 1989), pp. 81–2.

22. Cora Kaplan, 'Language and Gender', in *Sea Changes: Essays on Culture and Feminism* (London, 1986), p. 71.

23. This is the first of three generations of the Brangwyn family, progressively moving away from the security of land and church.

24. See W. J. McCormack, *From Burke to Beckett: Ascendency, Tradition and Betrayal in Literary History* (Cork, 1994), pp. 260, 277.

25. Davies, *A Reference Companion to Dylan Thomas*, p. 269.

26. Louis Simpson, *A Revolution in Taste: Studies of Dylan Thomas, Allen Ginsberg, Sylvia Plath, and Robert Lowell* (New York, 1978).

10

'Very profound and very box-office': the Later Poems and *Under Milk Wood*

JOHN GOODBY

I

There are several points in Dylan Thomas's third collection, *The Map of Love* (1939) – 'Once it was the colour of saying' and 'After the funeral' are the most obvious – at which a farewell to the modernism of his early work seems to be announced. Confirmation of the shift has been seen in *A Portrait of the Artist as a Young Dog* (1940), which has often been read as a substantially autobiographical reprise of Thomas's childhood and adolescence. In this version of events, the war poems of *Deaths and Entrances* (1946) are a diversion on the high road to that volume's final piece, 'Fern Hill', the realism of the later work, the poems of *In Country Sleep* (1952) and the radio work *Under Milk Wood* (1954).[1] Yet the insistence on a more or less clear progression from youthfully energetic solipsism to mature expansiveness and rootedness not only rests on diminishing some of Thomas's most powerful poems but also on the assumption of the self-evident realism of the later writings,[2] especially the later prose and *Under Milk Wood*, which are taken to confirm a movement towards the renunciation of modernist difficulty and embrace of locatedness.

It is certainly the case that Thomas's work took on a different focus as his raw material changed in the late 1930s. Ceasing to be the adolescent 'Rimbaud of Cwmdonkin Drive', he acquired with marriage a more or less stable relationship and responsibilities as a breadwinner for a growing family by the time World War II broke out in 1939. His new situation intensified his deep fears concerning the war, fears which did not disappear after 1945, but took on a new form with the onset of the Cold War and the emerging super-power balance of nuclear terror. At the same time, the perception of Thomas was changing. Always a rising star on the British poetry scene of the 1930s, his reputation reached its zenith in the late 1940s when, by common critical consent and in the absence of Auden, he was accepted as the country's outstanding poet. But while this much can be conceded, it should not be taken as licence to interpret change biographically, or even in terms of an altered subject matter. Instead, the personal and general literary dynamics which reshaped Thomas's poetic style need to be viewed in the light of their interaction with larger postwar cultural, social and histori-cal trends and developments. It is important to see that as its mag-nitude grew, the nature of Thomas's reputation altered, undergoing a *qualitative*, not simply a quantitative, change.

This alteration can be illustrated by comparing the audience of the first three collections with that of the later work. The early au-dience was, in the main, a small, self-constituted elite of *avant-garde* readers trained in the exacting techniques of close analysis, one which was not only accustomed to, but demanding of, formal and linguistic innovation. The war, however, marked the death of this *avant-garde* formation as it had been constituted in the 1920s and 1930s. After 1945 it was utterly reshaped by the democratising forces of the mass media and meritocratic educational reform, as at-tempts to diffuse 'high' culture became public policy. In the words of David Harvey, 'the "heroic" era [of modernism] came crashing to an end in WWII', to be followed by an institutionalised form which 'became hegemonic after 1945 [and] exhibited a much more comfortable relation to the dominant power centres in society . . . High modernist art, architecture, literature, etc. became establish-ment arts and practices in a society where a corporate capitalist version of the Enlightenment project of development for progress and human emancipation held sway as a political-economic dom-inant'.[3] This was coupled with a loss of nerve on the part of the European *avant-garde* – the spectacular barbarities of the war

having dealt a blow to its sense of a pioneering mission – just as its
centre of gravity was being relocated to the USA, and specifically
New York. One result of this, it has been plausibly argued, was a
loss of political radicalism.[4] The resultant anxiety was articulated
forcefully by Adorno and Horkheimer in their notion of a US
'culture industry' – Hollywood film, the music of Tin Pan Alley,
kitsch – which they saw swamping a high modernist art which
alone was able to articulate the profound alienation of modern life.[5]
It is with these developments in mind that we need to situate the
unique extent of Thomas's involvement in popular media (or
'culture industry') forms among poets of his generation.

Besides producing poetry, short stories and a novel, Thomas was,
variously, a writer of feature film and documentary scripts, radio
features and talks, and recorded his readings for gramophone, as
well as making two television broadcasts before his death in 1953.
This involvement is central to his reputation, and to the reception
and production of his later writings (and at a deeper level than, for
example, the benefit of scriptwriting experience for the dialogue of
Under Milk Wood). Rather than seeing the move as a populist con-
cession, or even a 'selling out', it is possible to regard Thomas as an
early example of a postwar writer producing different kinds of
work for disparate, seemingly incompatible audiences. As Steven
Connor suggests,

> The distinction between art and mere entertainment is personified in
> terms of a distinction between the active and autonomous reader and
> a mere member of a readership. Such a notion underlies much educa-
> tional theory and policy from the 1930s onwards. This idea is both
> contradicted and, in an intriguing sense, complemented by the
> modernist construction of the ideal reader of the future . . . In its
> way, the modernist ideal reader is an exact counterpart to the
> idealised reader of mass fiction; though each is defined against the
> other, each is also imagined as a wholly self-identical category, with
> no possibility of traffic or fraternisation between the two kinds of
> reader or readership. The central principle of Leavisite close reading
> [i.e.: that of an 'ideal reader of the future'] and the educational prac-
> tices founded upon it is that of irreversible evolution; having become
> a sensitive and flexible reader, one is supposed to be incapable,
> except in the case of pathological relapse, of reverting to one's earlier
> condition.[6]

In this context, Thomas appeared to be able to square the circle of
'mere entertainment' and high modernist difficulty. As with his

ambivalence concerning national identity and his queasy version of the suburban sublime, he appears again in the guise of a liminal, hybrid and fluid figure. 'Fraternisation' between different kinds of readership and texts came naturally, and respect for the 'modernist ideal reader' was strained, even in the earliest work, whose parodic aspect included the provincial writer's conflation of earnestness and mockery (Auden as 'the boy bushranger', Eliot as 'Pope Eliot'). The finely-balanced mixture of subaltern seriousness and outsider send-up shifted as the high/low art distinction – in terms of cultural change and personal involvement – began to blur. Thomas, who instinctively rejected the notion of 'irreversible evolution' in matters of taste, conspicuously problematised it, while at the same time seeming to insist on a distinction between his 'potboiling' prose and scripts and his poetry. This could be seen as the price he paid for rejecting the Auden School's linguistic transparency and discursivity, and the result was a body of work in which the left hand did not always fully know what the right hand was doing. Thomas, that is, adhered to a conception of poetry as a fundamentally lyrical, formally conservative if risk-taking linguistic practice to the end. Thus, while his anti-authoritarianism can be seen as admirable, the charge of 'pathological relapse' – David Holbrook's criticism being the most virulent case in point – was always likely to be levelled at him in a literary community which was to be dominated, for two decades after the war, by F. R. Leavis's moralised, petit-bourgeois version of modernist hauteur.

It could be argued, then, that if Thomas's writing reveals the process of exchange between different cultural levels, the novelty of the process meant that it could hardly theorise this in any explicit way. This is no reason to accept a narrative of humanistic evolution in which rural and childhood themes in Thomas's work are seen to offset the 'moral shock' of war and its aftermath. Such an account does not explain why, in Karl Shapiro's words, Thomas was able to achieve 'the impossible' in creating 'a general audience for a barely understandable poet' on his American tours.[7] Nor does it get to the heart of the issue identified by William Empson who, in discussing a proposed treatment by Thomas for a film of the life of Dickens, noted that the project would have been 'very profound and very box-office',[8] so suggesting a process which had deeper sources and more significant outcomes.

Set in the context of the institutionalisation of modernism, Thomas's enthusiasm for the new popular media cannot be seen as

merely populist, but also as a further development of the suspicion
he had always harboured against elitism. At the same time, his commitment to lyric, conceived as the form of writing making
maximum demands on its readership at all points, continued. The
apparent contradiction is made manifest as a crisis of authority and
language in the later poetry. But more than this, that poetry also
mediates a linguistic crisis, or crisis of representation, under the
pressure of deep and unprecedented social and historical anxiety. If
there is a greater sense of place in the later poems and a pastoral
thematics, these do not simply mean that '[a]s a convincing artist
[Thomas] needed a background'.[9] Words like 'convincing' and
'background' tend, in any case, to return us to biographical interpretation (how 'sincere' was Thomas?) as well as to the notion of
writing as quasi-pictorial reflection of reality ('mature' writing has
an ethical obligation to be representational). Moralistic interpretations, that is, are doomed to remain circular ones. Without denying
their relative clarity by comparison with the early work, the so-
called realism of the language of the most obviously 'located' poems
is continually shadowed by a linguistic excess which threatens inarticulacy, a dis-articulation of utterance. In a passage towards the
end of 'A Winter's Tale', this occurs at the point where the hermit
figure of the poem finally encounters the 'bride bird' he has
pursued, simultaneously dying and achieving salvation. The poem's
system of reference, it might be said, implodes:

> Listen and look where she sails the goose plucked sea,
>
>   The sky, the bird, the bride,
> The cloud, the need, the planted stars, the joy beyond
> The fields of seed and the time dying flesh astride,
> The heavens, the heaven, the grave, the burning font.
>   (CP, 102)

This kind of complexity results in an erasure of meaning through its
superabundance, a paradoxical fear that there may be no meaning,
that language may have lost its power to enact or signify at all.
Such anxiety is felt at the end of the poem in the image of 'the
whirl- / Pool at the wanting centre, in the folds / Of paradise, in the
spun bud of the world' (CP, 103). If, here, the fusion is a mystic-
sexual one, with the 'wanting centre' – the core of desiring, but
also a supreme linguistic lack creating the extraordinary verbal
'whirl- / Pool' around it – then it nevertheless anticipates the more

ominous 'yawning wound' in which all 'the world' (and word) will '[fall], silent as the cyclone of silence' (*CP*, 140), in 'In Country Sleep', and the similar 'whirlwind silence' of 'Over Sir John's hill' (*CP*, 144). 'Place' and 'realism', in the later poems, become ways of containing and anchoring the threat of lack and absence, the linguistic surplus a displacement of anxiety. This is why, *tonally*, the later poems are elegiac, the richness of linguistic compensation undoing itself, dissolving signification and authorial presence in the very process of proclaiming it. But although that anxiety inevitably takes linguistic form – language is always inadequate to its representations – it nevertheless mediates the historical threat of war and nuclear annihilation and the larger changes at work within and around the texts. In this light, rather than being seen as the culmination of a progress towards a whimsical realism, *Under Milk Wood* asks to be read through the poems rather than, as is usually the case, the other way round. Given the extent to which Thomas's reputation has been based on a valorisation of his performance of his self as *voice*, his 'play for voices' actually belongs, like the poems, to a wider debate in which questions are asked about personal utterance, the authenticity it is so often presumed to indicate, and the authority which it can legitimately be expected to bear.

II

Much has been made of the locatedness of the later poetry and of *Under Milk Wood*. Walford Davies, John Ackerman and others have, in their different ways, asserted the groundedness of the later work in the landscape of West Wales. Yet 'the pastoral' is not reducible to 'the rural', or even to the Church in its pastoral role; in its original, religious sense, it refers to the identification of Christ with the sacrificial Passover lamb of Jewish ritual which opened up a vein of pastoral typology deriving from Latin *pastor* as shepherd. When we use 'pastoral' of Thomas's later work, this original sense (but taking all humankind as a potential sacrifice to the forces of annihilation) must be borne in mind. Seamus Heaney is a good example of a critic who accepts the limited application of the term, and who consequently betrays the unease which results from the lack of specific 'rural' detail in Thomas's writing. Detecting a bogus note, Heaney believes that Thomas's relationship to the metropolis remained an essentially provincial one, with *Under Milk Wood* 'symptomatic of a not irreprehensible collusion with the stereotype of the voluble Taffy'.[10] For Heaney, a non-metropolitan writer must have a distinct notion of the validity of his region, 'revers[ing]' the 'Copernican' model of provinces revolving around the centre for a 'Ptolemaic' one in order to 'envisage the region as the original point'.

Yet the thoroughly Catholic-medieval religious co-ordinates of Heaney's thinking ('Ptolemaic' for 'Copernican' is more revealing of his own thinking than it purports to be of Thomas's) show his failure either to see pastoral in the larger sense, or to break with the centre–periphery paradigm which has until recently been the bugbear of criticism of regional or postcolonial writing. In fact, Heaney confirms that paradigm (he wants to 'reverse', or invert, rather than challenge its terms) because he believes, like many of Thomas's critics, that the 'mature' writer is necessarily 'rooted' in a given place. In offering, in the same essay, the example of Joyce as a 'regional redeemer', Heaney shows just how completely he misses historical context, Thomas's use of Christian typology *and* the extent to which, for authors like Joyce and Thomas, writing is not representation so much as an investigation of the ways in which language signifies, according to the revolutionary formal demands of modernist practice. If, by the same token, Thomas is no Joyce, and his revolution of the word hardly as resolute or as systematic, it is incumbent on the critic to place this in the larger context of the ebbing of high modernism throughout the 1930s and 1940s rather than simply ascribing it to differences in individual talent.

The lyrical-descriptive style, regarded as the first fruits of Thomas's dissatisfaction with modernist solipsism, is seen first in 'Poem in October', a birthday poem conceived as early as October 1939 (when he first lived in Laugharne), though largely rewritten in 1944. On its completion, Thomas described it as 'a Laugharne poem: the first place poem I've written' (*CL*, 518). The fragment of the poem surviving from 1939/40 actually mentions Laugharne by name, and inaugurates his consideration of the potential of place-and-landscape poetry. Exploration of this potential, shelved by the urgent demands of the Blitz poems of 1940–41, was taken up again in 1944, producing 'The Hunchback in the Park', 'A Winter's Tale' and 'Fern Hill', all of which appeared with 'Poem in October' in *Deaths and Entrances*. In the last poems, written between 1947 and

1952, the concern with location (and with childhood) was intensified, a concern shared with a number of contemporary radio and short prose pieces – 'Reminiscences of Childhood' (first version, 1943), 'A Child's Christmas in Wales' (1945), 'Holiday Memory' (1946) and 'Return Journey' (1947). 'Quite Early One Morning' (1945), which has a single narrative voice moving through a sleeping seaside town based on New Quay, weaving together the dreams of the town's inhabitants, brief comic character sketches and observations, is in a mixture of prose and verse. It is, in other words, clearly the main forerunner of *Under Milk Wood* (although that was more or less modelled on Laugharne, where Thomas returned to live in 1949). The seven completed poems of these years, then, do have a location-specific quality. 'Over Sir John's hill' (1949), 'Poem on his Birthday' (1951) and 'Prologue' (1952) allude to the Towy estuary at Laugharne and the Boathouse in which Thomas wrote. 'In Country Sleep' (1947) is full of the spinneys, dingles, hills, woods, birds and beasts of an idealised Carmarthenshire countryside. 'In the White Giant's Thigh' (1951) is, similarly, an exercise in the pastoral mode. Finally, if 'Do not go gentle into that good night' (1951) and 'Lament' (1951) are hardly 'place' poems, the first contains a 'green bay' (*CP*, 148), while the latter anticipates the places (Donkey Down, Goosegog Lane and Milk Wood itself) of Llareggub.

This locational specificity is vague, and works against incorporating the poems in a teleological model which would make them a kind of run-up to *Under Milk Wood*. Thus – if we except in the second half of 'Prologue' (which sets 'Wales in my arms' against 'the cities of nine / Day's night' [*CP*, 2, 1]) – there is only one Welsh placename in the later poems (the River Towy in 'Over Sir John's hill'), no use of dialect (except for 'gambo' [*CP*, 151]) and very few socio-cultural references ('the chapel fold' [*CP*, 148]). 'In the White Giant's Thigh' is something of a case in point. The title refers to a gargantuan figure cut into the chalk of a hillside at Cerne Abbas in Dorset. If the poem has place markers they are, then, English. Place, though, is more complex than first appears if we understand that the giant is both English (in England) and a pre-Saxon creation of the Celts (seen as forebears of the Welsh). There is a double subversion – of nationalistic Welshness through an English location, and of Englishness through Celtic origins – if we want to discover it, but the main point is that the poem itself doesn't rely on such an understanding. In the same way, any essential 'Welshness' of the countryside of 'In Country Sleep' or even 'Over

Sir John's hill', is largely beside the point; if there is any dominant location in Thomas's poetry it is the sea, a non-location redolent of margins, swamping, self-loss and erasure. 'In the White Giant's Thigh' and 'In Country Sleep' avoid it, although 'Poem on his Birthday' and 'Over Sir John's hill' run true to this marine form. (Thomas wrote in 1936 of the need to read his poetry 'literally' [CL, 301], and to resort to a pun of which he would have surely approved, he might have added that much of it has to be taken *littorally* too.) Even here the point is more a linguistic than a locational one and bears on the dilemma he outlined in a letter of May 1934: 'the sea is a sea of words ... I can't give actuality to these things' (CL, 138). If there is a typically British compromise in the later poetry it is one which, as with the parallel cases of John Nash and Benjamin Britten in other art forms, remains attached to its original modernist impulses. Landscape, such as it is, exists within frames of epistemological uncertainty and disjunct narrative strategies, as knowingly linguistic entities. Thus, the near-frenzied listing of idealised rural properties in 'In Country Sleep' – 'hearthstone', 'ganders', 'greenwood', 'hamlet', 'homestall', 'hobnail' (CP, 139–40) – is an example which at once betrays an unease concerning dis-locatedness *and* a foregrounding of that unease in order to turn it to baroquely exfoliating linguistic advantage. At the very least it amounts to the verbalising of new poetic terrain, not its description in any realist sense.

This is one reason why such poems also resist incorporation in one of the two main trends in British poetry of the 1940s, the Regionalist movement, which flourished in Wales, Scotland, Northern Ireland and the north of England. Alternatively, their impacted ambiguities, restraint and increasingly dense formal patterning sets them at odds with the expressionist romanticism of the other main movement of the day, the New Apocalypse group. This is not to say that Thomas did not share concerns with both. Regionalism was a response to the centralising grip exercised by the State in the course of prosecuting the war with maximum efficiency, a grip which continued after hostilities ceased. This centralisation fuelled cultural opposition after 1945, even for socialists such as Thomas who broadly welcomed the new majority Labour Government.[11] Yet if Regionalist grievance took the form of individualist protest via an assertion of the separate and unique identities of the component parts of the United Kingdom, Thomas was fully aware that a cultural regionalist agenda in Wales was inseparable from a political nationalist one which had no place for him as an English-speaking, London-published South Walian. It is no coincidence, for example, that the original plan for *Under Milk Wood*, 'The Town (or "Village") That Was Mad', was to have involved the harmlessly eccentric inhabitants of the town being labelled insane and then quarantined by a newly created Welsh national government. 'Welshness' in the later writing, then, tended to be tactical, politically neutral and consciously hybrid. Likewise, for all that they cited him as their chief inspiration, the naïvely Romantic response to postwar conditions of the New Apocalypse poets bears little resemblance to the dense complexity and lucid control of Thomas's poems.

III

Thomas published only seven new poems between *Deaths and Entrances* and his death in 1953. Apart from 'Prologue', written as a verse introduction for the 1952 *Collected Poems*, these were published separately as *In Country Sleep and Other Poems* in the USA in 1952. This relatively straightforward-seeming history is, inevitably, more tangled than it might appear. Crucially, Thomas claimed to regard 'In Country Sleep', 'Over Sir John's hill' and 'In the White Giant's Thigh' as three parts of a sequence which was to have been given an 'over-arching structure' (*CP*, 160) by a fourth poem, 'In Country Heaven'. This poem exists only in incomplete form, but was to have lent its name to the sequence as a whole. Thomas's account of the project, in a BBC radio broadcast of 25 September 1950 provides something of an explanation:

> The poem is to be called 'In Country Heaven'. The godhead, the author, the milky-way farmer, the first cause, architect . . . – He, on top of a hill in Heaven, weeps whenever, outside that state of being called his country, one of his worlds drops dead, vanishes screaming, shrivels, explodes, murders itself. And when he weeps, Light and His tears glide down together hand in hand. So, at the beginning of the projected poem, he weeps, and Country Heaven is suddenly dark . . . And the countrymen of heaven crouch all together under the hedges and, among themselves . . . surmise which world, which star, which of their late, turning homes, in the skies has gone for ever. And this time, spreads the heavenly hedgerow rumour, it is the Earth . . . It is black, petrified, wizened, poisoned, burst; insanity has blown it rotten . . . And, one by one, these heavenly hedgerow-men, who once were of Earth, call one another, through the long night, Light and

> His tears falling, what they remember . . . what they know in their
> Edenie hearts, of that self-called place.[12]

According to Thomas, '[T]he poem is made of these tellings', becoming 'an affirmation of the beautiful and terrible worth of the Earth. It grows into a praise of what is and what could be on this lump in the skies. It is a poem about happiness.'[13] However strange this remarkable mixture of quasi-sci-fi and pastoral might appear now, it made complete sense in the context of British writing of the time. Thomas's scheme clearly shares the contemporary apocalyptic tone. At the same time its religious terminology is, as Ralph Maud has pointed out, wholly secular.[14] This is significant, and not only because it reveals a continuity with the earlier poems. 'Over Sir John's hill' takes as one of its central pre-texts the passage in Matthew 10: 29 which asserts God's knowledge of even the death of the least of birds, the sparrow, combining it with the courtroom imagery of the 'just hill' and its 'black cap of jack-daws' and executioner hawk:

> Over Sir John's hill,
> The hawk on fire hangs still;
> In a hoisted cloud, at drop of dusk, he pulls to his claws
> And gallows, up the rays of his eyes the small birds of the bay
> And the shrill child's play
> Wars
> Of the sparrows and such who swansing, dusk, in wrangling hedges.
> (CP, 142)

'God' is referred to twice in the poem, and the poem's language is thoroughly eschatological: 'save', 'blest', 'mercy', 'souls', 'hymning', 'psalms' (CP, 142–4) and so on. As Maud notes, however, the sense of the poem works against the grain of its religious properties: 'Death is not just (or unjust), Sir John's hill is not judging, the heron is not holy, and God is not, in any meaningful sense, merciful.'[15] Thus 'Thomas's God, both in the prose account and in the poems, is not a religious entity at all in the normal sense of a presiding Being whose presence controls or at least justifies our existence . . . [He] does nothing to alleviate the absurdity of the position of rational man in an irrational universe . . . [He] has perhaps only one function: to make death less fearful.'[16] The poet's final claim to be 'grav[ing]' the birdsong 'for the sake of the souls of the slain birds sailing' (CP, 144) is not, in any salvational sense, true; rather he enacts it as a lyrical-elegiac trace in a world where even the vitalism of nature is a thing of the past. Neither the heron nor the observing poet, who is identified with it, can offer more than 'tell-tales' (*CP*, 143) (with a pun on 'tall', or untrue, tales), these couched in a superannuated language of a faith which has been invoked to represent the lack of any faith. In this, religious usage differs from the oppositional stance of the early poetry which, in its calculated blasphemies, acknowledged the residual power of institutional Christianity. 'Over Sir John's hill' is a 'swansing' (*CP*, 142) for the singing of swansongs, an elegy for the elegiac at least as much as it is an elegy proper. This can be blankly yet richly tragic, as here, or comically uncaring, as in *Under Milk Wood*, in which – to cite Nogood Boyo's words – most of the characters 'don't know who's up there and . . . don't care' (*UMW*, 29). If this is so, it is because the symbolism of doom and judgement, while not anchored to Christianity, finds its proper referent in 'the doomsday-explosion symbolism running throughout the poem'.[17] Religious symbolism is a sign of the poem's grasp of precisely the ungraspability of this unsymbolisable event.

For it is under the shadow of this ambiguous mediation of the postwar scene that, above all else, 'Over Sir John's hill', like 'In Country Sleep' and the other later poems, demands to be read. Nuclear extinction – a world which might be 'blown rotten' by 'insanity' – seemed a real possibility in 1947. Following the two atom bombs dropped on Hiroshima and Nagasaki, the USA began a series of tests on Bikini Atoll in the Pacific in 1946 and built up its nuclear arsenal. The USSR, exploding its first atom bomb in 1949, responded in kind. In 1952 the USA detonated the first H-bomb and the British their first atom bomb. The following year, the USSR tested its own H-bomb. Amid growing international tension, stoked by the Berlin Airlift of 1947, the victory of communism in China in 1949 and the 'hot war' beginning in 1950 in Korea, the Western powers experienced a domestic climate of anxiety, even paranoia. Thomas's letters reveal a response which is alternately flippant or darkly humorous, as he attempted to contain his underlying fears: so, writing to Oscar Williams in December 1945, he dismisses as unproductive 'two months when there was nothing in my head but a little Nagasaki, all low and hot' (*CL*, 576). The later poems are saturated with references to nuclear war. The 'hawk on fire' of 'Over Sir John's hill' is both part of threatened nature, but also an emblem of a bomber's atomic payload, complete with 'viperish fuse'[18] (*CP*, 142–3). 'Poem on his Birthday' is the poem which makes this fear most explicit, as might be expected of a self-elegy whose speaker, its author said, knows that '[h]is death lurks for him, and for all, in the next lunatic war' (*CP*, 254). In the poem,

> . . . tomorrow weeps in a blind cage
> Terror will rage apart
> Before chains break to hammer flame. .
> (*CP9*, 145)

That speaker

> . . . knows the rocketing wind will blow
> The bones out of the hills,
> And the scythed boulders bleed, and the last
> Rage shattered waters kick
> Masts and fishes to the still quick stars.
> (*CP*, 146)

'Still quick', of course, because the 'star' of Earth, as contemplated by its former inhabitants in Country Heaven, will finally have 'shrivel[led], explod[ed], murder[ed] itself'. Nor does it take much imagination to see in the last verse's 'mansouled, fiery islands' (*CP*, 147) not simply the cockle-pickers silhouetted on the mudflats of the Towy estuary, but also those other 'fiery islands' – Bikini, Eniwetok, Elugelab, Monte Bello – of the Pacific test ranges.[19] Such imagery is set against a darkness which is even more ultimate and 'all humbling' (*CP*, 85) than that foreseen in the Blitz poems and ranges from the 'dying' of the light (fading [as adjective], but also killing [as verb]) of 'Do not go gentle into that good night' (*CP*, 148), to the 'Daughters of Darkness' who 'blaze like Fawkes fires still' (*CP*, 152). These references are often positive in that they are set against 'darkness', although their pervasiveness calls attention to the possibility that, unlike the 'words' of the 'wise men' in 'Do not go gentle', they refer to a 'forked', that is duplicitous, 'lightning' (*CP*, 148), which may be that of the Bomb as well as that of illumination and insight. Similarly, the last lines of the first section of 'In Country Sleep' inextricably link the inevitable fall of 'the Thief' on the sleeping child with atomic destruction:

> as the star falls, as the winged
> Apple seed glides,
> And falls, and flowers in the yawning wound at our sides,
> As the world falls, silent as the cyclone of silence.
> (*CP*, 140)

More obliquely, but more pervasively, in the final lines of the poem's last section the child is told that 'you shall wake, from country sleep, this dawn and each first dawn, / Your faith as deathless as the outcry of the ruled sun' (*CP*, 142). There is a contrast being drawn here between 'the lawless sun' five lines before, where the adjective indicates the sun's ungovernability. With 'the ruled sun', however, the transitive form of the verb indicates human mastery of its energies; specifically, the phrase is informed by a knowledge that the processes by which the stars burn have been yoked to destructive purposes by man. The reading is borne out by the sun's response in an 'outcry' (*CP*, 142) – that is, its natural activity of *fostering* (rather than destroying) life on the earth – to man's perverse and terrifying misapplication of such forces. Of course, the 'sun' here is also the 'son' of an absent God – the sacrificial Christ – but this is not because the poem offers a religious consolation. Rather, the Christian allusions serve to emphasise the fact that this is a world in which man's own powers have become godlike, at the same time as supernatural control or sanction over them has ceased to exist. As a result the entire human race is potentially a burnt offering.

IV

Thomas's engagement with historical crisis is not confined to such allusions. Beyond them, the poems register a general crisis in postwar writing, that of how – in the aftermath of the death camps and Hiroshima – literature, as previously conceived, could happen at all. Such knowledge placed a question mark over the meaning and validity of human culture and posited a future which could now be abolished, for the first time and forever, by human agency. However obliquely, the poems bear witness to a crisis in *writing*, in representation itself, which these events created. Although Adorno's famous dictum that lyric poetry was 'barbaric' after Auschwitz[20] might seem at first glance to have little to do with Thomas, the anti-elegies of the Blitz had already shown him grappling with the limits of the poetic and attempting to find ways of representing the unrepresentable or, more accurately, representing its unrepresentability. The stylistic variety of the later poems – baroque clottedness, the thickening excesses and redundancies of the forms, style and language ('In Country Sleep' is perhaps the best example), flirtation with orotundity (in 'Poem on his Birthday'), sardonic directness

('Lament'), or a mixture of these ('Do not go gentle into that good night') – is a response to a compulsion to find ways of saying a new form of the unsayable. This aspect of the work can be read in the light of Jacques Derrida's point that there is in truth no choice about the possibility of the narration of nuclear apocalypse, since it is 'a phenomenon whose essential feature is that of being *fabulously textual*, through and through'.[21] As Connor comments, this is because there is

> no other mode in which to represent it other than fable and fiction. The nature of the event of absolute annihilation ... will be to have destroyed all possibilities of memorial or history, everything that would enable it to persist, or come into being as an event, which means that it can only be known in advance, in projections, predictions, and premonitory narratives. The paradox here is that an event or terminal eventuality which stands outside the continuum of history and narrative, in so far as it signals the obliteration of [these] can ... only ever be signalled by and within narrative itself. The intimate proximity of the end of the world which has characterised life since the end of the Second World War, making this period of history qualitatively different from that of any other ... means the habituation of a double-bind in which we simultaneously must and must not narrate a kind of absolute ending that we anyway both cannot and cannot not narrate.[22]

As we have seen, pastoralism rather than parabolism, exfoliation rather than minimalism was Thomas's response to a crisis of silencing in the form of an over-determined writing which, at every stage, threatens to collapse in on itself. Throughout the later poems, therefore, there is an anxiety about the fact of writing and the limits of language, an unease around which narrative organises itself. Each poem dramatises the desire to believe and the impossibility of believing; each turns on a paradox. 'In Country Sleep' thus begins with a father reading to his daughter at bedtime, in the guise of adult assurance:

> Never and never, my girl riding far and near
> In the land of the hearthstone tales, and spelled asleep,
> Fear or believe that the wolf in a sheepwhite hood
> Loping and bleating roughly and blithely shall leap,
>   My dear, my dear,
> Out of a lair in the flocked leaves in the dew-dipped year
> To eat out your heart in the house in the rosy wood.
>   (CP, 139)

The father is afraid that the child will fear a shadowy, undefined figure referred to as 'the Thief', and attempts to assuage that fear. But as the poem continues, the father gradually intuits that the daughter in fact desires the assault of the Thief, which signifies, after all, that her 'faith' is there to be stolen in the first place. This sheds light on the references within the poem to fairy stories, legends, myths and the 'fables [which] graze / On the lord's table of the bowing grass' (*CP*, 140). These are particularly dense in the opening of the second section of the poem, with its references to reindeer, 'the great roc' (of Sinbad's adventures), 'the nightingale's din and tale', 'The saga from mermen / to seraphim' (*CP*, 141). All of these on 'this night' 'tell of him', the 'Thief' (*CP*, 141), to whom the father must abandon his daughter. In these first six stanzas of the second section of the poem the speaker notably abandons the intimate second person address of the poem's first section for a near-frenzied third person mode, in a denial of his identification with the Thief, who threatens to exteriorise his own incestuous desires for 'The haygold haired, my love asleep' (*CP*, 141). Although, as James J. Balakier has pointed out, the poem is 'a Freudian catharsis in which the father may be seen spontaneously coming to terms with his daughter-fixation', it would be reductive to see it as merely this, just as it would be simplifying a deeper ambiguity to see the Thief as Time set against the Christ of the sleeping child's prayer.[23] Balakier is on surer ground when he sees the Thief as externalising 'whatever ... impedes a more natural state of existence', a Blakean figure paradoxically beneficial to the child because he will 'steal her old limited image of her self so that she can be liberated from captivity to dualities'.[24] Yet this psychological account is also incomplete insofar as it overlooks the linkage of the fate of the child's knowing innocence to that of the 'fall[ing]' world, and the way narrative and language themselves, 'the leaping saga of prayer!' (*CP*, 140, 141) and its idealised landscape, are seen to have failed, subordinated to 'the Thief', at the poem's point of crisis. It is the medium and 'design' of the poet himself which have succumbed here, as in 'A Winter's Tale', unable to intercede between his daughter and threat.

One final aspect of the late poems needs to be mentioned in connection with the anxieties outlined above, the relationship between high and low/popular cultural forms and Thomas's own later reputation; namely, the extent to which the process of story-telling is itself their subject. What is marked is their oral performance aspect, the emphasis on speech and recitation, which these poems conjure up. This, of course, is precisely what certain commentators have objected to in the later work. For the US poet-critic Cid Corman, 'The poet intones' rather too obviously, something he connects to Thomas's success on the lecture circuit: 'I suspect that the unusual "success" he has enjoyed (or possibly not enjoyed) has prodded him to repeat his past performances exclusively.'[25] The late poem of Thomas's which most invites these charges is 'Do not go gentle into that good night'. For Corman this has a notably 'hemmed and, unfortunately, also hawed structure', rhetorically deafened to any subtlety of effect as '[t]he set form [of the villanelle] treads on Thomas's feet'.[26] Arguably, however, 'Do not go gentle' is aware of its rhetorical devices, subverting them even as they are laid so magniloquently before their reader. Moreover, as with the other later poems, this one also turns on linguistic duplicity: like the speaker of 'Poem on his Birthday' (who both triumphantly *and* despairingly affirms that he will 'sail out to die' [*CP*, 147]), the narrator of 'Do not go gentle' urges its addressee to make death a moment of supreme vitality. So far so Yeatsian, perhaps, and the poem's vocabulary is studiedly that of Yeats's *Late Poems*: 'gay', 'fierce', 'burn', 'rave', 'wild', 'rage', 'curse' (*CP*, 148), while even the phrase 'good night' (*CP*, 148) has its Yeatsian pretext ('The second best's a gay good night, and swiftly turn away').[27] But it is precisely the density of these echoes which should alert us to something more at work in the poem than a spirit of rhetoric or tired pastiche (of Yeats, or of *King Lear* to cite Thomas's other obvious source). For one thing, the poem is distinctly at odds with any Yeatsian message that gaiety 'transfigur[es] all that dread',[28] and it is deliberately antiheroic in its use of Yeats's heroic trappings, ending as it does with an appeal to his father to 'curse' and 'bless' his son (*CP*, 148). And, in an attempt at reparation for his agonising inheritance, Thomas reverses the Biblical father–son relationship, for in the poem it is the father who is the Christ-son wounded 'on the sad height' (*CP*, 148) of the crucifixion of his death, as his son, now in the position of God the Father, unwillingly looks on. The poem seems a straightforward elegy for the father, but more than this it is an elegy for his father's voice, the voice which made Thomas so famous in his final years; a poem for reading aloud, it deliberately booms in the father's tones as handed down to his son. Like 'Poem on his Birthday', it could be said to be offered 'Faithlessly unto him' (the use of 'unto' pointing the indulgence in, and rejection of, a liturgical dimension) (*CP*, 146). Even 'Do not go gentle' has a root in miscegenation and mockery, albeit a grievous self-mockery, and it speaks with the ghost of a tongue in its hammy cheek. But this does not mean that it is not a true lament; rather, by challenging the conventional belief that such lushness is inappropriate, inauthentic, its gestures are made, paradoxically, all the more vulnerable and more moving. In this, the anguished repetitions of its villanelle form – *pace* Corman – are exactly right for its occasion:

> And you, my father, there on the sad height,
> Curse, bless, me now with your fierce tears, I pray.
> Do not go gentle into that good night.
> Rage, rage against the dying of the light.
>
> (CP, 148)

The very *vulgarity* of the poem, then – which is, paradoxically, what plain style-preferring critics like Corman are really objecting to – is made a source of strength, right down to the (grammatically) surplus second comma, with its effect of a catch in the throat, in the line 'Curse, bless, me now with your fierce tears, I pray'.

V

As has already been noted, the origins of *Under Milk Wood* lie in a piece conceived of as 'The Town (or Village) That Was Mad', in which the outside world's judgement on a settlement peopled by eccentrics would end up rebounding on it; it is the world which, in the eyes of the Llareggub population, and the listeners to the drama, would have been deemed to be 'mad'. It has been lamented that Thomas did not stick to this original plan, the belief being that this would have made for a more 'serious' work. But even if we discount much of this as speculation coloured by the tragedy of Thomas's early death, there remains the fact that the play is connected with the other later work, and that its dominant comic-fantastic tone contains, and is given its particular poignancy, by an awareness of darkness and death. The final words spoken by a character, after all, are those of Polly Garter: 'But I always think as we tumble into bed / Of little Willy Wee who is dead, dead, dead' (*UMW*, 62).

The preponderance of critical opinion on *Under Milk Wood* makes it an Arcadian, pastoral fantasy, yet the view of Llareggub as Edenic links it with the 'Edenie hearts' of the 'In Country Heaven' project, while its very eccentricity also makes it something of an embattled site. Thus, in a letter of 25 August 1939, from the same year and same eve-of-war contexts which shaped the later poetry, Thomas referred to Laugharne as 'a little Danzig' (*CL*, 401), referring to the port city which lay at the end of the 'Polish Corridor' dividing post-Versailles Germany, the territory whose invasion a few days later would trigger the British declaration of war on Nazi Germany. Nevertheless, *Under Milk Wood* is utopian, bracketing off as it does the more overtly social contexts shaping other work of the period even as it continues the later poems' series of self-dramatisations – as father, son, writer-elegist, 'Aesop fabling' (*CP*, 143), collier 'dying of downfall' (*CP*, 149) and Hardyesque churchyard sage. Thomas himself subtitled *Under Milk Wood* precisely as a 'play for voices', although play *of* voices might have been closer to the truth. What it presents is a consciously static structure which allows the temporary quarantining of the town (or its imaginative space) from social contexts in an unresolved and unresolvable linguistic 'play' in both senses of the word. The cyclical nature of the text's progression is the most obvious aspect of this, as it moves from the dreams of its characters in the 'starless and bible-black' small hours (*UMW*, 3), through the day and on to 'the second dark time this one Spring day' (*UMW*, 62). If the fact that this is Spring allows for optimism and the erotic energies which, repressed by the majority of characters but always endorsed by the narrating First Voice, inform the narrative, time as defined by authority is always as frozen as the hands of the clock stuck 'at half past eleven' in the Sailors Arms. Indeed, the two are dependent on each other; 'It is always opening time in the Sailors' Arms' (*UMW*, 28) suggests a perpetual loving embrace as well as pub doors eternally ajar to thirsty drinkers.

This comic tension between erotic promise and its refusal can be seen as the major theme of the work, its social critique as it were, and as the chief source of its popularity. As shamelessly as the *Carry On* films were to do a little later, Thomas draws upon a cultural sub-world of saucy seaside postcards, music-hall jokes, smutty ballads and the scandal sheets, containing these within an almost mathematically symmetrical web of relationships and fixed natures. Although the characters of the play exist within their own private worlds – nobody is influenced or changed by the actions of anyone else, as they are in true drama – they exist in strict relationship to others. The pairing off and matching is almost complete: Mog Edwards has (but only because he does not have) Myfanwy Price,

Utah Watkins has Mrs Utah Watkins, Organ Morgan has Mrs Organ Morgan, Bessie Bighead has Gomer Owen (although he is now dead), Butcher Beynon has Mrs Butcher Beynon, both have Lily Smalls who, in turn – albeit briefly – has Nogood Boyo. If Mrs Ogmore Pritchard has Mr Ogmore and Mr Pritchard, Dai Bread has, by way of contrast, Mrs Dai Bread One and Mrs Dai Bread Two. Cherry Owen is 'two husbands', the drunk and the sober, but both are loved by Mrs Cherry Owen. Polly Garter can have anyone – among them Mr Waldo, perhaps the most fluid character of all – but the man she wants, Little Willie Wee, is dead. Captain Cat has the same kind of frustrated yet pure relationship as Mog Edwards and Myfanwy Price, but as Laurence Lerner points out, 'Time does for [him] what distance does for [them]'.[29] Unattached characters tend to be defined, like some of these, in terms of their occupations, via an emblematic, metonymic naming: Evans the Death, Attila Rees, Lord Cut-Glass, Jack Black, Ocky Milkman. The nature of the exchanges between unidentified voices – the four Neighbours or the five Drowned – is choric, and adds to the feeling of fixation within a closed universe of types. The roots of frustration are equally timeworn and predictable – money (as in the case of Mog Edwards who 'hugs his lovely money to his heart' [*UMW*, 62] or class, as with Sinbad Sailors adoring the 'proud' schoolteacher Gossamer Beynon [*UMW*, 46]). While this might produce paralysis in a realist drama, it is not felt as such here by either characters or their audience; Mr and Mrs Pugh, as Thomas himself explained, are content, and can only be content, in their roles of nagging wife and prospective poisoner (*UMW*, xxxvi). To this extent, there is little to disturb the equilibrium of the emotional economy of the play.

This emotional economy, it might be said, is that of childhood. In *Under Milk Wood*, however, the child's-eye view, voyeurism, and refusal of what is usually defined as 'mature' sexuality is tempered, and even undermined. An adult sense of humour and irony is manifested in 'childish' verbal mischief. For all that it has been claimed that 'the good images perish with the rest' in the play,[30] it is the precision and unpredictability of the language which continually pulls the listener back from its own calculated lurches in the direction of lavish word-painting: the 'cold grey cottage pie' of 'shroud meat' lingeringly eaten by Mr Pugh and Mrs Pugh's draught of 'clouded peasoup water' (*UMW*, 47) are cases in point, unnervingly blending as they do the comic-descriptive and the disgusting-disturbing.

Similarly, Captain Cat occasionally reminds us that he is more than just a sentimental old observer:

> *The sun and the green breeze ship Captain Cat sea-memory again.*

CAPTAIN CAT
No, I'll take the mulatto, by God, who's captain here? Parlez-vous jig-jig, Madam?

(*UMW*, 37)

Where the language of the play might be viewed as self-indulgent it is important not only to remember the extent to which this is writing to be heard, rather than read, but also that its play is part of Thomas's desire to allow language something of its autonomy. In a dream-world, as Freud explained, connections are made through transference and seemingly trivial associationism; alliteration and pun bulk more centrally than causal logic. In this world, comedy acts as a continual rebuke to moralism, at times in an almost surrealist manner. The effectiveness of Thomas's blend of character, situation and comic timing hardly needs stressing:

> *From Beynon Butchers in Coronation Street, the smell of fried liver sidles out with onions on its breath. And listen! In the dark break-fast-room behind the shop, Mr and Mrs Beynon, waited upon by their treasure, enjoy, between bites, their everymorning hullaballoo, and Mrs Beynon slips the gristly bits under the tasselled tablecloth to her fat cat.*

[Cat purrs.]

MRS BEYNON
She likes the liver, Ben.

MR BEYNON
She ought to do, Bess. It's her brother's.

(*UMW*, 27)

It is the pause at the end of Mr Beynon's first sentence, and the casual nature of his second, which makes this so wonderfully funny, although the exchange also illustrates Thomas's unerring ear for normal speech – 'she ought to do', not the more standard 'she ought to' – and illustrates how he interweaves realism and near-surrealism. Another way of putting this would be to say that if the characters of the play and their routines are frozen and stereotypical, the language is anything but. Not only does it exhibit an empathic quality which draws us in – 'And listen!' – but it mixes different registers (condescending guidebook prose, punchline, innuendo – 'it's organ, organ all the time with him' [*UMW*, 36] – lyric, list, fantasy) in a manner which can only be called polyphonic.

The opening exchange is a good example. In it, the speakers introduce themselves and, involved in their own action, each other, acting in a sense as their own chorus, so that they are not simply addressing Captain Cat. It begins simply with the First Drowned asking 'Remember me, Captain?', but then starts weaving more complex patterns:

THIRD DROWNED
Hold me, Captain, I'm Jonah Jarvis, come to a bad end, very enjoyable.

FOURTH DROWNED
Alfred Pomeroy Jones, sealawyer, born in Mumbles, sung like a linnet, crowned you with a flagon, tattooed with mermaids, thirst like a dredger, died of blisters.

FIRST DROWNED
This skull at your earhole is

FIFTH DROWNED
Curly Bevan. Tell my auntie it was me that pawned the ormulu clock.

CAPTAIN CAT
Aye, aye, Curly.

SECOND DROWNED
Tell my missus no I never

THIRD DROWNED
I never done what she said I never.

FOURTH DROWNED
Yes, they did.

(*UMW*, 5)

The polyphony not only weaves between the various characters, but ties the exchange to the whole play. The 'ormulu clock', for example, looks forward to Lord Cutglass, while the 'skull at the earhole', as well as the Spoon River and Thomas Hardy connotations, also recalls Yorick's skull and Ariel's song for Ferdinand in *The Tempest*, mixing and confusing different cultural levels. Likewise the rhythms of the Fourth Drowned have the hypnotic appeal associated with verse, which continually disturbs prose rhythms, and not only in the Reverend Eli Jenkins' poem, which is presented, ironically, as one of the flattest stylistic episodes of the play (the end of each clause is anchored with a trochaic foot: 'flágon', 'drédger', 'mérmaid', 'blísters').

'Stereotypical', or 'caricature' have, of course, become something of a critical get-out clause in discussions of *Under Milk Wood*; as terms they are invariably undefined and generally taken to mean simply 'one-dimensional'. This touches on the reading of Thomas's career progress from solipsism to humanism, modernism to realism, isolation to communal warmth. *Under Milk Wood*, we should note, has never quite fitted this model, largely because of the stylistic and tonal peculiarities discussed above. Thus, Walford Davies has complained that 'One wishes he had compounded more community with the geography of the later phase, explored the reality for which *Under Milk Wood* was a variant caricature'.[31] But as with critical discussions of Dickens's work, it is worth paying a little more attention than is usually the case to Thomas's use of 'caricatures' or stereotypes.

One place to begin is with their function in modern popular cultural forms. The genre and sources of *Under Milk Wood* have been well investigated: the radio features blending comedy, fantasy and realism; the prose fictions; the day-in-the-life-of structure; the passages in letters which describe Laugharne and other places in terms of the kinds of eccentricities which characterise the population of Llareggub; Thomas's own gift for oral comic improvisation. Less attention has been paid to the context of radio production in the early 1950s and the parallels between *Under Milk Wood* and BBC radio comedy. This was in its fullest flowering between the 1940s and the 1960s, from the wartime show 'ITMA' and 'The Goon Show' in the 1950s, to 'Round the Horne' in the 1960s. Just how close Thomas came to writing a radio situation comedy can be seen in the letter of 1951 to Ted Kavanagh, the scriptwriter of 'ITMA', mooting their collaboration on a new comedy programme, provisionally titled 'Quid's Inn'. The eponymous inn which is the focus of the programme was to be located in a village ('Little Fiddle on the Grog or anywhere, though not, by God, that' [*CL*, 790]), and was to have been the place in which the two writers would bring 'all the rich, rooted, fruity past of the rural gallimaufry loud alongside with the world of to-now' (*CL*, 189). The terms of this description, as well as Thomas's reference to a number of stock characters who might have featured in 'Quid's Inn', irresistibly suggest the new genre of the open-ended series located in a fixed place, or soap opera, which first began around the time of *Under Milk Wood*, with 'The Archers' on radio and 'Coronation Street' (the name – coincidentally? – of one of the two main streets in Llareggub) on television.

In such multifarious forms, 'stereotype' cannot simply be taken as a synonym for 'one-dimensional'. Discussing the function of the stereotype in the context of colonialism, Homi Bhabha has noted that what is distinctive about it is not so much its one-dimensionality as the anxiety which lies behind its usage. That is, the stereotype 'is a form of knowledge and identification which vacillates between what is always "in place", already known, and something that must be anxiously repeated'.[32] For Bhabha, the stereotype is not so much a fixed quantity as an ambivalent *process*, the resort to which – such-and-such a kind of person is essentially unreliable, comic, obsessed with clocks (Lord Cutglass), Bach (Organ Morgan), beer (Cherry Owen) or whatever – reveals an angst-ridden attempt at *self*-definition by those who resort to them. Drawing on Lacanian psychoanalytic theory, Bhabha claims that the stereotype can be seen in relation to what Lacan calls the formative mirror phase in the development of the human subject, the point at which it realises itself from outside as a discrete, separate entity. This moment, for Lacan, is a problematic one; it allows self-identification, but also confrontation with the objects of the surrounding world. For Bhabha, these two kinds of identification – narcissism and aggressivity – are to be found exercised in relation to the stereotype 'which, as a form of multiple and contradictory belief, gives knowledge of difference and simultaneously disavows or masks it.'[33] We do not need to follow Bhabha to the function of the stereotype in colonial discourses to see how applicable the formulation is to the way in which the characters of *Under Milk Wood*, and the play itself, works. The plenitude and self-sufficiency of the stereotypes offered by Thomas (Captain Cat, Black Jack, Polly Garter) are continually threatened by the 'lack' he identifies, and this is the source of the undertow of melancholy in the play. The characters themselves are both 'rich' and 'thin', to use an older critical terminology, since '[s]tereotyping is not the setting up of a false image which becomes [a] scapegoat ... It is a much more ambivalent text of ... displacement, over-determination, guilt, aggressivity ... the stereotype is at once substitute and shadow.'[34]

There is no doubt, as Peter Lewis has claimed, that the history of *Under Milk Wood* amounts to 'one of the greatest literary and dramatic success stories of [the twentieth] century, and for something conceived as a radio play, it is unique'.[35] Its fame has led readers to view not only Thomas's other work, but also his life in terms of the play: blowsy, generous, boozy, comic, lewd – 'Oh, isn't life a terrible thing, thank God?' (*UMW*, 24) – but fundamentally decent and good-hearted. As such, *Under Milk Wood* works as a soap opera-cum-biodrama in the terms of Jacqueline Rose's formulation: 'Soap operas are one of the means of negotiating the stereotypes of the culture. They offer vicarious pleasure and invite moral judgement: sexual narrative as gossip ("so they gossiped gently on . . . as if [each event] had no beginning and no end"), morality as a form of licensed pleasure in itself.'[36] In this case arguing that Sylvia Plath can be considered neither victim nor aggressor, Rose concludes that the point is that '[h]er writing crosses the very boundary repeatedly marked out in her name' through the soap opera's either/or distribution of guilt and blame. In *Under Milk Wood*, of course, we have a soap opera structure in which guilt and blame – moral judgement – are both courted and conspicuously refused, as if Thomas recognises the trap of his own reputation and representations. Like Plath, Thomas's writing also transgresses the boundaries laid down for it. Despite their many differences, then, it may be no coincidence that a title which Plath used for both a poem and a short story – 'All the Dead Dears' – echoes Captain Cat's valediction at the end of his opening colloquy: 'Oh, my dead dears!' (*UMW*, 7).[37]

The investment in personal voice exemplified in *Under Milk Wood*, but also in the later poems, has been read retrospectively to cover all of Thomas's work (largely due to the potency of the myth of his last years in shaping reception). It can still be claimed, for example, that 'it is not as constructions or as sets of influences that we experience the poems. Their power comes from a unique and resonant voice.'[38] While such a claim fends off crudely sociological interpretations, it does so by evading issues like the importance of parody to modernism or the role of phonocentric prejudice in the reception of Thomas's work (phonocentrism being defined as belief in the absolute proximity of voice and being, of voice and the meaning of being, of voice and the ideality of meaning). The problem is the failure to specify what is meant by 'voice'. Actual performance? The 'voice effect' created by a given style? Or the more philosophical 'presencing' of the author? In Thomas criticism such vagueness leads to the conflation of the massive authority of the readings and personal legend with the poetry's sincerity (which, alternatively, is precisely an index of its speciousness). Thomas's own creative manipulation of the different senses of 'voice' *is* the secret of his later success; but it is for just this reason that criticism needs to avoid imprecision. Rather than succumbing to the authority of the poet's utterance, or to phonocentric naïvety, it is necessary to tackle them both as barriers to understanding and as keys to Thomas's critical fortunes. Thus the emphasis on voice – which at first glance seems to reveal the work as a form of deluded self-presencing – can itself be seen as resistant to incantational resonance and authority. The linguistic materialism of Thomas's writing and the theatrical qualities of his now-unfashionable reading style appear, at a deeper level, as providing fresh critical opportunity; for, if the voice strengthens the nostalgia for an ineradicable source of meaning prior to and constitutive of all sign systems, it nevertheless works, in its baroque richness, to present the materiality of the sign, pulling in the other direction against linguistic idealism and 'naturalness', sonorously overflowing any fixed order of meaning. The voice, indeed, alerts us to a central contradiction of the later work: the fact that far from obscurity and popularity functioning as opposed terms, in Thomas's case they are actually complementary.

NOTES

[In this essay, John Goodby challenges the assumption that there is a direct route from the inner landscapes of Thomas's early work to the later external and rural ones, and from these to the pastoral of *Under Milk Wood*. Focusing on the boundary-blurring aspects of Thomas's use of high and low, elite and popular cultural forms, Goodby argues against the humanist assumptions of this narrative which, he suggests, tend to overlook both the change in literary audiences after the Second World War and the questioning of the efficacy and meaning of literature as such in the new climate of nuclear anxiety. In this reading, the later work is seen as part of a wider crisis of writing which generated a style both accessible and excessive, at once saturated with religiosity and determinedly secular. For Goodby, Thomas's use of voice is an aspect of a calculated self-display and self-quizzing of which the poet himself is ambiguously aware, as he turns 'vulgarity' to moving purpose in a poem such as 'Do not go gentle into that good night'. The same kind of linguistic excess, although in a more relaxed mode, is seen as energising Thomas's most famous work, *Under Milk Wood*. Goodby claims the play may also be read as a precursor of soap opera, radicalising the tendency to see it as merely reflecting Thomas's own personality. Here as elsewhere, Goodby is concerned to prevent us reading the work in terms of the life, discussing the 'stereotypes' of the play's characters in the more complex sense of the term defined by the postcolonial theorist Homi Bhabha. Eds]

1. Walford Davies, for example, has claimed that Thomas is 'experientially most at sea in the "war casualty" poems *Deaths and Entrances*', while 'additional poems in [the manner of "After the Funeral"] might be counted among the literary casualties of the war.' '[A]ll at sea', however, is precisely the no-place where so many of the poems actually *are*, and are happy (not) to be. See Walford Davies, '*The Wanton Starer*', in *Dylan Thomas: New Critical Essays*, ed. Walford Davies (London, 1972), pp. 149, 161.

2. See, for an example of this unproblematic approach to realism, Annis Pratt, *Dylan Thomas's Early Prose: A Study in Creative Mythology* (Pittsburgh, 1970), p. 151.

3. David Harvey, *The Condition of Postmodernity: An Enquiry into the Origins of Cultural Change* (Oxford, 1992), p. 35.

4. Jacqueline Rose, *The Haunting of Sylvia Plath* (London, 1992), p. 191.

5. Theodor W. Adorno, *The Culture Industry: Selected Essays on Mass Culture*, ed. J. M. Bernstein (London, 1991), pp. 85–93.

6. Steven Connor, *The English Novel in History: 1950–1995* (London, 1996), p. 22.

7. Karl Shapiro, 'Dylan Thomas', in *Dylan Thomas: A Collection of Critical Essays*, ed. C. B. Cox (Hillsdale, NJ: 1966), p. 179.

8. William Empson, '*Collected Poems* and *Under Milk Wood*', in Cox, *Dylan Thomas*, p. 86.

9. Davies, '*The Wanton Starer*', p. 149.

10. Seamus Heaney, 'The Regional Forecast', in *The Literature of Region and Nation*, ed. R. P. Draper (London, 1989), p. 13.

11. There was a contradiction at the heart of Regionalism, best embodied by John Hewitt, the Northern Irish poet, since where localism shaded into demands for political autonomy it could be seen as support for backwardness and isolation (as with the Stormont regime in Northern Ireland, for example).

12. Dylan Thomas, *Quite Early One Morning* (New York, 1960), pp. 178–9.

13. Ibid., p. 180.

14. Ralph Maud, *Entrances to Dylan Thomas' Poetry* (Pittsburgh, 1966), pp. 103–10.

15. Ibid., p. 109.

16. Ibid., p. 112.

17. Ibid., p. 107.

18. 'Viperish' is also, of course, a grimly retrospective self-reference to 'The force that through the green fuse'.

19. Similarly in 'In Country Sleep' we find 'pounded islands' (*CP*, 140).

20. Theodor W. Adorno, *Prisms*, trans. Samuel and Shierry Weber (London, 1967), p. 34.

21. Jacques Derrida, 'No Apocalypse, Not Now (full speed ahead, seven missiles, seven missives)', trans. Catherine Porter and Philip Lewis, *Diacritics*, 14 (1984), 23.

22. Connor, *The English Novel in History*, pp. 202–3.

23. James J. Balakier, 'The Ambiguous Reversal of Dylan Thomas's "In Country Sleep" ', *Papers on Language and Literature*, 32: 1 (1996), 33.

24. Ibid., 39, 41.

25. Cid Corman, 'Dylan Thomas: Rhetorician in Mid-Career', in *Dylan Thomas: The Legend and the Poet*, ed. W. D. Tedlock (London, 1960), p. 227.

26. Ibid., p. 226.

27. *W. B. Yeats: The Poems*, ed. Richard J. Finneran (Basingstoke, 1983), p. 227.

28. Ibid., p. 294.

29. Laurence Lerner, 'Sex in Arcadia: *Under Milk Wood*', in Davies, *Dylan Thomas*, p. 274.

30. Geoffrey Thurley, *The Ironic Harvest: English Poetry in the Twentieth Century* (London, 1974), p. 126.

31. Davies, 'The Wanton Starer', pp. 160–1.

32. Homi K. Bhabha, *The Location of Culture* (London, 1994), p. 66.

33. Ibid., p. 77.

34. Ibid., pp. 81–2.

35. Peter Lewis, 'The Radio Road to Llareggub', in *British Radio Drama*, ed. John Drakakis (Cambridge, 1981), p. 75.

36. Rose, *The Haunting of Sylvia Plath*, p. 6.

37. Ibid., p. 1.

38. Dylan Thomas, *Selected Poems*, ed. Walford Davies (London, 1993), pp. xxxvi–xxxvii.

Further Reading

OTHER WORKS BY DYLAN THOMAS

Thomas's writings have suffered over the years from haphazard editorial attention and the items below contain material not included in the list of works cited at the beginning of this volume. The first two items contain statements by Thomas on his own poetic practice; the others give a valuable insight into his development as a poet and work in other media.

Quite Early One Morning (London: Dent, 1952).
Early Prose Writings, ed. Walford Davies (London: Dent, 1971).
The Notebook Poems 1930–34, ed. Ralph Maud (London: Dent, 1989).
The Poems, ed. Daniel Jones (London: Dent, 1982).
The Broadcasts, ed. Ralph Maud (London: Dent, 1991).
Selected Poems, ed. Walford Davies (London: Dent, 1993).
The Filmscripts, ed. John Ackerman (London: Dent, 1995).

BIBLIOGRAPHY

James A. Davies, 'Dylan Thomas', *Annotated Bibliography of English Studies* (Abingdon: Swets and Zeitlinger, 1997).
Georg Gaston, *Dylan Thomas: A Reference Guide* (Boston: G. K. Hall, 1987).
John Harris, *A Bibliographical Guide to Twenty-four Modern Anglo-Welsh Writers* (Cardiff: University of Wales Press, 1994).
Ralph Maud, *Dylan Thomas in Print: A Bibliographical History* (with Appendix) (London: Dent, 1970).

BIOGRAPHY AND CRITICISM

Part of the problem with writing on Thomas in the past, as outlined in the Introduction, has been the unthinking conflation of criticism and biography. To some degree, our yoking together of the two kinds of writing here has to reflect this; for example, both of the *Companions* listed below contain potted biographies and critical accounts of the writings. Paul Ferris's biography is more complete than Constantine Fitzgibbons's somewhat romanticised account, although it is at times over-judgemental and lacks insight into the poetry. Walford Davies's 1986 study is currently the most accessible short introduction to Thomas's work for the beginner. John Ackerman's *Companion* is a lucid overview of all of Thomas's writings, while James A. Davies's *Reference Companion* is a useful source of additional material. Although dated, William York Tindall's *Guide* is the only poem-by-poem exegesis available, and provides information crucial to an understanding of many of the more difficult early poems.

John Ackerman, *A Dylan Thomas Companion* (Basingstoke: Macmillan Press – now Palgrave, 1991).

John Ackerman, *Welsh Dylan* (Bridgend: Seren, 1997).

James A. Davies, *A Reference Companion to Dylan Thomas* (Westport, CT: Greenwood Press, 1998).

Walford Davies, *Dylan Thomas* (Milton Keynes: Open University Press, 1986).

Paul Ferris, *Dylan Thomas* (Harmondsworth: Penguin, 1978).

Constantine Fitzgibbon, *The Life of Dylan Thomas* (London: Dent, 1965).

Barbara Hardy, *Dylan Thomas's Poetic Language: The Stream That is Flowing Both Ways* (Cardiff: University College, Cardiff, 1987).

Ralph Maud, *Entrances to Dylan Thomas's Poetry* (Pittsburg: University of Pittsburg Press, 1963).

Ann Elizabeth Mayer, *Artists in Dylan Thomas's Works: Adam Naming and Aesop Falling* (Montreal and Kingston: McGill University Press, 1995).

William T. Moynihan, *The Craft and Art of Dylan Thomas* (Ithaca, NY: Cornell University Press, 1968).

Annis Pratt, *Dylan Thomas' Early Prose: A Study in Creative Mythology* (Pittsburg: University of Pittsburg Press, 1970).

William York Tindall, *A Reader's Guide to Dylan Thomas* (Syracuse, NY: Syracuse University Press, 1996).

COLLECTIONS OF ESSAYS

None of these essay collections is wholly satisfactory. There are, though, a few good articles in each which can be read with profit. E. W. Tedlock's collection contains one of the few genuinely insightful discussions of Thomas's poetry written in his lifetime, by David Aivaz. C. B. Cox contains short pieces by William Empson and an early essay by Raymond Williams on *Under Milk Wood* which is perhaps the best place to begin a study of the play. Walford Davies's book, as might be expected of a Thomas scholar, contains many of the most substantial essays available; particularly useful is C. J. Rawson's which contains an unparalleled range of reference to other English poetry and deploys more positively the neo-Augustan criteria applied by Donald Davie and the Movement poets to Thomas, while Alastair Fowler's reading of 'Fern Hill' is a quasi-structuralist, exhaustively detailed reading of the poem. Georg Gaston's is the most uneven of the collections listed (and displays considerable critical naïvety considering its date of publication), but – like Tedlock – it includes testimony by a number of US poets to Thomas's transatlantic influence. The best essay in Alan Bold's book is included in this volume.

Alan Bold (ed.), *Dylan Thomas: Craft or Sullen Art* (London and New York: Vision and St. Martin's Press – now Palgrave, 1990).

C. B. Cox (ed.), *Dylan Thomas: A Collection of Critical Essays* (Hillsdale, NJ: Prentice-Hall, 1966).

Walford Davies (ed.), *Dylan Thomas: New Critical Essays* (London: Dent, 1972).

Georg Gaston (ed.), *Critical Essays on Dylan Thomas* (Boston, G. K. Hall, 1989).

E. W. Tedlock (ed.), *Dylan Thomas: The Legend and the Poet* (London: William Heinemann, 1960).

OTHER RECOMMENDED READING

The books and articles listed below include material on Dylan Thomas and discuss the work in the broad context of modern literature. These items also provide an insight into the changing critical reception of Thomas's writing, from the 1950s to the present.

John Bayley, *The Romantic Survival* (London: Constable, 1957).

Tony Conran, *Frontiers in Anglo-Welsh Poetry* (Cardiff: University of Wales Press, 1997).

Neil Corcoran, *English Poetry since 1940* (London: Longman 1993).

Donald Davie, *Articulate Energy : An Inquiry into the Syntax of English Poetry* (London: Routledge & Kegan Paul, 1955).

James A. Davies, 'Questions of Identity: Dylan Thomas, the Movement, and After', in *Appropriations and Impositions: National, Regional and Sexual Identity in Literature,* ed. Igor Navrátil and Robert B. Pynsent (Bratislava: Nàrodné literáne centrum, 1997), pp. 118–29.

R. P. Draper, *An Introduction to Twentieth-Century Poetry in English* (Basingstoke: Macmillan Press – now Palgrave, 1999).

William Empson, *Argufying,* ed. John Haffenden (London: Hogarth Press, 1988).

Seamus Heaney, 'Dylan the Durable? On Dylan Thomas', in *The Redress of Poetry* (London: Faber, 1995), pp. 124–45.

Philip A. Lahey, 'Dylan Thomas: A Reappraisal', *Critical Survey,* 5:1 (1993), 53–65.

Peter Elfed Lewis, 'The Radio Road to Llareggub', in *British Radio Drama,* ed. John Drakakis (Cambridge: Cambridge University Press, 1981), pp. 72–110.

Don McKay, 'Crafty Dylan and the "Altarwise" Sonnets', *University of Toronto Quarterly,* 55 (1986), 375–94.

J. Hillis Miller, *Poets of Reality: Six Twentieth-Century Writers* (Cambridge, MA: Harvard University Press, 1966).

Blake Morrison, *The Movement: English Poetry and Fiction of the 1950s* (London and New York: Methuen, 1980).

Paul. C. Ray, *The Surrealist Movement in England* (Ithaca, NY: Cornell University Press, 1971).

Louis Simpson, *A Revolution in Taste* (New York: Macmillan Press – now Palgrave, 1978).

Jon Silkin, *The Life of Metrical and Free Verse* (Basingstoke: Macmillan Press – now Palgrave, 1997).

M. Wynn Thomas, *Corresponding Cultures: The Two Literatures of Wales* (Cardiff: University of Wales Press, 1999).

Notes on Contributors

Stewart Crehan is Senior Lecturer in English at Manchester Metropolitan University and has taught in Northern Ireland and at the Universities of Zambia, Turin, Swaziland, Transkei, Huddersfield and Sheffield Hallam. His interests include the eighteenth century, Romanticism, critical theory and modern African literature. His publications include *Blake in Context* (Dublin, 1984). He is currently completing two books, one on African writing, the other entitled *Narratives of Master and Servant*, and is also working on a study of poetic and economic discourse from Pope to Rossetti.

James A. Davies was Senior Lecturer in English at University of Wales, Swansea. He has been Visiting Professor at Baylor University, Texas and is the author of *John Forster: A Literary Life* (Leicester, 1983), *The Textual Life of Dickens's Characters* (Basingstoke, 1989) and *A Reference Companion to Dylan Thomas* (Connecticut, 1998).

Walford Davies was Senior Lecturer in English Literature at St Anne's College, Oxford. His work on Dylan Thomas includes two critical studies of the poet: *Dylan Thomas* (Milton Keynes, 1986) and *Dylan Thomas* (Cardiff, 1990). He is also the editor of *Early Prose Writings* (London, 1971), *Dylan Thomas: New Critical Essays* (London, 1972), *The Collected Stories* (London, 1983), *Deaths and Entrances* (London, 1984), and with Ralph Maud, *Collected Poems* (London, 1988). His editions of *Dylan Thomas: Selected Poems* and *Under Milk Wood* are published by Penguin (Harmondsworth, 2000).

John Goodby is Lecturer in English at the University of Wales, Swansea. He is co-editor with Maurice Scully of *Colonies of Belief: Ireland's Modernists* (London, 1999) and author of *Irish Poetry Since 1950: From Stillness into History* (Manchester, 2000). He has published widely on British and Irish poetry and is a member of the ESRC Transnational Communities Programme Axial Writing project. He is currently working on a study of Dylan Thomas's poetics.

Katie Gramich is Staff Tutor for English at the Open University in the South-West, Bristol. She is the co-editor of *Dangerous Diversity: The Changing Faces of Wales* (Cardiff, 1998) and the general co-editor of the Honno Classics series, which brings works by neglected Welsh women writers back into print. Her edition of Allen Raine's *Queen of the Rushes* appeared in this series in 1998.

Ivan Phillips is a Lecturer in Digital Culture at the University of Hertfordshire. He has published articles on Thomas Chatterton, Thomas

MacGreevy and Seamus Heaney, and is currently working on a study of British poetry of the 1940s. His own poetry has appeared in a number of journals, including *The Honest Ulsterman*, *The North*, *Thumbscrew* and *The Wide Skirt*.

Stan Smith is Professor of English at Nottingham Trent University. His publications include *Inviolable Voice: History and Twentieth-Century Poetry* (Dublin, 1982), *W. H. Auden* (Oxford, 1985), *Edward Thomas* (London, 1986), *W. B. Yeats: A Critical Introduction* (Basingstoke, 1990), *The Origins of Modernism: Eliot, Pound, Yeats and the Rhetoric of Renewal* (Hemel Hempstead, 1994) and *W. H. Auden* (Southampton, 1997). He is General Editor of the Longman Critical Readers series and Longman Studies in Twentieth-Century Literature. He is currently working on the sequel to *The Origins of Modernism*; the new book, of which his essay here is an excerpted chapter, is called *Ruined Boys: W. H. Auden and the Lineages of Modernism*.

Steve Vine is Lecturer in English at the University of Wales Swansea. He is the author of *Blake's Poetry: Spectral Visions* (London, 1993), *Emily Brontë* (New York, 1998), and edited the Penguin edition of D. H. Lawrence's *Aaron's Rod* (Harmondsworth, 1995). He is currently working on *Literature in Psychoanalysis: A Practical Reader*, and a study of the Romantic and Postmodern sublimes.

Chris Wigginton is Head of the School of English and Communication at Trinity College, Carmarthen. He is currently completing a monograph on Dylan Thomas for Northcote House and the British Council, and is also working on a study of early twentieth-century writing.

Jeni Williams is Lecturer in English at Trinity College, Carmarthen. Her publications include *Interpreting Nightingales: Gender, Class, Histories* (Sheffield, 1997). Forthcoming are studies on *Alice's Adventures in Wonderland* and *Women in Love*, the child in Kate Roberts and Dylan Thomas (*Welsh Writing in English*) and the place of dialect in Chaucer's *Reve's Tale*.

Index

Aberpennar, Davies, 188
Ackerman, John, 103n, 156n, 197, 221, 222
Adelphi, 8
Adolescence, 4–5, 8, 16, 21, 22, 28, 29–34, 36, 37, 51, 57, 69, 94, 158, 175, 185, 188, 192
Adorno, Theodor W., 194, 205
Aeschylus, 79
Alice in Wonderland, *see* Carroll, Lewis
Alice books, *see* Carroll, Lewis
Alvarez, Al, 6
Amis, Kingsley, 5, 6, 10, 159–61, 170n
Angier, Natalie, 79
Anschluss, 126
'The Archers', 215
Arnold, Matthew, 97
The Ashes, 126
Auden, W. H., 3, 10, 13, 18, 20–45 *passim*, 67, 86, 87, 159, 193, 195
Auschwitz, 205
Austen, Jane, 1

Bakhtin, Mikhail, 3, 99, 169
Balakier, James J., 207
Barker, George, 87, 124–6
Bartok, Béla, 102
Bassnett, Susan, 171
Bataille, Georges, 139n
Bateson, F. W., 109
Baudrillard, Jean, 128, 133–5
Bayley, John, 6, 73, 111, 223
BBC, 10, 131, 133, 201, 214

Beauvoir, Simone de, 68–9, 79
Beckett, Samuel, 8, 133
Belsen, 163
Belsey, Catherine, 47
Benjamin, Walter, 88
Bennett, Tony, 103n
Berlin Airlift, 203
Berth, Edouard, 42n
Betjeman, John, 46
Bhabha, Homi, 10, 11, 12, 14, 164, 169, 170n, 215, 218n
The Bible, 35, 40, 73, 89, 152, 166
  Ezekiel, 20
  Habakkuk, 30, 43n
  John, 28
  Matthew, 202
  Old Testament, 72
  Revelation, 28
  St Paul, 39, 40
Bikini Atoll, 203, 204
Bildungsroman, 173–4, 188
Blaen Cwm, 163–4
Blake, William, 127, 137, 165, 166, 207
Blakeston, Oswell, 81
The Blitz, 127, 129, 130, 136, 151, 155, 164, 198, 204, 205
The Boathouse, 138, 199
The Body, 9, 14, 30, 31, 48, 51, 52–3, 54, 55, 62, 66, 67, 68, 73, 74, 76, 80, 81–2, 95, 96, 97, 125, 126, 129, 130, 133, 140, 141, 142, 152, 153, 154, 176, 182
Bold, Alan, 223

227

Botteghe Oscure, 40–1
Botting, Fred, 96, 190n
Bowen, Elizabeth, 14
Bradbury, Malcolm, 86
Breton, André, 88
Brewer's Dictionary of Phrase and Fable, 43n
Brinnin, John Malcolm, 47, 122n
Britten, Benjamin, 200
Brownjohn, Alan, 46
Byron, George Gordon, sixth baron, 96

Caetani, Princess, 40–1
Cameron, Norman, 34
Caplan, Cora, 187
Carmarthenshire, 91, 108, 162
Carroll (Lewis), 173
    Alice in Wonderland, 174
    Through the Looking-Glass, 121
Carry On films, 210
Carson, Ricks, 150
Cerne Abbas, 199
Chapman, Max, 81
Childhood, 16, 17, 21, 25, 27, 28, 32, 33, 37, 47, 50, 52, 57–8, 62, 63n, 69, 76, 83, 93, 110, 158, 164, 165, 166, 167, 172–89 *passim*, 192, 195, 211
China, 203
Christianity, 20, 23–4, 26, 28, 29, 39, 66, 72–3, 75, 80, 89, 93, 94–5, 97, 142, 198, 201–2, 203, 205, 207, 208
Cixous, Hélène, 65–7, 79, 81, 83
Clare, John, 165
Clarke, Gillian, 69
The Cold War, 17, 138, 193, 203
Coleridge, Samuel Taylor, 32
Comfort, Alex, 50–1
Communism, 23, 24, 25, 40, 63, 88, 126, 203
Connolly, Cyril, 32, 42, 170n
Connor, Steven, 194, 206
Conrad, Joseph, 90
Conran, Tony, 11–12, 89, 92, 93, 174, 179, 184, 190n, 223
Corcoran, Neil, 3, 16, 133, 223

Corman, Cid, 208, 209
Coronation Street, 17, 215
Cox, C. B., 222, 223
Cox, R. G., 158, 170n
Crawford, Robert, 92
Crehan, Stewart, 3, 13–14, 46–64, 96, 101, 102n
Crompton, Richmal, 173
Cwmdonkin Drive, 106, 115, 167, 193

Dali, Salvador, 88, 89
Danzig, 210
Davie, Donald, 6, 48, 112–14, 117, 222, 223
Davies, Aneurin Talfan, 122n
Davies, James A., 5, 6, 9, 10, 102n, 158–71, 178–9, 221, 222, 223
Davies, Russell, 3, 50
Davies, Walford, 2–3, 9, 17–18, 30, 34, 35, 36, 94, 99, 101, 102n, 106–23, 140–1, 156n, 168, 196, 197, 214, 218n, 221, 222
Davis, Alex, 102n
Day-Lewis, Cecil, 86, 87
Deconstruction, 39, 72, 76, 95, 96, 205, 216–17
The Depression, 86, 91, 106
Derrida, Jacques, 95, 206
Dickens, Charles, 195, 214
Disney, 33
Dodgeson, Charles Ludwidge, *see* Carroll, Lewis
The Domestic, 15, 72, 76, 83n, 106–7, 129, 130, 140, 163, 164, 166, 175, 176, 178, 179, 180, 185, 186, 187, 189n, 203, 206–7
Donne, John, 88, 140–2
Doolittle, Hilda (H. D.), 14
Douglas, Keith, 15, 128, 132, 133, 135
Doyle, Arthur Conan, 97
Draper, R. P., 223
Dresden, 127
Duck, Donald, 33, 34
Dyment, Clifford, 87

Easthope, Antony, 49, 81
Elegy, 14, 73, 76, 124–5, 133,
        135, 137, 138, 141, 148, 149,
        150, 151, 152, 153, 154, 155,
        197, 202, 203, 205, 208
Eliot, George, 66, 165
Eliot, T. S., 13, 14, 32, 77, 85–6,
        88, 90, 92, 97, 99–100, 102,
        114, 115, 116, 118–19, 120,
        121, 159, 165, 169, 195
Ellis, Havelock, 125
Elugelab, 204
Empson, William, 6, 86, 139n,
        195, 222, 223
Engels, Frederick, 62, 64n
Eniwetok, 204
Enright, D. J., 6, 160
Ernst, Max, 88
Evans, Caradoc, 78, 90–1, 93, 161
Ezekiel, *see* The Bible

Faber (and Faber), 90
Family, 15, 16, 20, 23, 33, 35–8,
        39, 44n, 58, 60, 61, 73, 76,
        107–8, 129, 163, 164, 165,
        179, 180, 186, 187, 206–7,
        208–9, 210
Fascism, 56, 63n, 86, 87, 92, 126,
        136, 178
Fernhill, 108, 162–3
Ferris, Paul, 5, 39, 45, 58, 61, 92,
        122n, 163, 221, 222
Fitzgibbon, Constantine, 5, 32, 33,
        44–5, 126, 221, 222
Fourth International, 88
Fowler, Alastair, 112, 222
Freud, Sigmund, 3, 22–3, 41–2n,
        57–62, 63n, 87, 121n, 125–6,
        129, 148, 156, 188, 212, 207
    Chronos, 36–7
    Oedipus, 13, 16, 23, 33, 36, 42n

Gascoyne, David, 87, 117
Gaston, George, 221, 222, 223
Gender, *see* Sexuality and gender
Genet, Jean, 65, 66
Germany, 210
Ghosts 16, 31, 146, 186
Gibbons, Stella, 93

Goebbels, Joseph, 127, 131
Goodby, John, 17, 192–220,
        217–18n
'The Goon Show', 17, 214
The Gothic, 2, 13, 14, 67, 82, 85,
        87, 93, 94, 96–7, 98, 102n,
        126, 174
Gower, 131, 184
Goya y Lucientes, Francisco José,
        36
Graham, Colin, 12–13
Gramich, Katie, 5, 13–14, 16, 17,
        65–84, 102n, 189n
Grand Guignol, 80
Graves, Robert, 5, 10, 96
Greenway, Betty and William,
        173, 174
Grierson, Herbert, 88
Grigson, Geoffrey, 5, 22, 26, 42n,
        43n
Guernica, 127

Habakkuk, *see* The Bible
Hall, Stuart, 162
Hamlet, *see* Shakespeare, William
Hardy, Barbara, 222
Hardy, Thomas, 77, 165, 210, 213
Harris, John, 189n, 190n, 221
Harvey, David, 193
Hawkins, Desmond, 38
H-bomb, 203
Heaney, Seamus, 197–8, 223
Hewitt, John, 218n
Hiroshima, 127, 162–4, 203
History, *see* Politics and history
Hitler, Adolf, 56, 126, 127, 135
Hoffman, Ernst Theodor
        Amadeus, 61
Holbrook, David, 2, 3, 10, 47, 57,
        195
Hollywood, 194
Hopkins, Gerard Manley, 30, 31,
        112
Horizon, 130
Horkheimer, Max, 194
Horlicks, 126
Hornick, T., 61
Houdini, Harry, 41
Housman, A. E., 55

Hughes, Ted, 6,
Hughes, Trevor, 22, 26, 32, 34, 125
Hulme, T. E., 97
Huxley, Aldous, 82
Hyde Park, 131

Imagism, 115, 141
Ireland, 162
Irigaray, Luce, 79–80
'ITMA', 17, 214

James, Henry, 89, 117, 174
Jenkins, Lee, 102n
John, see The Bible
Johnson, Pamela Hansford, 23–5,
    26, 29, 32, 38, 42, 44, 58,
    80–1, 82, 125
Jones, Daniel, 106
Jones, David, 7, 90
Jones, Glyn, 34, 81, 126, 161
Jones, Jack, 161
Joyce, James, 8, 16, 65, 66, 90, 97,
    110, 187, 198
Jung, Carl, 57

Kavanagh, Patrick, 162
Kavanagh, Ted, 214
Keats, John, 96, 137–8
Kermode, Frank, 90
Keyes, Sidney, 15, 128, 132, 135,
    137
Kincaid, James, 172, 174
King Lear, see Shakespeare,
    William
Kipling, Rudyard, 25
Korea, 203
Kristeva, Julia, 101, 188
Krober, Karl, 190n

Labour Government, 162–3, 200
Labour Party, 56
Lacan, Jacques, 15, 150, 153,
    156n, 188, 215
Lahey, Philip A., 223
Language and style, 2, 4, 6, 14, 15,
    16, 17, 18, 21, 30, 48, 50, 51,
    54, 56, 57, 63n, 74, 86, 89, 90,
    92, 93, 95, 96, 98, 99, 100,
    101, 102, 107, 109–17, 120,
    121, 122n, 124, 125, 127, 128,
    131, 136, 137, 142, 155, 158,
    159, 160, 166, 168, 180, 195,
    196, 198, 200, 205–6, 208,
    209, 211–14, 216, 217n
Larkin, Philip, 1, 6, 46, 159–60,
    170n
Larrissy, Edward, 190n
Laugharne, 138, 198, 199, 210,
    214
Lawrence, D. H., 24, 25, 27, 28,
    33, 58, 67, 77, 82, 86, 91,
    97–8, 137, 165, 187
Leavis, F. R., 47, 194, 195
Lehmann, John, 159
Lerner, Laurence, 211
Levinson, Marjorie, 104n
Lewis, Alun, 15, 128, 132, 133,
    135
Lewis, Jane, 190n
Lewis, Peter, 216
Lewis, Peter Elfed, 223
Lewis, Saunders, 8, 19, 93
Lewis, Wyndham, 23–4, 42n, 86,
    97
The Listener, 29
Llewellyn, Richard, 161
London, 10, 91–2, 114, 128, 129,
    130, 147, 149, 160, 161, 163,
    176
London Mercury, 32–3
Louis, Joe, 126
Lucy, Sean, 162
Lurie, Alison, 173
Luftwaffe, 156

Mabinogi, 108
Machen, Arthur, 97
Macherey, Pierre, 89, 103n
MacDonald, Ramsay, 56
McCormack, W. J., 191n
McDonald, Peter, 104n
McFarlane, James, 86
McKay, Don, 223
MacNeice, Louis, 6, 13, 87, 125
Magritte, René, 89
Mallarmé, Stéphane, 98
Mankovitz, Wolf, 158, 170n
Mansfield, Katherine, 97, 184
Marshfield, 128
Mathias, Roland, 103n

Matthew, *see* The Bible
Maud, Ralph, 4, 30, 34, 35, 36, 122n, 202, 221, 222
Mayer, Ann Elizabeth, 222
Mayhead, Robin, 158–9, 170n
Mellors, W. H., 158, 170n
Melville, Herman, 89
Meredith, George, 129
Miller, J. Hillis, 54, 223
Modernism, 2, 7–8, 12, 13, 14, 17, 18, 23, 48, 65, 66, 83n, 85, 86, 87, 90, 92, 93, 96, 97, 98, 101, 102, 110, 114, 115, 116, 119, 121, 164, 165, 187, 192, 193, 194, 195, 198, 200, 214, 216
Monte Bello, 204
Morris, William, 97
Morrison, Blake, 159, 223
Motion, Andrew, 139n
The Movement, 6, 49, 122n, 159–60, 162, 170n, 222, 223
Moynihan, William T., 222

Nabokov, Vladimir, 174
Nagasaki, 162–3, 203,
Nairn, Tom, 13
Napoleon (Bonaparte), 56
Narrative, 17, 30, 59, 71–3, 76, 93, 99–100, 101, 106, 112, 115, 117, 118, 119, 120, 121, 172–89 *passim*, 206, 207, 216
Nash, John, 200
Nature, 8, 17, 33, 51, 52, 55, 59, 59, 67, 68, 71, 74, 77, 97, 100, 130, 138, 163, 167, 178, 199, 200, 203
Neil, Michael, 60, 61
The New Apocalypse group, 33, 200, 201
New Country, 13, 31, 40, 86, 87, 96, 100, 102n
New Quay, 163, 199
New Signatures, 86
New Verse, 26, 30, 42, 87, 125
New York, 193
News of the World, 185, 186
Nietzsche, Friedrich, 24
Norris, Leslie, 175, 177–8
Northern Ireland, 218n

Nuclear warfare, 127, 138, 162, 163, 193, 197, 203–5, 217n

Old Testament, *see* The Bible
Olson, Elder, 46
Orpheus, 41
Orwell, George, 17, 172, 183–4, 189n
Owen, Wilfred, 127
Oxford English Dictionary, 21, 22

The Pastoral, 17, 166, 196, 197, 198, 199, 202, 206, 209, 217n
Pater, Walter, 97
Paul, St, *see* The Bible
Paulin, Tom, 138n
Peach, Linden, 174, 175
Pendine Sands, 138
Petrarch (Francesco Petrarcha), 187, 191n
Phillips, Ivan, 15, 124–39
Pierce, Lynne, 169
Pinkney, Tony, 97
Plath, Sylvia, 79, 216
Plomer, William, 86
Poetics, 6–7, 14, 46–63 *passim*, 86, 87, 100, 101, 108, 109, 117, 118, 119, 120, 121, 122n, 143, 144, 158–65, 192, 194, 195, 221, 222
Politics and history, 47, 50, 56, 57, 63, 86, 87, 88, 89–90, 93, 96, 102n, 106, 121n, 126, 127, 129, 130, 139, 146, 162, 163, 178–9, 193, 196, 198, 210
Popular Culture, 17, 27, 48, 75, 81, 89, 97, 126, 185, 186, 194, 207, 210, 217, 218n, 221
Porteus, H. G., 4
Porthcawl, 177–8
Postcolonial Criticism, 1, 7, 8–13, 16, 92, 96, 104n, 122, 162, 164, 169, 170n, 173, 174, 189n, 198, 215, 218n
  hybridity, 8–13, 14, 16, 18, 92, 102n, 122, 195, 201
Poststructuralism, 1, 15, 49, 53, 57, 133–5, 138n, 140–56 *passim*, 196–7, 205–6, 217, 218n

Pound, Ezra, 24, 86, 90, 97, 114
Pratt, Annis, 218n, 222
Psychoanalysis, 4, 8–9, 13, 15, 23, 28, 31, 33–4, 38–9, 40, 42n, 47, 49, 54, 55, 57–8, 59, 60–1, 62, 63, 82, 87, 93, 94–5, 99, 101, 107, 121n, 125–6, 128–9, 135, 138, 145, 147, 148–9, 153, 156n, 174, 186–7, 188, 196–7, 215
Punter, David, 97, 190n

Raban, Jonathan, 46
Ramazani, Jahan, 148–9, 156n, 157n
Rawson, C. J., 222
Ray, Paul C., 223
Reed, Henry, 128
Reid, Alastair, 122n
Regionalism, 4–5, 7–13, 17, 18, 85, 87, 89, 90, 91, 92, 96, 97, 102, 110, 111, 173, 198, 200, 218n
Revelation, see The Bible
Rilke, Rainer Maria, 137
Rimbaud, Arthur, 34, 41, 89, 115, 193
Roberts, Kate, 183–4
Roberts, Michael, 32–3
Roget's Thesaurus, 110
Romanticism, 6, 32, 49, 50, 52, 54, 55, 66, 77, 83n, 89, 102, 103n, 121, 159, 161, 172, 173, 200, 201
Rose, Jacqueline, 173, 216
'Round the Horne', 214
Rousseau, Jean-Jacques, 95
Ruskin, John, 97
Russian Formalists, 93

Sacks, Peter, 149–50
Said, Edward, 9–10, 190n
St Paul, see The Bible
Saussure, Ferdinand de, 101
Scrutiny, 158–60
Selfridges, 131
Seven, 34–5
Sexuality and gender, 2, 9, 14, 16, 17, 24, 28, 30, 38, 52, 53, 57, 59, 60, 65–83 passim, 85, 86, 93, 94, 95, 96, 101, 103n, 107, 122n, 128, 129, 130, 172, 174, 175, 176, 177, 178, 179, 180, 183, 185, 186, 187, 188–9, 190n, 196–7, 210, 211, 216
Shakespeare, William, 1
    Hamlet, 153, 213
    King Lear, 208
    The Tempest, 213
Shapiro, Karl, 195
Shelley, Mary, 96
Shelley, Percy Bysshe, 52
Silkin, John, 224
Simpson, Louis, 188, 224
Sitwell, Edith, 98, 162–4,
Skelton, Robin, 87, 139n
Smith, Stan, 3, 13, 16, 20–45, 41n, 43n, 102n
Spivak, Gayatri Chakravorty, 190n
Socialism, 24, 25, 34, 56, 86, 87, 91, 96, 162, 163, 183, 194, 200
Sophocles, 23
Sorel, Georges, 23, 42n
Soviet Writers Congress, 56
Spender, Stephen, 46, 48, 86, 87, 170n
Spengler, Oswald, 23
Stalin, Joseph, 56
Stein, Gertrude, 98
Stone, Patsy, 159
Story, Mark, 171n
Strand Films, 133
Stravinsky, Igor, 102
Strewwelpeter, 29, 60, 94
Style, see Language and style
Surrealism, 13, 54, 85, 87, 88, 89, 93, 99, 116–17, 118, 133, 175, 178, 188, 189n
Sutton, J. B., 159–60
Swansea, 18, 42n, 85, 91, 106, 108, 131, 160, 167, 182, 184, 185, 193
Symbolism, 17, 62n, 78, 115, 116, 118, 119, 121
Symons, Julian, 9

The Tempest, see Shakespeare,
    William
Tennant, David, 162
Thomas, Aeronwy, 39
Thomas (Macnamara), Caitlin, 39,
    44n, 108, 163
Thomas, D. J., 58, 60, 61, 107–8,
    163, 165, 179
Thomas, Dylan, Works:
    'A Child's Christmas in Wales',
        76, 199; 'A grief ago', 120;
        'A process in the weather of
        the heart', 55, 122n, 143;
        'A Refusal to Mourn the
        Death, by Fire, of a Child in
        London', 37, 50, 51, 54,
        133, 136–7, 148, 149–51,
        152, 153; 'A saint about to
        fall', 38; 'A Story', 16, 176,
        177–83, 184, 185, 186,
        188; 'A Vest', 176; 'A Visit
        to Grandpa's', 186; 'A
        Winter's Tale', 196–7, 198,
        207; *Adventures in the Skin
        Trade*, 75–6, 176; 'After the
        funeral (In memory of Ann
        Jones)', 47, 51, 54, 73–5,
        192; 'All all and all', 50,
        51, 61; 'Altarwise by
        owl-light', 88–9, 112–14,
        120; 'Among those Killed in
        the Dawn Raid was a Man
        Aged a Hundred', 132–3,
        141, 148, 151, 153; 'An
        Adventure from a Work in
        Progress', 59, 60;
        'And death shall have no
        dominion', 50, 51, 136;
        'Answers to an Enquiry',
        99, 121, 123; 'Author's
        Prologue', 109; 'Ballad of
        the Long-legged Bait', 59,
        67; 'Before I knocked', 16,
        38, 94, 108, 111, 119;
        The Broadcasts, 221;
        'Ceremony After a Fire
        Raid', 15, 133, 136, 151–5;
        Collected Letters, 5, 23–7,
        28–9, 32–4, 35, 38, 47, 48,
        49, 54, 56, 73, 81, 82–3,
        87, 89, 95, 96, 98, 99,
        100, 106–7, 108, 115,
        120, 125, 126–7, 129, 130,
        131, 143, 144, 146, 151,
        155, 162, 163, 164, 183,
        198, 210, 214; *Collected
        Poems, 1934–52*, 2, 5, 34,
        68, 107, 158, 170n, 201;
        Collected Stories, 59;
        'The conversation of
        prayers', 142–3; *Deaths
        and Entrances*, 15, 35, 37,
        140–57 *passim*, 192, 198,
        201; 'Deaths and
        Entrances', 130, 131–2,
        133, 146–7, 149, 151;
        'Do not go gentle into that
        good night', 51, 78, 136,
        138, 199, 204, 206, 208–9,
        217n; 'Do you not father
        me?', 22; 'The Dress', 72;
        Early Prose Writings, 221;
        18 Poems, 26, 56, 87,
        102n, 129; 'The Enemies',
        71; 'Extraordinary Little
        Cough', 80, 184; 'Fern
        Hill', 3, 8, 11, 62, 63n,
        162–9, 179, 192, 198, 222;
        The Filmscripts, 221; 'Find
        meat on bones', 51; 'The
        Followers', 16–17, 177,
        184, 185–9; 'The force that
        through the green fuse',
        52–4, 55, 59, 69; 'From
        loves's first fever', 49; 'The
        hand that signed the paper',
        127; 'Hold hard, these
        ancient minutes', 99;
        'Holiday Memory', 76,
        199; 'Holy Spring', 35;
        'The Horse's Ha', 71–2;
        'How shall my animal',
        53–4, 60, 109; 'How Soon
        the Servant Sun', 98;
        'The Hunchback in the
        Park', 198; 'I dreamed my
        genesis', 61, 108;
        'I fellowed sleep', 16;

Thomas, Dylan, Works: (*continued*)
'If my head hurt a hair's foot',
38, 73, 74; 'I have longed to
move away', 107; 'I, in my
intricate image', 30–1, 48, 54,
108, 114; 'I make this in a
warring absence', 32; *In
Country Heaven*, 16, 77, 78;
'In Country Heaven', 201,
209; *In Country Sleep* ,
39–40, 192; 'In Country
Sleep', 16, 39, 197, 199, 200,
201, 203, 204–5, 206; 'In my
craft or sullen art', 137–8;
'In the beginning', 61; 'In the
White Giant's Thigh', 5, 75,
76–8, 138, 199, 200, 201,
204; 'Into her lying down
head', 129–30; 'I see the boys
of summer', 16, 26–7, 29, 55,
61, 68–71, 94; 'Just Like
Little Dogs', 174, 176;
'Lament', 199, 206, 210;
'The Lemon', 97; 'Lie Still,
Sleep Becalmed', 61; 'Light
breaks where no sun shines',
48, 119; 'Love in the Asylum',
145; *The Map of Love*, 4, 14,
93, 101–2, 178–9, 192;
'Memories of Christmas', 29;
'The Mouse and the Woman',
72–3; 'My hero bares his
nerves', 95; 'My world is
pyramid', 46, 82; Notebook
poems (*The Notebook Poems,
1930–34*), 107, 115, 221;
'Now', 98; 'On a Wedding
Anniversary', 132; 'Once
below a time', 60, 61; 'Once it
was the colour of saying',
192; 'On the Marriage of a
Virgin', 129; 'The Orchards',
72, 82; 'Our eunuch dreams',
48; 'Over Sir John's hill', 138,
197, 199–200, 201, 202–3,
210; 'The Peaches', 75, 182,
185; 'Poem on his Birthday',
34–5, 110, 199, 200, 203,
205, 208; 'Poem in October',
37, 198; *The Poems*, 221;
Poet in the Making, 4;
*Portrait of the Artist as a
Young Dog*, 75, 93, 158, 174,
176, 192; 'Prologue', 164,
199, 201; 'Prospect of the
Sea', 78; 'Quid's Inn',
214–15; 'Quite Early One
Morning', 29, 199, 221;
'Reminiscences of Childhood',
199; 'Return Journey', 29,
199; 'The School for Witches',
71–2; *Selected Letters*, 5, 40;
Selected Poems, 3, 221;
'Should lanterns shine', 119;
'Sixteen Comments on
Auden', Thomas's
contribution (*New Verse*), 20;
'The spire cranes', 57, 120;
'Then was my neophyte', 36;
'This side of the truth', 36,
54; 'The Town (or "Village")
That Was Mad', 201, 209;
'The True Story', 71; *Twenty-
five Poems*, 94, 101, 102n;
Under Milk Wood, 1, 4, 8,
17, 66, 81, 129, 131, 138,
192, 194, 197, 199, 201, 203,
209–17, 222; 'Vision and
Prayer', 73; 'The Visitor', 72;
'We lying by seasand', 116;
'When I woke', 34–5, 61;
'When, like a running grave',
29–30, 48, 60, 61, 99, 117;
'When once the twilight
locks', 51, 52, 109; 'Where
once the waters of your face',
100–1; 'Where Tawe Flows',
174, 176; 'Who Do You Wish
Was With Us', 174, 184;
'Why east wind chills and
south wind cools', 60;
'The Woman Speaks', 75, 81
Thomas, Edward, 26, 165
Thomas, Gareth, 90
Thomas, Llewelyn, 36, 38, 44n
Thomas, M. Wynn, 166, 224
Thomas, R. S., 82, 160
Thurley, Geoffrey, 6

Thwaite, Anthony, 6
Tindall, William York, 2, 147, 156n, 168, 222
Tin Pan Alley, 194
Tottenham Court Road, 131
Towy, River, 199, 204
Toynbee, Philip, 170n
Traherne, Thomas, 165
Treece, Henry, 32–3, 47, 82, 122n, 126–7
Trick, Bert, 25, 26, 28, 126
Trollope, Anthony, 35, 165
Trotsky, Leon, 63n, 88

USA, 18, 108, 162–3, 194, 203
USSR, 203

Valéry, Paul, 115
Vaughan, Henry, 164, 166
Versailles, Treaty of, 210
Vine, Steve, 15, 138–9n, 140–57
Voice and performance, 14, 18, 36, 47, 50, 68, 75, 100, 143, 153, 155, 158, 177–8, 181, 197, 207–9, 210, 216–17

Wales, 26, 91, 111, 128, 130, 159, 160, 163, 165, 166, 197, 199, 200
Waller, Fats, 163
Waller, Gary, 191n
Watkins, Vernon, 4, 14–15, 35, 44n, 47, 130, 159–60, 166
Wayne, John, 178

The Welsh language, 7, 8, 11, 89, 91–2, 107–8, 109, 111, 121n, 172, 179, 180, 183–4
The Welsh Marches, 169
Welsh nationalism, 92, 94, 104n, 199, 200
Wigginton, Chris, 1–19, 13–14, 16, 85–105
Williams, Gwyn A., 91
Williams, Jeni, 16, 42n, 83n, 172–91
Williams, Oscar, 162–3, 165, 203
Williams, Raymond, 222
Wilson, Elisabeth, 190n
Witness 14, 55, 132
Wollstonecraft, Mary, 66
Woolf, Virginia, 1, 187
Wordsworth, William, 38, 66, 77, 165, 166
World War I, 23–5, 26, 91, 127–8
World War II, 14–15, 86, 102, 126, 127, 129, 130, 131, 132, 133, 135, 136, 137, 138, 140–56 *passim*, 162, 163, 164, 193, 195, 200, 206, 210, 217n, 218n

Yeats, W. B., 20–1, 44n, 78, 114, 115, 116, 118, 119, 126, 208

Young, Alan, 55

Žižek, Slavoj, 153